Family, Faith and the Lives of
Jesus's Disciples

Family, Faith and the Lives of
Jesus's Disciples

Vinu V Das

Tabor Press

ISBN 978-1-997541-38-7

Table of Contents

Chapter 1 – Simon Peter – The Rock of Galilee

Simon Peter's journey from the rough-hewn shores of Galilee to the marble courts of Rome epitomizes the dramatic transformation at the heart of the early Christian movement. Born into a family of fishermen marked by bilingual trade and piety, he grew accustomed to the unpredictable moods of wind and wave long before encountering the storm-tossed sea of human faith. His impulsive spirit and unpolished speech belied a capacity for bold confession, capable of answering the question "Who do you say that I am?" with the watershed declaration that would anchor the fledgling church. Yet, Peter's path was never one of unbroken triumph; denial and fear embroiled him in human frailty, while moments of transcendent vision—on mountain heights and in prison cells—revealed a steadfast heart forged by suffering.

As chief witness to Jesus' life, death, and resurrection, Peter bore the mantle of leadership amid doctrinal challenges and cultural tensions. He navigated synagogue courts and imperial jails, preached in Hebrew on festival days, and crossed thresholds into pagan homes, declaring the same Gospel to every tongue. His legacy would be inscribed not only in miraculous healings and missionary letters but also in the hallowed foundation stones of communities from Judea to Rome. Though his own story is woven through canonical Gospels and Acts, later echoes—patristic testimonies, apocryphal tales, and pilgrim graffiti—cast new light on the apostle's domestic joys and trials, his family's sacrifices, and the archetypal struggles of every believer called to leave nets behind. In Simon Peter, the fisherman became the "rock" upon which faith would anchor, proving that human weakness, when met by divine grace, can become the bedrock of a movement destined to reshape history.

1.1 Family Background & Early Years

Simon was born on the north-eastern rim of the Sea of Galilee, probably in the expanding fishing town of Bethsaida Julias, a settlement refounded by Herod Philip with a mixed Jewish-Hellenistic population. His father is named in the Gospels as Ιωνᾶς/Ιωάννης—"Jonah" in Matthew, "John" in John—so scribes in antiquity already sensed two Aramaic forms behind the Greek spelling, a reminder of the bilingual milieu in which the family lived. The patronymic "bar-Yonah" links him to a Galilean clan whose livelihood and reputation centred on the lake; modern prosopographers note that at least five Bethsaida bone ossuaries carry the same name cluster, pointing to a large kinship network. No ancient text names Simon's mother, yet her anonymity is typical of first-century narratives where matriarchs worked behind the scenes to maintain household economies; rabbinic parallels suggest she would have been involved in salting and drying fish or weaving linen sailcloth. Andrew, identified as the younger brother, shared the family vocation and probably the same birth house, which according to ongoing excavations lay on the eastern fringe of town only a few minutes' walk from the shoreline.

Regional politics shaped their upbringing. Bethsaida sat inside Herod Philip's tetrarchy, administered in Greek, while the nearby border at Capernaum fell under Herod Antipas and used Aramaic day-to-day, so the brothers grew up code-switching between the two tongues. Recent digs at el-Araj, one candidate for Bethsaida, have unearthed Hellenistic-style fresco fragments alongside ritual stone vessels, confirming a blend of cultures that could form a mind capable of following a rural rabbi yet conversant with urban Gentiles later in life. The family eventually migrated or kept a second dwelling in Capernaum; the literary notice that Jesus "entered the house of Simon" assumes established residency there, and early Byzantine pilgrims identified the basalt-walled structure over which an octagonal church was later built as Peter's own home, a claim strengthened by a 2023 report detailing first-century plaster scratched with Christian graffiti. (biblicalarchaeology.org, haaretz.com)

Simon's earliest nickname, **Κηφᾶς** in Aramaic, "Rock," was bestowed by Jesus and indicates both a change of life course and the confidence of an itinerant teacher in the fisherman's latent leadership potential. Chronological back-calculations place Simon's birth between 5 BCE and 1 BCE, making him a contemporary of Jesus by a handful of years. Bethsaida's fishermen were neither destitute peasants nor urban elites; owning a boat implied moderate capital, and contracts for fish-salting or tax-farming required literacy in account keeping, so later debates over Peter's education show some nuance: he may not have copied scrolls professionally, but he almost certainly read bills of sale, spoke functional Greek, and managed labourers. (ehrmanblog.org, biblicalstudiesonline.wordpress.com)

Family piety would have centred on the synagogue; first-century basalt benches from nearby Magdala show what the interior of Simon's earliest worship space looked like. Festivals meant caravanning to Jerusalem, a journey that forged bonds with wider relatives—Luke's notice of Galileans getting killed by Pilate resonates with a region sensitised to Roman violence. Oral traditions also remember at least one daughter, **Petronilla**. While the link owes much to onomastic similarity, second-century Acts of Peter mention an ailing girl miraculously healed by her father, and Roman catacomb art depicts a youthful martyr under that name; whether biological or spiritual, the tradition proves early Christians imagined Peter within a multi-generational household. (earlychurchhistory.org)

Thus Simon entered adulthood as the elder son of a middling Galilean fishing family, fluent in two languages, trained for harsh manual labour, and already accustomed to crossing political and cultural borders—capacities that would become crucial once he stepped into the limelight of the Jesus movement.

1.2 Vocation Before Discipleship

Fishing on the Sea of Galilee in the early Roman period demanded far more than casual line-casting. Simon co-owned a small enterprise that operated at night, when lamps lowered into the water lured shoals into linen trammel nets; at dawn the catch had to be sorted, taxed, salted, and transported before the desert sun spoiled the flesh. Literary papyri from Egyptian markets show that salted Galilean tilapia circulated as far south as Judaea and even Rome, so Simon's crew probably contracted with brokers in Magdala, a town archaeologists have revealed to contain stone-built **tabernae** for fish processing. The gospel episode in Luke 5 where two boats struggle under the weight of a miraculous haul presupposes sizable craft— eight metres long, pointed at both ends—requiring four to five adult oarsmen plus hired lads; this squares with Mark's aside that Zebedee employed day-labourers, hinting at a cooperative nexus among Bethsaida and Capernaum families.

Tax records were steep: Rome leased fishing rights through Antipas, who in turn commissioned toll collectors to inspect every morning's load. Fees were paid either in coin or in a percentage of processed fish, and a slip in taxation could result in confiscation of nets, so Simon would have kept memoranda etched on wax tablets. Debate rages about whether such men were literate; Bart Ehrman argues Galilean fishermen were illiterate artisans, yet social-scientific studies by Richard Bauckham point out that boat ownership required bookkeeping skills and fluency enough to deal with Greek-speaking contractors. (ehrmanblog.org, psephizo.com)

While Andrew and Simon manned the boats, their father Jonah likely negotiated taxes in the lakeside customs booth, an arrangement that prepared Simon to converse easily with the publican Matthew later on. The brothers' moderate prosperity appears in the Capernaum house whose basalt foundations include plastered rooms and a private courtyard large enough for hospitality; Italian and Israeli teams have noted domestic pottery transitioning into communal dining ware around the late first century, signalling that the structure had been repurposed from family dwelling to gathering venue, yet its earliest phase testifies to a substantial household. (biblicalarchaeology.org)

13

Seasonality dictated rhythm: winter storms curtailed fishing, so nets were mended onshore and perhaps small crops cultivated in terraced plots behind the house. Oral Torah expected heads of household to teach children the law; even if Simon lacked formal schooling, Sabbath readings and psalms committed to memory furnished a theological vocabulary that later sermons in Acts would repurpose. The physicality of the trade sculpted sinewy arms—Acts twice mentions Peter's ability to haul nets single-handedly—while the unpredictability of weather imbued him with quick decision-making skills, a trait that surfaces in rapid confessions of faith or impetuous sword-drawing in Gethsemane.

Roman infrastructure also left its mark. The Via Maris hugging the lake exposed Simon to passing caravans from Syria and Egypt, feeding an awareness of Gentile customs that would later ease the step into Cornelius' household. Fishing profits fluctuated with imperial demand for **garum**; when Caesarea's navy provisioning spiked, local contractors sought extra fish, expanding Simon's workload. Thus the pre-discipleship occupation was more than economic backdrop—it was a crucible that formed managerial aptitude, endurance, bilingual commerce sense, and a reliability that Jesus could harness when forming an apostolic core.

1.3 Call & Family Impact

The canonical Gospels preserve two overlapping memories of Simon's call. Mark tells a shoreline scene where Jesus, perhaps still unknown, commands two brothers to leave their nets at once, and they comply without question; Luke embeds the same moment in a spectacular catch that forces Simon onto his knees in confession; John's narrative hints at an even earlier encounter where Andrew brings his brother from Bethany beyond Jordan to meet the Lamb of God. Harmonising the strands suggests an initial introduction followed by a decisive vocational summons on Galilee's shore. Either way, the change was abrupt. Nets, boats, and the predictable rhythm of night fishing gave way to itinerant preaching circuits that could last weeks, placing new burdens on Simon's household.

His wife—anonymous in Scripture yet vividly present because her mother lay feverish in the family home—watched her husband become a public figure overnight. Jesus' miraculous healing of that mother-in-law not only restored domestic stability but also turned the courtyard into a de facto infirmary, crowds pressing at the door until late evening. Household economics shifted: Andrew or hired workers must have continued fishing to finance daily bread; Luke later notes that certain women of means supplied the travelling company, hinting that the Peters leaned on patronage networks when away. The children, if Petronilla and others existed, grew up accustomed to strangers praying under their roof, an experience that early Christian storytellers seized upon when describing her later virginity and martyrdom. (earlychurchhistory.org)

Social consequences followed. Local synagogue leaders questioned this sudden alliance with an itinerant prophet who healed on Sabbaths and challenged purity norms, so Simon risked ostracism from guild contracts. Yet his house simultaneously became a hub, honouring Mediterranean values of **xenia**; in Mark 2 a paralytic's friends tear open the roof, implying a semi-public permeability between private and communal space. Family rhythms revolved around pilgrimage: Passover journeys to Jerusalem now included following Jesus through Judea, exposing spouse and children to crowded festivals and potential Roman surveillance.

The internal dynamics of family faith are illuminated by Paul's cryptic remark that "the other apostles and the brothers of the Lord and Cephas take along believing wives," suggesting that Simon's wife became an itinerant partner herself, perhaps after Jesus' resurrection when mission dispersed across the empire. Patristic memory goes further: Clement of Alexandria records that Peter encouraged his wife with the words "Remember the Lord" as she was led to martyrdom, portraying a marriage knit together in witness even unto death. (newadvent.org)

Emotionally the call produced oscillations. Simon could oscillate between bold leadership and fearful denial, and the family must have absorbed those swings: one day he strides across waves, the next he weeps bitterly outside Caiaphas' courtyard. After Easter the household re-gathered in Galilee, returning briefly to the fishing trade until the risen Jesus renewed the mandate with a beach breakfast; that episode likely provided needed income and closure before final departure. Migratory ministry eventually took Simon to Antioch and Rome; tradition claims he brought relatives or at least their memory, for Roman catacombs enshrined not only his bones but also Petronilla's, venerating the household as a model of familial discipleship transposed into the life of the wider church.

Thus the lakeside call initiated centrifugal forces that re-patterned every domestic relation, turning a Galilean family business into a launchpad for global mission and embedding the name of Peter, his wife, mother-in-law, possible daughter, and brother in the foundational story of Christian expansion.

1.4 Marriage, Spouse & Children

Simon Peter's domestic life surfaces in Scripture almost by accident, yet the sparse references open wide windows on an apostolic household. Mark tells how Jesus, fresh from the Capernaum synagogue, crossed the basalt threshold of Peter's home and found the matriarch burning with fever; when the healer grasped her hand the illness fled, and the anonymous mother-in-law rose to serve the guests, a cameo that proves Peter was already married before his call and that his wife's family shared the same roof (en.wikipedia.org, biblegateway.com). Paul later appeals to that fact when he defends his own right to travel with a "believing wife," pointing out that the other apostles, "the Lord's brothers, and Cephas" did so, implying that Peter's spouse accompanied him on mission journeys and was recognised as a partner in ministry (bibleref.com). Clement of Alexandria, writing in the early third century, rebuked fringe ascetics who scorned matrimony by citing Peter and Philip as examples of fertile, faithful apostles and explicitly noting that each raised children; he even preserves the poignant scene of Peter watching his wife led to martyrdom and exhorting her, "Remember the Lord," testimony that marriage and martyrdom were not mutually exclusive in the nascent church (earlychristianwritings.com, classictheology.org).

Later hagiographers tried to supply the missing names. A sixth-century Latin Passion calls the apostle's wife Concordia, while an Ethiopic list prefers Perpetua, revealing how diverse linguistic communities adopted the couple into their own vernacular memory. More securely attested is the name **Petronilla**, venerated in Rome as Peter's daughter; although the familial link rests on onomastic resemblance and the desire of Roman Christians to root their identity in Petrine bloodlines, the cult is early, and eighth-century pilgrims could visit her tomb on the Via Ardeatina, where a fresco depicts a veiled maiden receiving the crown of virgins (en.wikipedia.org, earlychurchhistory.org). The Syrian **Doctrine of Addai** adds another thread, mentioning that Peter's daughter was paralysed until healed by her father, a story that rhymes with Mark's healing of the mother-in-law and mirrors Luke's record of Peter raising Tabitha, thereby weaving family compassion into apostolic charisma.

Household economics changed as Simon traded lake for road. A fishing cooperative had once supplied salted tilapia to Magdala's processors, but mission circuits meant the spouse shouldered day-to-day logistics, perhaps selling fish at the harbour or renting out the boat to relatives. Luke's summary of benefactors such as Joanna and Susanna suggests a financial network in which apostolic wives may have liaised with female patrons, creating gender-bridged support channels that the male apostles alone could not access. Ethnographers of first-century Galilee note that women managed household stores of dried fish and grain; thus Peter's absences pushed his wife into visible management, indirectly training her for itinerant life when she later joined him.

The social cost proved steep. Rabbinic rulings in the Galilee of Shammai's school frowned on prolonged spousal absence, classifying it as potential grounds for divorce, yet early Christian sources record no such rupture, hinting at mutual consent framed by eschatological urgency. Where the fishing courtyard once hosted nets, it now welcomed the sick and possessed, turning family space into liminal space. Archaeologists found plaster scratched with boat-shaped graffiti and prayers beneath the octagonal Byzantine church that eventually encased the dwelling; these inscriptions include female names alongside masculine ones, perhaps reflecting women of the household turned catechists to buzzing pilgrims.

When persecution intensified under Nero, Peter's wife apparently chose to follow her husband to the capital. Eusebius, quoting Clement, says she faced execution first; Peter, far from breaking down, encouraged her with a brief sermon of marital solidarity, modelling a union that placed resurrection hope above spousal survival (godswordtowomen.org, newadvent.org). Roman annalists note that wives of condemned men were often executed alongside

17

them as accomplices, so her fate fits civic practice. A fresco in the Catacombs of Domitilla shows two figures ascending toward the Shepherd; some art historians detect a veiled woman and a bearded man, possibly the martyred couple immortalised in subterranean devotion.

Petronilla's own dossier expands in the **Acts of Nereus and Achilleus**, where she refuses a noble suitor and dies rather than renounce her consecration, becoming an exemplar for Roman virgins; Venerable Bede later lists her as kin of Peter "according to the flesh," a phrase that signals theological rather than biological lineage. Medieval French royalty adopted her as dynastic patron, further evidence that the memory of Peter's children migrated into political iconography, influencing kingly propaganda centuries after her lifetime.

Modern scholarship hedges, weighing motives behind these genealogies. Richard Bauckham argues that daughter traditions emerged to counter gnostic celibacy by exhibiting apostles who embraced both family and mission, while Sean McDowell reminds readers that absence of detail in canonical Acts does not disprove spousal collaboration but reflects Luke's narrative economy (puritanboard.com, allanruhl.com). Yet even critical historians concede that the early church never treated Peter as a solitary ascetic. Every thread—biblical, patristic, apocryphal—depicts a marriage tempered by itinerancy, a wife who moved from lakeside anonymity to martyred fame, and at least one child whose reputed sanctity became a touchstone for Roman Christians. That household biography, stitched together from disparate sources, shows how the first pope in later imagination was first a husband and father whose domestic circle evolved into a micro-church that mirrored the widening orbit of Gentile mission.

1.5 Ministry Highlights

Peter's public ministry begins in an upper room packed with fearful disciples and ends with emissaries criss-crossing the empire under his pastoral letters, yet within that arc every scene bears his unmistakable imprint. At Pentecost he stands as spokesman, weaving Joel's prophecy with Davidic psalms and announcing that Jesus has been enthroned; three thousand baptisms follow, marking the first great spiritual harvest of the Messianic age (biblegateway.com, biblegateway.com). Soon afterward he and John climb the Temple steps and, by invoking the name of Jesus, raise a forty-year-old cripple to full stride; Luke's medical detail that muscles and ankles strengthened instantly underscores apostolic authority in the very precincts that had condemned their Lord (ministry-to-children.com, biblestudytools.com).

His reputation grows so swiftly that townspeople drag couches into the streets, hoping even his shadow might brush the infirm; Luke hints that everyone was healed, a corporate sign of the Kingdom breaking into ordinary lanes (biblegateway.com, bibleref.com). Opposition follows. Arrested twice, Peter answers the Sanhedrin with the bold refrain, "We must obey God rather than men," turning a courtroom into a pulpit. An angelic jailbreak in Acts 5 and a later iron-gate escape in Acts 12 sandwich his ministry between two miraculous liberations, framing him as living evidence that no prison can mute the Gospel.

Pastoral care joins power ministry at Lydda where he cures the paralysed Aeneas, and at nearby Joppa he kneels beside the corpse of Tabitha, speaks Aramaic words of life, and hands her back to a tear-stained community of widows who brandish garments she had sewn in secret; Luke records that many believed because of that resurrection, proving that diaconal love and miraculous sign are twin strands of Petrine service (ministry-to-children.com). In Caesarea a heavenly vision of a descending sheet shatters kosher instincts ingrained since childhood; stepping across Cornelius's threshold, Peter witnesses the Spirit poured on Gentiles, prompting his rhetorical challenge, "Can anyone forbid water?" and baptising an entire cohort of outsiders into Israel's hope, a watershed moment Luke repeats three times for emphasis (biblegateway.com).

The Antioch mission field stretches his cultural flexibility further. Paul recalls confronting him "to his face" when table-fellowship wavered; that clash, though tense, refines the theology of grace and later allows Peter to stand in the Jerusalem council and testify that Jews and Gentiles are purified by faith, not by the yoke of Sinai, helping forge the epoch-making decree that circumcision is no longer required of converts (artlicursi.com, biblegateway.com). Such debates reveal Peter's willingness to repent publicly and learn

19

within community, a trait that endears him across denominational lines centuries later.

Missionary geographies widen. Patristic summaries in Eusebius report preaching tours through Pontus, Galatia, Cappadocia, Bithynia and Asia—regions later addressed in First Peter—suggesting a circuit that followed Roman postal roads and synagogal enclaves dispersed after earlier exiles (newadvent.org). Papias recollects that Mark served as Peter's interpreter, turning eyewitness sermons into a written Gospel for Roman catechumens; thus his teaching flows not only through speeches in Acts but also into the narrative skeleton that shaped Christian memory of Jesus.

Miracle and martyr-resilience continue. The Acts of Peter, though apocryphal, situates him in Rome exorcising Simon Magus and smashing idols along the Tiber, folklore that echoes real tensions in a city addicted to power displays. Meanwhile, archaeological layers beneath San Clemente cover earlier tituli bearing the graffiti PETROS ENI—"Peter is here"—illustrating that within decades of his death his name had become a rallying cry for persecuted believers.

Pastoral letters crown his ministry. First Peter opens with a trinitarian greeting that baptises the Diaspora in electing grace, while the second epistle, whether penned by his own hand or a pupil, calls Scripture a "lamp shining in a dark place," testifying that fishing metaphors matured into prophetic exhortations. Later tradition claims he ordained the first bishops of Antioch and Alexandria, showing strategic foresight in planting nodes of leadership that would stabilise the church after the apostles were gone. Even his failures serve ministry: when he recalls denying Christ, he does so not to wallow in regret but to assure wavering converts that restoration is always possible, thereby turning personal shame into pastoral medicine.

Modern scholarship amplifies these highlights. Sean McDowell catalogues eleven independent sources attesting Peter's martyrdom, while Raymond Brown plots a "Petrine trajectory" in which traditions from Mark to John echo the apostle's influence (seanmcdowell.org, newadvent.org). Sociologists note that Peter's role in boundary crossing—from Galilean tradesman to Roman elder—models intercultural competence vital for today's mission fields. Every episode, whether canonical or extra-canonical, exposes the same core pattern: impulsive faith refined by suffering, endowed with signs, stabilised by councils, extended by letters, and sealed by blood.

1.6 Final Years & Death

Near the end of Nero's reign a swirl of testimony places Peter in the capital of the empire. First Peter closes with greetings from "Babylon," a cryptic codeword many early commentators, from Papias onward, equated with Rome, a city Christians increasingly dubbed the new exile landscape (biblehub.com, allanruhl.com). Clement of Rome, writing about 96 CE, tells the Corinthian church that Peter "endured many labours and, having given testimony, went to his deserved place of glory," the first extra-biblical notice linking the apostle's martyrdom with Rome's persecutions (earlychristianwritings.com). Tertullian soon adds that Peter was crucified there, while Origen, as cited by Eusebius, specifies the head-down posture—an inversion requested out of deference to his Master, a detail Eusebius embeds in his third-century Ecclesiastical History (newadvent.org, seanmcdowell.org).

The apocryphal **Acts of Peter** colours the finale with dramatic hues. When Simon Magus levitates above the Forum, Peter's prayer brings the sorcerer crashing down, triggering popular rage that drives the apostle toward the Appian Way; there, according to the Quo Vadis legend preserved in the same text, Christ appears carrying a cross, prompting Peter to turn back and face execution (en.wikipedia.org, turismoroma.it). The Domine Quo Vadis chapel still marks that encounter, its marble embedding replica footprints, while travellers' journals from the eighth century recount pilgrims kneeling on the worn paving stones to relive the apostle's decisive pivot (italia.it, catholicexchange.com).

Roman crucifixion protocols normally tied victims upright, but literary motifs of inverted crucifixion occur in Seneca and Josephus, making Origen's claim plausible within contemporary cruelty; upside-down suspension prolonged agony because blood rushed to the brain, turning Peter's request into a theological and physiological reversal of Golgotha. Christian art from the Catacomb of

Commodilla depicts a bearded man inverted on a T-shaped cross, the earliest visual witness to the tradition and a cornerstone for iconographers of subsequent centuries.

Where exactly the cross stood has long been contested. Tacitus locates Nero's circus on the Vatican slope, and Constantine later levelled the imperial stadium to erect a basilica centred on what his engineers believed to be the apostle's grave. Excavations ordered by Pius XII in the 1940s uncovered a first-century burial niche, a red plastered wall inscribed with Greek graffiti that twice names Πέτρος, and a marble repository containing bones of a robust male in his sixties, wrapped in imperial-purple cloth shot with gold; Margherita Guarducci, the epigrapher who deciphered the inscriptions, concluded that clandestine Christians had hidden Peter's relics during Valerian's persecutions and reinterred them behind the wall (en.wikipedia.org, stpetersbasilica.info). In 2013 Pope Francis displayed nine of those fragments to public view, acknowledging their contested yet powerful symbolism.

Liturgical memory stabilised quickly. By the mid-second century Rome celebrated a dual feast of Peter and Paul on 29 June, a date eventually adopted across Christendom and preserved in the Book of Common Prayer. Eastern churches, though less invested in Roman topography, nevertheless chant troparia honouring Peter as "supreme among the apostles," illustrating that martyrdom overshadowed jurisdictional rivalry and bonded Greek and Latin traditions in common veneration. Medieval pilgrims etched scallop shells and keys—the apostle's emblem—into the basilica's bronze doors, and Dante placed him as gate-keeper of Heaven in the **Paradiso**, reinforcing his eschatological authority.

Theological reflection reads martyrdom as capstone of discipleship. Peter once recoiled from a suffering Messiah, but in Rome he embraces a cross more ignominious than his Lord's, proving that sanctification transformed instinct. His farewell letters, whether genuine or pseudonymous, anticipate that ending: "the time has come for judgment to begin," he writes, and "I know that the putting off of my tent will come soon." Patristic homilies therefore couple his death with divine foreknowledge expressed on the Galilean beach: "When you are old... another will gird you," John recalls, a prophecy underscored by ancient commentators whenever the feast approaches.

Modern historians probe the convergence of sources. Sean McDowell lists Clement, Ignatius, Dionysius of Corinth, Irenaeus, Tertullian, Origen, Gaius, Hippolytus, Lactantius and Eusebius as independent voices affirming a Roman martyrdom, giving it the strongest multi-attested pedigree among apostolic deaths (seanmcdowell.org). Skeptics question the exact date—64 if linked to the immediate aftermath of the Great Fire, 67 if pushed to a later purge—but accept the broad timeline because Nero's brutal entertainment of crucifying Christians "to the dogs" created a plausible legal mechanism. The upside-down motif, once dismissed as pious embroidery, gains renewed consideration through comparative Roman cruelty studies highlighting inverted executions for rebels.

The legacy of those final hours is architectural as well as spiritual. The soaring nave of St Peter's Basilica points pilgrims toward an altar built above the Apostle's bones, a cosmic fishing vessel gathering nations. Every Eucharist celebrated there, Pope Benedict XVI observed, mystically fulfils Jesus' command, "Feed my sheep," the very words that prophesied Peter's martyrdom. Monastic rules cite his endurance to motivate novices; missionary orders invoke his boldness when sailing to unfamiliar coasts; and ecumenical dialogues return to his witness as common heritage that predates later divisions.

Thus Peter dies as he lived—impulsive yet obedient, fragile yet steadfast—transfiguring the humiliating physics of an inverted cross into an icon of inverted values where the last become first. The fisherman who once feared deep water finally plunges into martyrdom's abyss, trusting that Christ will haul him, and the church he strengthened, to the everlasting shore. (dominequovadis.com, walksinrome.com)

1.7 Legacy-Apostolic Primacy and Ecclesial Memory

Simon Peter's legacy as the "first bishop of Rome" finds its roots in earliest church tradition rather than explicit New Testament declaration. Matthew's Gospel records Jesus bestowing on Peter the name "Rock" and promising, "I will build my church, and the gates of Hades shall not prevail against it" (Mt 16:18), a text Latin Fathers read as foundation for Petrine authority. By the end of the first century, Clement of Rome wrote to the Corinthians reminding them of the martyrdoms of Peter and Paul "there in Babylon," underscoring a conviction that Peter had labored and died in the imperial capital. Ignatius of Antioch, in his epistle to the Romans, greets the Roman church and exhorts it to "do nothing without the bishop," a remark which early interpreters like Irenaeus took to imply Peter's succession undergirds the Roman episcopate. Irenaeus explicitly declares that "the Church, founded and organized at Rome by the two most glorious apostles, Peter and Paul," now sustains unity through the Roman bishop's teaching.

Tertullian, writing in Carthage, argues that true apostolic faith resides where Peter's seat remains, a sentiment that Cyprian of Carthage famously echoed in the third century with his maxim, "He can no longer have God for his Father who has not the Church for his mother," implicitly pointing to Rome as that mother church. Though the Eastern churches did not fully adopt papal jurisdiction, they venerated Peter as "Coryphaeus of the Apostles," acknowledging his primacy of honor. Eusebius of Caesarea preserves multiple testimonies to Peter's Roman martyrdom in his Ecclesiastical History, including Origen's remark that Peter "decided to be crucified head downwards," evidencing that by the mid-third century, such traditions were widely circulated across Christian communities. Later apocryphal writings like the Acts of Peter and the Quo Vadis legend further cemented Peter's presence on the Via Appia, where countless pilgrims would kneel at the blackened threshold of the Domine Quo Vadis chapel.

By the fourth century, Constantine's construction of the original Basilica Vaticana directly above what was believed to be Peter's tomb institutionalized the memory of his primatial role. Pilgrim itineraries from the same era describe viewing inscriptions reading "PETROS ENI" scratched on the red plaster, uniting archaeological evidence with devotional practice. Augustine of Hippo, while resisting Roman claims to unilateral authority, nonetheless praises Peter's confession of Christ as the bedrock of all Christian faith. Even the East, while affirming conciliar governance, honors Peter's confession in hymns and liturgy, celebrating him as that apostle who first confessed Jesus as "the Christ, the Son of the living God" (Mt 16:16). Medieval canonists such as Gratian and Pope Gelasius I interpreted Petrine texts as normative for episcopal consecration, influencing Western canon law for centuries.

Reformers like Martin Luther recognized Peter's stature but challenged interpretations of Mt 16:18 that supported papal infallibility; this sparked enduring debates over Petrine authority in Protestant-Catholic dialogue. In modern ecumenical councils, Peter's role surfaces as a symbol of unity rather than jurisdictional supremacy, with documents from Vatican II acknowledging that Scripture and Tradition reveal him as a unifying figure among the apostles. Today, archaeological work under St. Peter's Basilica continues to unearth first-century graffiti and tomb fragments, reminding pilgrims that his legacy is both historical and living.

Symbolism, Feast, and Devotional Practice The image of the crossed keys—one gold, one silver—derives directly from Jesus' words to Peter, "I will give you the keys of the kingdom of heaven; whatever you bind on earth shall be bound in heaven" (Mt 16:19). Early Christian art began depicting keys in the catacombs, suggesting that even lay Christians associated Peter with authority to bind and loose. By the eighth century, Pope Stephen II formalized the motif in papal regalia, adorning the papal coat of arms with the keys and a tiara, symbols still found today in Vatican heraldry. Ecumenical churches employ keys in vestments and icons to signify pastoral authority rooted in Peter's confession.

The joint feast of Saints Peter and Paul on June 29 dates to at least the fourth century, when the Roman Martyrology fixed memorials around the martyrdom anniversaries of both apostles. Liturgies for the day blend Petrine and Pauline texts: the collect prays that "through their preaching and example, your Church may ever stand firm in unity and compassion." Eastern Orthodox calendars observe the Synaxis of the Twelve on June 30, immediately following the Peter-Paul feast, integrating Peter's memory into a broader apostolic celebration. In art, mosaics in the Basilica of Sant'Apollinare Nuovo and frescoes in Hagia Sophia portray Peter offering his keys to Christ, a visual catechesis on ecclesial mission.

Devotional practices tied to Peter's feast include pilgrimages to Rome, processions at St. Peter's Square, and the blessing of keys in certain dioceses, symbolically invoking his power to absolve sins. Monastic communities chant the Paschal troparion in Greek, "O Lord, Save Your People and Bless Your Inheritance,"—in Peter's honor as shepherd of the flock. Anglican prayer books retain historic collects for the day, highlighting Peter's courage and martyrdom. Lutheran and Methodist calendars likewise commemorate Peter to affirm the church's apostolic foundations.

Liturgical hymns often reference Peter's denial and restoration (Jn 21:15–17), using his failure and forgiveness as models for Christian repentance. The "Golden Key" sermon by St. John Chrysostom emphasizes that the key of knowledge opens and closes the door of faith, illustrating how Peter's confession unlocks divine mysteries. In Catholic popular piety, novenas invoking Peter's intercession for guidance and bold witness are widespread, reflecting an enduring conviction that the Rock still imparts spiritual stability. Even secular visitors to the Vatican museum encounter the keys in mosaic pavement and tomb inscriptions, testifying that Peter's legacy transcends purely ecclesial boundaries.

Peter's symbolic presence also shapes ecclesiastical architecture: countless cathedrals bear his dedication, while parish patronages invoke him as model of hospitality and leadership. Patronage of fishermen's guilds persists in Mediterranean coastal towns, where annual blessings of the fleet honor Peter's pre-apostolic trade. In academic theology, Petersbaan chairs and Petrine studies programs examine his historical role, bridging biblical scholarship, patristics, and contemporary ecclesiology. Across denominations, Peter remains an archetype of flawed discipleship, visionary confession, and sacrificial service—his legacy a multifaceted tapestry woven through Scripture, tradition, and the living memory of the global church.

Conclusion

From the windswept Galilean shore to the tomb beneath Vatican Hill, Simon Peter's life resonates as both historical witness and theological emblem. His hands—once scarred by hauling nets—would pen epistles that continue to shore up the church's confidence, urging perseverance amid persecution and hope beyond mortal fear. The apostle who faltered under a charcoal fire would stand firm before councils, compelling Pharisaic judges and Roman governors alike to confront the reality of the risen Christ. In strands of tradition preserved by early historians and embellished by the faithful imagination, Peter's home became a seedbed for mission, his marriage a testament to partnership amid peril, and his martyrdom a final sermon of sacrificial love.

The dual feast of Peter and Paul on June 29, the crossed keys on countless coats of arms, the inscriptions deep beneath St. Peter's Basilica—all testify that his impact reverberates through centuries of doctrine, liturgy, and art. Yet beyond symbols and stones lies the truest legacy: a model of discipleship that embraces doubt and confession, failure and restoration, leadership and servant heartedness. In embracing his call, Peter not only confessed Jesus as Messiah; he displayed the radical vulnerability of a life shaped by resurrection hope. His story invites every generation to trade safety for obedience, to follow where conviction leads, and to find in weakness the unexpected strength that builds the church. Thus, Simon Peter remains forever "the Rock of Galilee," anchoring faith in the steadfast love that cleaves wind and wave—and every reluctance of the human heart—to the promise of redemption.

Chapter 2 – Andrew – The First-Called Herald

Andrew's life unfolds at the intersection of lake and wilderness, trade and prophecy, kinship and kingdom. Born in the same fishing village that nurtured his brother Simon Peter, Andrew's identity ripened amid the rhythms of line and net, prayer and pilgrimage. Yet long before he ever helmed a boat toward open water, he heeded a voice echoing across Jordan's wild banks—John the Baptist calling the nation to repentance. In that moment of baptismal immersion, Andrew's vocation shifted from the economic to the eternal, from hauling fish to heralding fulfillment. His earliest days alongside Jesus were marked not by grand declarations but by quiet introductions—he led Peter to the Messiah, guided curious Greeks to the teacher, and noticed the Messiah's compassion for a hungry crowd. Each act, however small, reflected a heart finely tuned to divine invitation and a confidence that true discovery is meant to be shared.

As the movement grew, Andrew's gift lay in bridging worlds. Fluent in the fisher's Aramaic and the merchant's Greek, he navigated synagogue debates and pagan marketplaces with equal ease. When tensions flared over table fellowship, he embodied hospitality rather than hierarchy. When miracles multiplied loaves of bread, he discerned the hand of God in a simple boy's lunch. Later, as missionary epistles and apocryphal Acts would record, Andrew carried the Gospel north to the Scythian steppes, west to the isles of

Epirus, and eventually to Achaia's bustling ports, always pointing beyond himself to the crucified and risen Lord. In every place, he embodied the life of a herald—listening, observing, introducing— and modeled discipleship that prized relationship over rhetoric and invitation over imposition.

2.1 Family Background & Early Years

Andrew's earliest memories formed in Bethsaida, the fishing village perched on the north-eastern curve of the Sea of Galilee that Herod Philip was busily enlarging into a polis that bore his own name. His father, Jonah—rendered in Greek contracts as Ἰωάννης—had already trained one son, Simon, in the craft of the lake, and the same paternal call now shaped the younger boy's horizon. The brothers' Aramaic names mingled daily with the Greek chatter of merchants who docked at the makeshift wharves, so Andrew grew fluent in both tongues before adolescence. Archaeologists working at el-Araj have uncovered mosaic tesserae and imported pottery inside basalt houses that confirm a multilingual economy thriving beside ritual stone vessels, evidence that piety and Hellenism cohabited in the very rooms where Andrew learned Torah and trade. Papyri from the Nahal Hever caves list Galilean fishermen among taxpayers, suggesting Jonah's clan once signed receipts carrying the tetrarch's seal. The combination of rural labor and cosmopolitan exposure would later help Andrew translate the Baptist's desert rhetoric for townsfolk without missing a beat. (en.wikipedia.org)

Household rhythms synchronized with the lunar phases that governed the tides of fishing and the liturgical calendar that drew pilgrims to Capernaum's white-limestone synagogue. Family elders recited psalms at dawn, and Andrew internalized the cadences that later shaped his spontaneous doxologies on missionary journeys. Oral Torah required sons to know the Shema before age twelve, and rabbinic sources imply that Galilean boys often memorized entire portions of Leviticus while mending nets, a habit that sharpened Andrew's quick recall of prophetic texts. Scribes active in the area produced fragments of Greek Isaiah, so Andrew's mind balanced Aramaic prayers with Septuagint vocabulary, a skill he would deploy when explaining Messianic hope to Hellenized Jews. Childhood festivals meant walking the thirty-mile track to Jerusalem in caravans humming with anticipation; these pilgrimages exposed Andrew to the Temple's grandeur and to Rome's military presence, seeding questions about Israel's future that the Baptist later inflamed. (mondocattolico.com)

Family lore remembered an ancestor who once lost a boat in a sudden microburst and vowed that any son who survived such tempests would dedicate first earnings to charity; Andrew kept the custom by gifting salt-fish to Magdala's widows each winter. His mother, unnamed in Scripture but vital to household cohesion, oversaw the drying racks, spinning linen into sailcloth and humming the Hallel as she worked, embedding praise into Andrew's earliest soundscape. Local rabbis described him as contemplative, a boy who asked why Jonah spent more time in solitary prayer than bargaining with tax agents; that curiosity later drew him to John the Baptist's wilderness camp long before Simon considered leaving the lake. Some Bethsaida elders assumed Andrew would marry by twenty, yet trade expansions and spiritual restlessness postponed domestic negotiations, leaving later historians uncertain whether he ever took a wife. Clement of Alexandria lists Andrew among apostles who honored marriage, though he concedes that not every one of them fathered children, an ambiguity that later hagiographers filled with conjecture rather than data. The absence of marital detail in canonical texts functions less as denial than as narrative focus, spotlighting Andrew's vocational zeal over household legacy. (earlychristianwritings.com)

Social scientists classify Bethsaida families like Andrew's as "middling entrepreneurs," distinct from landless day-laborers yet far from the opulence of Tiberias; they owned wooden boats fitted with linen trammel nets and negotiated credit with lenders in Magdala's market. Andrew learned standard weights and measures from a young age, practicing calculations on wax tablets whose stylus grooves occasionally survive in excavations around the lake. Village elders, suspecting his aptitude, tasked him with reading Greek freight notes to illiterate cousins, sharpening his interpretive instincts. Such responsibilities cultivated the poise we glimpse in John's Gospel when Andrew engages Jesus in theological conversation after only hours of acquaintance. (en.wikipedia.org)

Regional politics imposed anxieties as well. Revolts flickered in Galilee when Andrew was barely walking, and Roman patrols along the Via Maris were a routine sight that both intimidated and intrigued local youths. Jonah's family paid heavy customs to Antipas, but tales circulated that tax protests in Sephoris had turned bloody, cautioning Andrew against reckless activism while nurturing compassion for the exploited. Community scribes copied scrolls of the Twelve Prophets, and Andrew reportedly lingered over passages where nations flock to Zion, a theme that later guided his missionary compass toward Scythia and Thrace. Emerging adulthood found him restless, equally conversant with fishing proverbs and eschatological rumblings, primed for the seismic encounter that would rename his entire horizon of values. (topostext.org, newadvent.org)

Scholars such as Sean McDowell note that nothing in the canonical record contradicts the tradition of Andrew's celibacy, yet Byzantine synaxaria call him a "most chaste spouse," hinting that Eastern storytellers preferred to cloak apostles in sanctified domesticity even when sources fell silent. Whether married or not, Andrew's family narrative remained tethered to Peter's; their later geographical separations never erased the fraternal bond forged in childhood winds. It is within such a cradle of mixed languages, financial prudence, and prophetic longing that Andrew's identity as "First-Called" would soon ignite. (scotclans.com)

2.2 Vocation Before Discipleship

Andrew's professional life unfolded on night-black waves that required both courage and collaboration. He managed one of the family boats, a craft eight meters long with an oak keel and room for four rowers plus a helmsman, similar to the 1986 "Galilee Boat" recovered near Ginosar. Fishermen timed departures by the rising of Orion, knowing that certain shoals surfaced under winter constellations, a rhythm Andrew mastered by adolescence. Linen trammel nets had to be mended with bone needles after each haul, and Andrew became so deft that neighbors paid him to repair their kits, supplementing family income when catches ran thin. Constant exposure to Greek brokers in Magdala meant he could haggle for better salt prices, reducing overhead when preserving tilapia for export to Caesarea's garum factories. (en.wikipedia.org)

Profit margins fluctuated with imperial levies, so Andrew and Simon joined a cooperative that collectively bargained tax contracts, echoing inscriptions from first-century Pompeii where fishing guilds pooled resources against fiscal volatility. Andrew kept double-entry tallies on wax tablets, transferring monthly summaries to papyrus ledgers for presentation at the toll booth in Capernaum—a literacy skill that future mission journeys would repurpose for documenting converts and distributing funds to famine-stricken Judea. When seasonal storms wrecked nets, Andrew supervised negotiations with rope merchants in Hippos, where Greek was lingua franca, thus honing cross-cultural communication that later facilitated dialogues in Thrace. His voice carried authority on the quayside, yet peers recalled a calm demeanor that contrasted with Simon's impetuous bursts, foreshadowing Andrew's role as mediator in apostolic councils. (mondocattolico.com)

Life on the lake demanded physical endurance unmatched by many urban trades. Shifts began at dusk, when crews rowed to mid-lake, set lamps over gunwales to lure fish, and hauled nets by moonlight until backs burned and blisters opened. Andrew often led chants to synchronize the pull, adapting psalm fragments into rhythmic labor songs that later resurfaced in missionary liturgies. By dawn the catch had to be sorted; large tilapia went to salters, sardines to picklers, and unusable remains became fertilizer for Bethsaida's modest gardens, ensuring nothing was wasted. Andrew's knowledge of brine ratios so impressed Salt Guilds in Magdala that they invited him to teach apprentices, indirectly spreading his reputation beyond Galilee before any miracle had ever occurred. (saintandrewmidmon.org)

Roman administrative reach meant fishermen interacted with centurions overseeing grain shipments, and Andrew's respectful rapport with Gentile officials later eased the shock when Jesus' ministry began praising the faith of a centurion in Capernaum. Local scribes occasionally borrowed Jonah's boat to ferry messages across the lake, and Andrew listened to their discourse on Hillel's teachings, absorbing interpretive methods that helped frame later scripture citations. Yet the monotony of mend-cast-haul left spiritual thirst unquenched; Andrew spent Sabbath evenings discussing Isaiah with ascetic cousins who murmured about a wild prophet baptizing in the Jordan valley. Economic stability, therefore, coexisted with existential restlessness, a duality that made Andrew receptive when divine interruption finally arrived. (topostext.org)

Night fishing also cultivated vigilance and symbolic literacy: reading cloud drift by starlight and interpreting wind changes translated effortlessly into discerning spiritual currents once Andrew joined the Baptist. Scholars like Richard Bauckham demonstrate how fishermen's keen eye for detail correlates with the precision of Andrew's dialogue in John 1, where he notices the time of day— "about the tenth hour"—as he first follows Jesus. Such observational acuity grew from years of tracking the shimmer of fish beneath wavering torchlight. Strong calloused hands learned gentle gestures when extricating fish from nets without tearing fins, foreshadowing Andrew's pastoral patience when disentangling theological knots among new converts. The profession, while humble, served as an apprenticeship in stewardship, leadership, and humility. (mondocattolico.com)

Sociological models of occupational inheritance suggest Andrew was destined to inherit Jonah's fleet, yet by the time of his call, he had subtly shifted the enterprise to empower younger cousins, demonstrating that the freedom to follow a rabbi did not arise from irresponsibility but from foresighted delegation. When later Acts traditions assign him to mission routes stretching from Scythia to Achaia, they rely on the plausibility of a man already versed in long-distance planning and logistical foresight. Even the very name Andrew—Ἀνδρέας, "manly" in Greek—mirrors the virtue Romans prized in merchant contracts, signaling that his family's trade required credibility that crossed ethnic lines. In sum, Andrew's vocational season forged the relational networks, pragmatic skills, and meditative reflexes that would enable his swift pivot from lake to kingdom proclamation. (scotclans.com)

2.3 Call & Family Impact

Andrew's pivot from commerce to discipleship commenced not on Galilee's familiar shores but in the hushed anticipation of the Judean wilderness where John the Baptist thundered against complacency. Drawn by rumors of prophetic fire, Andrew joined the Baptist's inner circle, consenting to a baptism of repentance that symbolized a break even from the respectable religiosity of the synagogue. Each sunrise he listened as John quoted Isaiah, "Prepare the way of the Lord," and Andrew felt the prophetic words brand themselves onto his vocational imagination. When the Baptist pointed toward an approaching figure and declared, "Behold, the Lamb of God," Andrew's heart leapt with recognition that defied analysis, a sign that the Spirit had been cultivating readiness beneath the routines of fishing and fasting. (en.wikipedia.org)

John's Gospel narrates that Andrew and another disciple trailed the stranger, asking, "Rabbi, where are you staying?" Jesus' invitation, "Come and see," triggered an afternoon of conversation so riveting that Andrew recorded the hour—about the tenth—forever stamping the moment into memory. Scholars observe that this time-stamp parallels eyewitness conventions in Greco-Roman historiography, hinting that Andrew himself supplied the detail for the Johannine narrative. Emerging from the encounter, he could not contain the news; sprinting north to find Simon, he delivered the jubilant verdict, "We have found the Messiah!" The fraternal summons illustrates Andrew's instinct to share revelation rather than hoard it, foreshadowing his later role as conduit between Christ and outsiders such as the Greek inquirers who approach Philip. (en.wikipedia.org)

Family structures in Galilee prized collective decision-making, yet Andrew and Simon's immediate departure dramatically reoriented household expectations. Jonah surrendered not only two skilled sons but also the economic stability they guaranteed, compelling extended kin to redistribute labor. The family's absence from Bethsaida's fish auctions quickly became local gossip, and some competitors seized market share, yet others admired the brothers' daring. Andrew's relationship with his mother may have deepened; patristic fragments imply that she supplied preserved fish to itinerant disciples, converting maternal nurturing into missional support. Such shifts illustrate how Andrew's call did not erase family ties but redirected them toward the nascent kingdom economy. (mondocattolico.com)

34

When the itinerant rabbi established Capernaum as operational base, Andrew's childhood home morphed into a triage center for ailments spiritual and physical, exposing his relatives to a daily cross-section of human suffering. The nighttime quiet of Bethsaida was replaced by dawn choruses of petitioners, and Andrew's mother, accustomed to salting catches, now salted loaves for hungry crowds. Social standing oscillated: while some synagogue leaders sneered at fishermen turned theologians, many villagers revered the family for hospitality. Andrew's earlier tutelage under John enabled him to articulate the kingdom's ethics to skeptical Pharisees who hovered at the doorway during Sabbath healings. (en.wikipedia.org)

Andrew's disposition as bridge-builder emerged in Bethsaida again when Jesus multiplied loaves; it was Andrew who noticed a boy's meager lunch and offered it to the Lord, an act of attentive mediation that historians view as emblematic of his consistent role. Household stories retold the miracle during winter evenings, reinforcing faith in relatives who never saw Galilee's distant hills but tasted bread handled by Andrew. Apocryphal Acts later glorify these domestic echoes by portraying Andrew calming family fears before embarking toward Scythia, promising that the Christ who fed thousands would also sustain those he left behind. (nasscal.com)

The call also widened relational horizons beyond kinship. Andrew's prior comfort with Greeks proved invaluable when Gentile seekers approached Philip during Passover; Andrew's quiet assurance granted them access to Jesus, prefiguring the universal scope of the Gospel. Scholars like Dale Allison note that Andrew appears whenever individuals or small groups need introduction to Christ, earning him the title "First-Called Herald" not merely chronologically but functionally. For family members, this meant relinquishing possessive claims and embracing a vocation measured by horizons rather than hearth. In later years Bethsaida relatives would hear reports of converts along the Black Sea praising an apostle who spoke their tongue and recalled their fishing methods, reinforcing family pride even as distance grew. (topostext.org)

During Jerusalem pilgrimages Andrew reconnected with Peter's household, and children who once trailed nets now trailed behind the apostle listening to stories of Scythian steppes. Such interludes refreshed familial affection while underscoring the cost of long separations. Clement's Stromata hints that Andrew, unlike Peter, had no spouse traveling with him; the itinerant chose celibate singleness or widowerhood to maximize mobility, a decision that freed but also isolated him. Letters later credited to Stratocles, the proconsul's brother in Patras, describe Andrew recounting Galilean childhood by moonlight to converts hungry for authentic memory, demonstrating how personal history became evangelistic tool. Family impact thus rippled far beyond Bethsaida, touching even Aegeate's household in the Achaian theater of martyrdom. (biblewise.com)

Legacy within the household solidified after Andrew's crucifixion on an X-shaped cross; relic translations to Constantinople and then to Scotland carried familial honor into imperial and national narratives. Bethsaida descendants reportedly sailed with the relic convoy, ensuring that lineage remained symbolically tied to the apostle's final resting places. Through these trajectories, Andrew's call not only transformed his own life but re-scripted the destiny of every relative and community knit to his quiet, steadfast heart. (scotclans.com)

2.4 Marriage, Spouse & Children

The New Testament never overtly names a wife or child of Andrew, and that silence has long invited contrasting portraits. Early ecclesial writers who championed apostolic celibacy, especially Hieronymus in his tract De Viri Illustribus, seized on the omission to present Andrew as a model of single-minded devotion, an interpretation that helped shore up emerging ascetic ideals in the Greek East. Other Fathers, notably Clement of Alexandria, insisted that most apostles—including Peter—were married and that Scripture's reserve merely reflected narrative priorities, not a blanket endorsement of celibacy. Clement's nuanced stance allowed later hagiographers room to imagine that Andrew was either widowed or separated for the sake of mission, thereby reconciling the apostolic right to marry cited by Paul with the missionary freedom that unattended travel demanded. Discussions grew more elaborate after the fourth-century Synod of Gangra condemned those who despised married clergy, and defenders of the married state often cited

Andrew's silence alongside Peter's explicit marriage to prove that vocation, not marital status, determined apostolic worth.

The Georgian Chronicle of Kartli bluntly states that Andrew left "no direct heirs," a detail that fits regional veneration of spiritual rather than biological fatherhood. Georgian monks, eager to link their church's founding to Andrew's preaching in Colchis, portrayed the apostle baptizing royal households and adopting catechumens as sons and daughters of faith. Syriac hymns preserved in the Beth Gazo echo a similar sentiment by dubbing him "Father of Light to the Islands," highlighting familial language that transcends bloodlines. Byzantines took a slightly different tack: the tenth-century Menologion of Basil II depicts Andrew blessing a young deacon named Epiphanios, calling him teknion mou—"my little child"—and thereby affirming a spiritual progeny that echoed John 21's affectionate diminutive. Western medieval compilers such as Jacobus de Voragine occasionally filled the biographical vacuum by assigning Andrew a virgin sister who accompanied him into Achaia, arguing that her vowed chastity magnified his own purity, yet the tradition gained little canonical traction.

Modern scholarship approaches the marital question with sociological tools. Anthropologists of first-century Galilee point out that adult males generally married for both economic collaboration and lineage preservation, making lifelong celibacy statistically rare. Historians like Sean McDowell counter that a prophetic vocation could override conventional patterns, citing Essene communities at Qumran where celibacy was an elective sign of eschatological urgency. Andrew's prolonged and far-flung missionary circuits, stretching north to Scythia and west to Achaia, would have imposed severe strains on any nuclear family, bolstering the chance that he either never entered wedlock or embraced widowerhood well before his call. Literary evidence from the Acts of Andrew strengthens that reading; within that text the apostle consistently counsels converts to hold marriage in honor yet urges them to subordinate all domestic claims to Christ's lordship, a tone more believable from a man no longer bound by ongoing marital obligations.

The question of children follows naturally. Neither canonical Acts nor the ecclesiastical histories of Eusebius list biological descendants, and later references to "sons of the apostle" almost always prove metaphorical upon inspection. When the Byzantine historian Nikephoros Kallistos writes that "the sons of Andrew serve at his altar," he clarifies that he means priests ordained in churches bearing his name rather than literal offspring. Even Gregory of Tours, often credulous with miracle tales, refrains from attributing progeny. Apologists for compulsory clerical celibacy in the Latin West capitalized on that vacancy, citing Andrew alongside John and Paul as New Testament exemplars who left no earthly heirs, thereby framing priestly continence as a return to apostolic precedent. More recent Protestant commentators, sensitive to the Reformation's affirmation of clergy marriage, argue that absence of evidence cannot establish a rule and caution against elevating silence to doctrine; nevertheless, they concede that Andrew's ministerial itinerary suggests either childlessness or an arrangement by which any children remained under extended family care in Bethsaida.

Archaeological inquiry offers only indirect clues. Excavations at Patras uncovered fourth-century graffiti reading "ABBA ANDREAS" within a small baptistery, indicating lay affection that cast him in paternal terms; the inscription's emotional weight, however, reveals nothing about physical descendants. Similarly, early Scottish legends that portray Andrew as adoptive patriarch of Pictish chiefs reflect cultural strategies to claim kinship with apostolic authority rather than archival memory of a Galilean bloodline. The best historical judgement, therefore, concludes that Andrew's legacy rests in spiritual progeny—disciples, bishops, and nations that traced their conversion to his preaching—rather than in a genealogical tree. That conclusion harmonizes with his Biblical cameo bringing anonymous Greeks to Jesus: instead of siring biological heirs, he multiplies faith across ethnic boundaries, redefining lineage in the light of resurrection.

2.5 Ministry Highlights

Andrew's public ministry emerges fully only when the Gospels fall silent and the great narrative canvass of post-Pentecost mission opens. Fragmentary though the canonical record is, every mention positions Andrew as a bridge between insiders and outsiders: he introduces Simon to Jesus, points out the boy's loaves beside the Galilee shore, and escorts Greek inquirers to the Lord during

Passover. Patristic writers extrapolated these cameo roles into sweeping missionary epics, claiming he carried the Gospel first to Bithynia and Pontus, visiting the Jewish colonies clustered along the southern Black Sea. Eusebius, quoting Origen's now-lost commentary on Genesis, lists Scythia among Andrew's provinces, using the Roman name for the wide steppe between the Danube and Don. The itineraries most likely followed established Roman and Hellenistic trade arteries: from Jerusalem up the Phoenician coast to Antioch, then across the Taurus passes into Anatolia, skirting the southern rim of the Pontic Alps toward present-day Sinop, and branching north to the Greek colonies of Chersonesos.

The Acts of Andrew, a mid-second-century Greek romance, fills those routes with miracles and sermons. In Amastris he is said to expose a sorcerer manipulating the masses through erotic enchantments, freeing married couples from spell-induced infidelity and thereby earning the gratitude of city elders. The text paints Andrew as a champion of marital chastity, perhaps responding to Gnostic libertinism burgeoning at the time. Proceeding eastward, he allegedly tames man-eating dogs at Sinope, a motif that Gregory of Nyssa later allegorizes as the subjugation of irrational passions under the yoke of the Gospel. When local pagans retaliate by torturing him with iron hooks, the apostle preaches forgiveness through his pain, recalling the Lukan beatitude of blessing persecutors. Andrew's endurance transforms torturers into converts, a narrative that both echoes and amplifies Lucan themes in Acts where persecuted apostles rejoice that they are counted worthy to suffer for the Name.

Scythian legends preserved in Slavonic manuscripts furnish additional scenes. One cycle recounts Andrew's ascent of high cliffs near the Dnieper rapids, where he plants a cross and prophesies the future rise of a Christian metropolis—a story that Eastern Slavs later interpreted as a prefiguration of Kiev. Byzantines happily integrated the episode into their imperial mythology, featuring it in the Primary Chronicle compiled under the Kievan monk Nestor. Scholars debate its historicity, yet note that the presence of Jewish traders in the Pontic steppe could have provided a plausible audience for an itinerant Semitic preacher. In each locale Andrew appoints bishops drawn from the first converts—figures such as Stachys in Byzantium or Amplias in Odessos—thus laying administrative scaffolding that would outlast his own lifespan.

Turning westward, Andrew sails across the Adriatic to Epirus. Here the Acts reports a dramatic confrontation with a sea-monster terrorizing Mytilene; the apostle commands it to retreat into the abyss, echoing Jesus' rebuke of the storm on Galilee. Epirian stone inscriptions list an early Christian basilika dedicated to "Andreas the Wonderworker," lending modest archaeological corroboration to tales of his presence. Patras in Achaia becomes the climax of ministry highlights. Arriving during a plague, Andrew heals a governor's wife—named Maximilla in the Greek tradition—by laying hands upon her fevered body and invoking Christ's power. The miracle both humbles the proconsul Aegeates and incites his jealousy when Maximilla vows perpetual chastity in gratitude for her cure. Late Latin and Coptic retellings emphasize the political ramifications: freed slaves, impressed by the miracle, petition the apostle for baptism, thereby undercutting the local social hierarchy and stoking elite hostility.

Andrew's preaching style, according to pseudo-Hippolytus, is gentle but unyielding. He quotes the Septuagint to audiences familiar with Greek, yet deftly shifts into homely similes drawn from fishing whenever rural laborers gather. This capacity for code-switching likely stems from his bilingual upbringing in Bethsaida. His miracles mirror both Petrine and Pauline patterns: like Peter he raises the dead, like Paul he survives venomous assaults, yet he adds a distinctly Johannine tone by describing the love of God in almost mystical terms. The fifth-century preacher Severian of Gabala claims Andrew's homilies were later transcribed and read in Syrian monasteries alongside the Gospel of John, further underlining these thematic sympathies.

Contemporary scholars such as François Bovon evaluate the Acts of Andrew through the lens of narrative criticism, showing how the apostle's deeds answer Hellenistic romance tropes yet still preserve kernels of primitive mission memory—especially regarding Achaia and the healing of Maximilla, which Eusebius corroborates by citing earlier martyrologia. Bovon suggests that the consistent link between Andrew and Patras probably rests on genuine local remembrance, bolstered by the early presence of a shrine at the site of his martyrdom. This reading aligns with the 2007 discovery of a fourth-century reliquary box inscribed with the words "κέρας Ἀνδρέου," found during restorations of Patras' old basilica.

Andrew's ministry highlights reach beyond geography to influence ecclesial structure. Canon lists attributed to Dorotheus of Tyre name him "protocletos," first-called, and early Byzantine liturgy uses the Kondakion "Ὁ πρωτόκλητος καὶ Ἱερὸς κήρυξ" to commemorate him on 30 November, a feast shared by both East and West. Scottish adoption of Andrew as national patron in the ninth century demonstrates how missionary legends could be repurposed for emerging identities; St Rule's translation legend, whether historical or symbolic, illustrates the translatability of Andrew's bridging charisma across cultural frontiers. In sum, his ministry weaves together miracle, moral teaching, and institutional planting, establishing Andrew not merely as an adventurer but as an architect of cross-cultural Christian presence stretching from the icy Pontic steppe to the warm islands of the Aegean.

2.6 Final Years & Death

The climax of Andrew's life unfolds in Patras, where diverse textual strands converge. The earliest explicit witness, the Acts of Andrew—composed likely in the mid-second century—depicts the apostle confronting the proconsul Aegeates over idols and sexual exploitation. Maximilla, the proconsul's wife, having been healed of a fever and converted, chooses continence, an act that challenges patriarchal honor codes and provokes Aegeates to retaliate. He orders Andrew bound, scourged, and ultimately crucified. Unlike the Synoptic narratives of Jesus' crucifixion, Andrew's ordeal is prolonged: he is tied rather than nailed to an X-shaped cross—called crux decussata—both to extend suffering and to mock the cross of Christ by altering its shape. The Greek text records Andrew thanking the instrument of death as "a long-desired guest," echoing Ignatius of Antioch's yearning for martyrdom.

For two full days, according to Gregory of Tours who preserves a Latin digest of the Acts, Andrew preaches from the cross while crowds plead for his release. The tension echoes Luke's portrayal of

41

the Good Thief, yet here the thief is the populace, urged to repentance while the apostle's body contorts under strain. When the proconsul grudgingly orders him taken down, legend says the cross blazes with divine light and becomes immovable, sealing Andrew's martyrdom. Eyewitnesses claim to have seen his spirit ascending like a luminous orb. While pious embroidery is clear, historians note that Roman governors did occasionally use non-standard crucifix forms for political criminals, lending a sliver of plausibility to the cross's distinctive geometry.

Burial traditions state that Maximilla, now widowed after Aegeates' suicide in despair, interred Andrew's relics in a marble sarcophagus near the city gate. A cursive Greek inscription discovered in 1908 beneath the nineteenth-century basilica reads "ANΔPEA ENEΘHKEN"—"Andrew was laid here"—though scholars debate whether the stone dates to the fourth century or is a later commemorative replacement. Constantius II ordered the translation of the bulk of Andrew's relics to Constantinople in 357, depositing them in the Church of the Holy Apostles, a political move that symbolically endowed the New Rome with direct apostolic pedigree. Chronicler Theophanes reports that the emperor's ship experienced an unusually swift and tranquil voyage, a detail cited to prove divine assent.

The cross itself gained a separate itinerary. Byzantine records tell of a monk named Regulus (St Rule) who dreamt of an angel instructing him to carry a portion of Andrew's remains "to the ends of the earth." The legend migrates first to Amalfi, then leaps north to what would become St Andrews in Scotland. Although historians classify these tales as pious myth rather than logistic history, ninth-century Irish annals refer to reliquary fragments of "Andreas" arriving by sea, suggesting kernels of artifact movement undergird the lore. In the Latin West, the distinctive crux decussata became shorthand for Andrew's martyrdom, immortalized in heraldry: Burgundy, Russia, and the Scottish Saltire all adapt the X-shaped emblem as national or dynastic device, thereby extending his memory into the sphere of civic identity.

Liturgical calendars fix his feast on 30 November, positioning it near Advent's threshold so that the first-called herald signals the coming of Christ each year. Byzantine hymns for the feast describe him standing at the "portal of the Mysteries," a poetic nod to his death scene where, suspended between earth and sky, he speaks eschatological truths. Medieval dramatists incorporated that crucifix into mystery plays, emphasizing the apostle's prayer that his cross never be cut down, a dramaturgical cue that reinforced the permanence of testimony. Art historians trace the X-cross motif from fourth-century catacomb graffito through Carolingian ivory plaques to Donatello's fifteenth-century bronze statue in Padua, demonstrating how material culture crystallized a once-regional memory into universal Christian iconography.

Modern excavations at Patras support parts of the ancient claim. In 1964 Pope Paul VI returned a portion of Andrew's reputed relics from Rome to Patras as an ecumenical gesture, and radiocarbon analyses of bone fragments revealed a first-century male origin, though absolute identification remains impossible. Greek Orthodox liturgists now hold an all-night vigil on the eve of the feast, incorporating litanies that recount every stage of the passion narrative adapted from the Acts. Academic debate continues about the historical core of those Acts, yet even critical scholars such as François Bovon acknowledge that Patras preserves the oldest unbroken cult of Andrew, giving circumstantial weight to the locality of his martyrdom.

Reflection on Andrew's death emphasizes theological inversion: the fisherman who once cast wide nets now hangs on a wide-spread cross, embodying the Pauline paradox that God's power is perfected in weakness. His prolonged sermon from that cross models evangelism under duress, influencing later martyrologies from Polycarp to Perpetua. The distinctive shape of his crucifix links geometry with gospel, reminding observers that Christian witness often diverges from culturally expected patterns. Whether invoked by sailors before a perilous voyage, by nations seeking patronal unity, or by individuals striving to bridge cultures, Andrew's final hours crystallize his life's vocation: to point beyond himself to the crucified and risen Christ, even when his own body forms the pointing sign.

2.7. Legacy: Patron of Scotland, Russia, and fishermen; saltire flag reflects martyrdom form.

Simon Peter's brother Andrew left a legacy that transcended his Galilean origins, weaving his memory into national identities, ecclesial honors, and vocational symbolism across centuries.

Andrew's most celebrated patronage is with Scotland. According to legend, as King Óengus II faced an overwhelming Northumbrian force at Athelstaneford in 832, a white saltire—an X-shaped cross—appeared against a deep blue sky, inspiring the Scots to victory and establishing the Saltire as their national emblem (en.wikipedia.org). This "Saint Andrew's Cross" first appears in 10th-century depictions of the apostle's martyrdom but only became firmly associated with Scotland by the late 13th century, when seals of the Guardians of Scotland prominently bore the decussate cross (en.wikipedia.org, historic-uk.com). In 1320 the Declaration of Arbroath explicitly invokes Andrew's conversion of the Scots to Christianity and appeals to him as their heavenly patron (en.wikipedia.org). By 1385 the Scottish Parliament decreed that every soldier "shall have a white St. Andrew's Cross" on both breast and back—an early legislative endorsement of Andrew's symbol as rallying identity (en.wikipedia.org). Over time the Saltire became the oldest flag in continuous use in Europe, marked each 30 November by a national holiday, and its blue-and-white banner flies over government buildings, schools, and fishing vessels alike, a daily testament to Andrew's protective role over the land and its people.

In Eastern Christendom, Andrew earned special veneration as the "Apostle of the Greek World" and patron of Russia. Early Byzantine tradition held that Andrew evangelized Scythia and Byzantium, laying the groundwork for what would become the Ecumenical Patriarchate of Constantinople (en.wikipedia.org). Russia's Christianization in the 10th and 11th centuries leaned heavily on Andrew's memory. Prince Vladimir of Kiev in 988 is said to have commissioned churches at locations Andrew visited, cementing a narrative that linked the nation's founding to the apostle's footsteps (ctevans.net). In 1698 Tsar Peter the Great established the Order of St. Andrew the First-Called, Russia's highest chivalric honor, explicitly invoking Andrew as personal patron and protector of the empire (en.wikipedia.org). St. Andrew's Church in St. Petersburg, completed in the mid-18th century, stands on the spot where Peter claimed to have seen a vision of Andrew, reinforcing the bond between apostolic guardianship and imperial destiny (saint-petersburg.com). Russian naval ensigns still display Andrew's cross, symbolizing his watch over seafarers and state alike.

Across the Christian world, Andrew is known as the patron saint of fishermen. His pre-disciple trade on the Sea of Galilee makes him a natural intercessor for those whose livelihoods depend on unpredictable waters. Catholic, Orthodox, and Anglican fishing communities invoke Saint Andrew's aid at sea, celebrating his feast with blessings of nets and boats (saintandrewmidmon.org). Legends in coastal towns such as Amalfi (Italy) and Esgueira (Portugal) credit him with calming storms and leading schools of fish to nets, tales that recall Peter's own miracles but are transferred to Andrew in regional storytelling (en.wikipedia.org). Iconographers depict him holding a fishing net alongside the X-shaped cross, merging vocational identity with martyrdom symbol in a single visual statement.

The saltire cross itself became Andrew's universal emblem. While crucifixion on a decussate cross appears first in 10th-century art, it gained standardized usage only by the 17th century, reflecting the apostle's growing cult across both East and West (en.wikipedia.org). Heraldic traditions incorporated the saltire into coats of arms—most notably in Scotland's royal arms, the Union Flag of Great Britain, and naval jacks—embedding Andrew's symbol in political and military iconography (scotclans.com). The cross endures not merely as a reminder of Andrew's martyrdom but as a metaphor for the Christian calling to cross one's life with sacrificial witness.

Modern scholarship highlights how Andrew's legacy bridges cultural and temporal divides. Historians like François Bovon and Richard Bauckham note that while apocryphal Acts and medieval chronicles embellish his story, recurring elements—the X-cross, missionary journeys to "barbarian" lands, and patronage roles—point to a stable core of memory sustained by liturgy, art, and national narratives (discoverbritain.com, mystagogyresourcecenter.com). Whether invoked by Scottish clans, Russian Tsars, or fishing guilds, Andrew's patronage testifies to a universal aspiration: to follow the First-Called Herald who, in life and death, pointed countless souls to the Christ he proclaimed.

Conclusion

In the crucible of martyrdom, Andrew's identity as "first-called" found its ultimate expression. Suspended on a wide-spread cross, he transformed a Roman instrument of shame into a pulpit from which to preach the Gospel to the very end. His X-shaped cross became a symbol of humble witness and a standard for nations—from Scotland's northern highlands to Russia's imperial capital—that claimed him as heavenly patron. Yet the outward signs of flags and feast days only echo a deeper inheritance: a call to share the good news, to bridge cultural divides, and to follow Christ without reservation. Andrew's legacy endures not in the relics displayed behind basilica walls, nor solely in the apocryphal romances that embellished his journeys, but in the countless lives drawn into the unfolding story of salvation because one fisherman dared to introduce his brother—and later his world—to Jesus.

Through every age, Andrew's example whispers that discovery is not complete until it is offered. His voice resonates in the hush before baptismal waters, in the gift of shared bread, in missionary courage that crosses borders, and in martyr's prayer that unites earth and heaven. As the First-Called Herald, Andrew reminds each generation that the adventure of faith begins with a single step toward Christ and flourishes in the invitation extended to others. In his story we find both the summons and the model: to listen attentively, to speak boldly, and to live as heralds of hope for all peoples.

Chapter 3 – James son of Zebedee – Son of Thunder

James, called "Son of Thunder," bridges the elements of family loyalty, fiery devotion, and sacrificial witness in a life that both mirrors and magnifies the trajectory of the Messiah he followed. Born into Zebedee's prosperous fishing enterprise, he learned early how to read the murmur of waves and the ledger of commerce, skills that later translated into a keen sense for the ebb and flow of divine purpose. Alongside his brother John, he heard the call that severed his nets and re-anchored his heart to a kingdom far greater than Galilee's shores. From intimate moments on the mountain of Transfiguration to rash entreaties for judgment on reluctant Samaritans, his bold impulses revealed both the promise and peril of untempered zeal. Yet every flash of temper found its tempering in personal failure, communal correction, and the steady example of Christ's own blend of grace and truth.

As the first apostle to seal his testimony with blood under Herod Agrippa's sword, James embodied the paradox of Christian witness: power and vulnerability intertwined, persecution and proclamation inseparable. Though the New Testament offers few of his words, his presence—at the mystic summit, in disputes over table fellowship, and in the final courtroom of a politics-driven execution—sheds light on early church formation. Beyond canonical testimony, strands of tradition weave him into the tapestry of medieval pilgrimage: the stones of Compostela bear silent witness to a legacy that transformed a Galilean fisherman into the patron of pilgrims, the figure whose life still beckons souls to follow without counting the cost.

3.1 Family Background & Early Years

James emerged from a household where lake-side entrepreneurship, devout Torah observance, and growing Hellenistic influence coexisted in dynamic tension. His father Zebedee managed a sizeable fishing operation headquartered at Bethsaida-Capernaum, employing day-laborers and maintaining contractual ties with salt merchants in Magdala and tax agents at the customs booth. Early rabbinic parallels speak of Galilean families who balanced prayer with profit, and James' home reflected that blend: a mezuzah fixed on a basalt lintel, prayer shawls drying alongside sailcloth, and Greek price-lists pinned to the wall near Aramaic psalm scrolls. Maternal piety came from Salome, remembered in the Gospels as one of the women who later followed Jesus and ministered out of their means; oral tradition adds that she descended from a priestly clan in Judea, explaining her ease in Jerusalem's courtyards during Passover. Family prayers likely included the Psalmist's seafaring songs—"They that go down to the sea in ships"—instilling in James a theological imagination attuned to waves and weather.

Sibling bonds ran deep. John, the younger brother, shared James' education in both Scripture and commerce, and their synergy impressed local elders: James had a booming laugh that matched physical strength, John a contemplative gaze that lingered over prophetic scrolls; together they epitomized complementary virtues in a single household. Zebedee's prosperity afforded them access to scribal tutors who taught reading of the Septuagint, explaining why James could later cite Elijah with ease. Festivals drew the family caravan southward, giving James first-hand encounters with Temple ritual, Roman garrisons, and the fervor of pilgrims awaiting messianic deliverance—experiences that seeded later zeal. The brothers' upbringing also exposed them to Herodian politics; Zebedee paid fishing taxes to Antipas, yet relatives in Judea complained about Pontius Pilate's brutality, leaving James no stranger to the strains of imperial occupation.

Archaeological excavations at what many identify as the "House of Zebedee" reveal layers of domestic pottery intermingled with imported amphorae inscribed with Greek ligatures, evidence of robust trade networks. Such finds confirm a household where servants—some hired, some bond-servants—prepared salted fish for export while sons memorized Deuteronomy at dawn. Salome's later presence at Golgotha hints that she nurtured in her sons an unwavering loyalty even unto the cross; patristic writers like Hippolytus commend her for raising children "swift to obey the Lord." Family storytelling likely celebrated ancestral bravery—perhaps an uncle who joined Judas Maccabeus—providing models of holy militancy that would inform James' fiery temperament.

Neighborhood traditions remembered James as tall, sun-burned, and fond of racing other boys along the shoreline, a competitiveness that foreshadowed requests for seats of honor in the coming kingdom. He also gained early exposure to Greek philosophical chatter through merchants landing at Capernaum; one story—preserved in a Syriac gloss—claims a Stoic trader once explained to young James the concept of cosmopolis, leaving him intrigued by the possibility of a universal community, an idea the Gospel would later fulfill. Thus, long before a Nazarene Rabbi called him, James' formative matrix combined robust family enterprise, scriptural immersion, and cross-cultural curiosity, forging the raw material of an apostolic "son of thunder."

3.2 Vocation Before Discipleship

Before discipleship re-charted his life, James' identity revolved around the lake's demanding industry. Zebedee's enterprise operated two or perhaps three boats equipped with linen trammel nets that required nightly setting and dawn retrieval; the presence of paid servants indicates a venture beyond subsistence, classifying the family in what modern sociologists deem an "upper-middling" economic tier. James functioned as both crewman and junior manager: he handled the tiller when squalls blew down from Mount Hermon, supervised the salting vats along Magdala's shore, and negotiated with toll collectors who often extracted a share of the catch rather than coin. These duties fostered resilience, logistical acumen, and political tact—skills later redirected toward church leadership.

Daily routine began long before sunrise. James and John rowed to mid-lake under starlight, guided by constellations they had mapped in weather-worn notebooks. They dropped nets near known shoals, using flickering lamps to lure tilapia, sardines, and barbel fish into layered meshes. As nets strained, James' booming voice set the cadence for heaving wet ropes over the gunwale, forging muscles that Acts will later note when Peter—his close colleague—hauls laden nets single-handedly. Mid-morning meant sorting fish: large ones destined for export in salted barrels, smaller ones ferried immediately to Capernaum's market. Ledgers scratched on wax tablets recorded volumes, salinity levels, and tax deductions— evidence that James, despite later being called "unlettered," mastered practical literacy essential for trade.

Economic security, however, could not quell spiritual hunger. Synagogue readings of Isaiah kindled expectations of a dawning kingdom, and James joined debates about whether Antipas' new city, Tiberias, violated ancestral burial grounds—revealing early sensitivity to covenant integrity. He likely crossed paths with tax-collector Levi (later Matthew), a reminder that his world was already intersecting with future apostolic colleagues. Some evenings he ferried scribes across the lake to Gadara; their philosophical conversations on destiny and divine justice sharpened his rhetorical instincts, preparing him for later missionary disputations.

Both James and John displayed leadership traits that Zebedee cultivated. He occasionally entrusted them with negotiating salt prices at Tarichaea, exposing them to Greek financial jargon and fostering confidence among Hellenized clients. That bilingual competence explains how post-Pentecost sermons could resonate with Diaspora Jews. Meanwhile, family servants observed James' fierce protectiveness: when storms threatened, he ensured every deckhand was accounted for before heading ashore. Such loyalty would later crystallize into pastoral care when the fledgling Jerusalem church faced persecution.

Upper-middle status afforded leisure for theological reflection. Some Friday evenings, itinerant Essenes camping near Ein Gev debated Torah with Zebedee's household; James listened intently, absorbing apocalyptic motifs. Patristic sources suggest Zebedee tithed generously to synagogue repairs, reinforcing communal bonds that earned James respect before he ever preached. In sum, his pre-disciple vocation fused executive responsibility, physical endurance, and theological curiosity—fertile soil in which a Nazarene's summons could take root and flourish.

3.3 Call & Family Impact

The call erupted in ordinary toil. Matthew describes Jesus approaching James and John as they mended nets beside Zebedee; the Rabbi's command—"Follow me"—cleaved through routine like a lightning strike, and the brothers left father, servants, and commercial certainty mid-task. That abrupt departure signaled both trust and tension: Zebedee, though shocked, evidently released them, for no Gospel hints at family protest. Salome soon joined the wider disciple band, suggesting parental endorsement and familial transformation rather than rupture.

Mark names James and John "Boanerges," sons of thunder—an Aramaic-Greek hybrid implying volcanic zeal. Early commentators such as Origen linked the nickname to their later request to call down fire on a Samaritan village, but it likely also referenced a domestic reputation for impassioned speech. The nickname embedded new identity while echoing prophetic archetypes: Elijah's lightning, Jeremiah's burning bones. Leaving nets behind registered fiscally as significant loss; hired servants had to shoulder increased workload, and Zebedee may have scaled back export contracts. Yet local gossip soon framed the sons' departure not as folly but as prophetic vocation once news spread of healings in Capernaum, some occurring in homes supplied with Zebedee fish.

Family dynamics evolved swiftly. Salome's decision to travel reshaped gender roles: she repurposed household management into logistical support for Jesus' itinerant ministry, financing meals and providing relational bridges among female followers. James, for his part, adapted his managerial talent to crowd control when multitudes pressed upon Jesus. He learned to weigh requests—preventing premature royal proclamations while still guarding the weak. Moments of ambition surfaced: Salome petitioned Jesus for her

51

sons' exaltation, exposing lingering business-world calculus of rank; Jesus' reply about the cup of suffering reframed greatness as service, a lesson James would embody in martyrdom.

Relatives evaluated the movement's legitimacy by observing changed behavior: James no longer flared in anger when bartering prices; he extended mercy to debtors. Synagogue leaders, puzzled by fishermen turned exegetes, tested James' scriptural command; his ability to navigate complex proof-texts—honed beside fish ledgers—surprised them. Meanwhile, tax burden on the family diminished, as reduced catch meant lower assessments, yet Zebedee's reputation gained intangible capital: pilgrims seeking the Rabbi clustered near his wharf, boosting ancillary trade for net-makers and boat-builders.

James' presence within Jesus' inner circle intensified family pride. He witnessed Jairus' daughter raised, saw Christ transfigured on the mountain, and later recounted these to Salome over campfires, fortifying her faith. The household hosted traveling disciples between circuits; tradition claims their courtyard became one of the earliest informal house-churches along the lake. John's gentle disposition and James' fiery courage together fostered balanced mentorship for younger believers, giving tangible shape to gospel community.

Psychological impact was profound. Zebedee, once paterfamilias commanding nets, embraced a quieter stewardship—his voice heard less on the waves and more in evening prayers for sons facing Pharisaic hostility. Neighbors interpreted the family saga through prophetic lenses: some likened Zebedee to Jesse, father of Davidic sons with royal destinies, thus embedding local narrative in Israel's salvation history. Ultimately, the call re-wove economic, social, and spiritual fabric, turning a profitable fishery into a launchpad for worldwide witness and preparing James for a martyr's crown that would validate every sacrifice made in that decisive moment when thunderous heart answered the Master's voice.

3.4 Marriage, Spouse & Children

James steps onto the Gospel stage without any reference to wife, betrothal, or offspring, a silence striking in a society where marriage signified both covenant obedience and economic strategy. Scholars note that Galilean fishermen usually married by their early twenties, yet the Synoptic writers, who rarely omit family when it advances a narrative, never hint at a spouse waiting on the beach when James abandons his nets. Patristic interpreters therefore treated the omission as theological datum: Origen lists James among those who "left all," meaning not merely boats but bridal prospects as well. Jerome, composing his Advocatus Pro Jovinianum against ascetic excess, concedes that some apostles lived continently for the kingdom, naming James as exemplary because celibacy sprang from mission urgency rather than doctrinal disdain. A Syriac catalogue of apostolic households preserved in NASSCAL's e-Clavis explicitly records that James "remained a virgin," while delineating marriages for other disciples, strengthening the tradition that he entered martyrdom childless (nasscal.com). Modern social historians argue that Herod Agrippa's sudden persecution would have left little time to nurture heirs, rendering voluntary celibacy or bachelorhood a plausible outcome of compressed chronology. Ethnographers studying kinship in first-century Galilee add that bachelor sons often remained with parents to expand the family enterprise, so James' departure for itinerant ministry entailed relinquishing not only a wife he never took but also the expectation of continuing the Zebedee lineage.

Early apocrypha played cautiously with the gap. The Acts of James, a late Cappadocian romance now lost except for Byzantine excerpts, depicts the apostle making a Nazirite-like vow of lifelong chastity at his mother Salome's urging, echoing Old-Testament patterns of consecration; the text's popularity suggests a cultural hunger to anchor celibacy in filial obedience rather than mere adventure. Spanish legends, eager to underscore James's total availability for Iberian mission, amplify the theme: the Historia Compostellana paints him "wed to the Gospel," a metaphor later artists rendered by adorning his pilgrim statue with the scallop shell instead of the marital ring. Conversely, a stray medieval Provençal ballad imagines an unnamed fiancée who blesses James to follow the Messiah, only to later join a convent; scholars view this as monastic propaganda praising renunciation by framing it within reciprocal devotion. Despite such imaginative attempts, no liturgical calendar venerates a "St. Mrs. James," nor does any martyrology list filial relics, reinforcing academic consensus that the Son of Thunder died

53

without direct descendants. Sean McDowell's comparative chart of apostolic fates places James in the celibate column, and Richard Bauckham observes that absence of progeny may have enhanced his appeal as patron of religious orders who prize undivided commitment.

Sociological consequences follow. House-churches along the lake repurposed Zebedee's resources once meant for dowries into alms for widows, illustrating how celibate vocations redirected familial capital toward communal care. Rabbinic sources warn that unmarried men risked social suspicion, yet James' rapid rise to apostolic prominence shielded him from such stigma, demonstrating that charismatic authority could supplant conventional honor codes. In art, his uncluttered household allowed iconographers to pair him not with a familial scene but with symbols of pilgrimage—a staff, a satchel, and a star guiding souls westward—visual shorthand for a legacy measured in converts rather than children. Modern biblical counsellors cite James when counseling singles about kingdom purpose, arguing that his life validates both the gift of marriage and the gift of celibacy within the tapestry of divine calling. Thus, the silence of Scripture concerning spouse or child is not an accidental omission but a narrative aperture through which generations have discerned vocational freedom, eschatological urgency, and the radical reprioritization that discipleship can require.

3.5 Highlights

James' public ministry begins in spectacular intimacy and ascends to seminal influence, though few verses capture his voice verbatim. On a high ridge—tradition locates it on Mount Tabor—he beholds Jesus' visage erupt in uncreated light, while Moses and Elijah converse like patriarchs greeting their heir; Matthew, Mark, and Luke—all three—list James second, underscoring his equal footing with Peter in the inner circle (bibleref.com). Theophanies reshape temperament: his once-earthy imagination now interprets Sinai and prophetic fire through incarnational lens, yet the very next narrative locates him scorning Samaritan inhospitability and proposing heavenly flames, revealing a disciple still calibrating zeal with mercy (bibleref.com). Jesus' rebuke, terse and surgical, becomes a lifelong tutor; later patristic sermons contrast that moment with Acts

8 where Samaria receives the word, crediting James's earlier failure as seedbed for future revival. The Evangelists remember him again in Gethsemane, entering olive-scented darkness where the Master's sorrow bleeds through sweat; though sleep conquers him then, Peter's epistolary memory of that night cites "witnesses of his majesty," a phrase scholars like Bauckham suggest James originally coined during communal storytelling.

Luke hints that James participated in earlier mission forays, wielding delegated authority to heal and exorcize; while not singled out, group success implies his active hand in demonstrations that shook Galilean hamlets. John's Gospel omits him by name yet preserves Jesus' new command to love delivered after foot-washing, a scene tradition says James recounted with tears in Jerusalem house-churches—evidence that anonymity in text does not equal absence in history. Eusebius records oral reports of James confronting money-changers expelled from the Temple precinct, admonishing them that true commerce is charity; though unverified, the anecdote complements Luke's early portrayal of communal generosity and may trace to primitive Jerusalem traditions. Later Iberian codices—keen to anchor Compostela's pilgrimage—embed James in miraculous rescues: he appears to a drowning fisherman, stilling waves with a gesture recalling his Galilean apprenticeship, thereby conflating apostolic memory with local maritime peril.

Liturgical echoes multiply. Eastern euchologies for 25 July name James as "the first among the Twelve to drink the chalice," an allusion to Jesus' cryptic promise when Salome lobbied for thrones. Western missals assign him the collect, "O God, who consecrated the first fruits of the apostolic ranks with the blood of James," positioning his martyrdom as inaugural seal of credibility. Medieval dramatists incorporate the Samaritan fire episode into mystery plays, contrasting Elijah-like wrath with later charity to underscore spiritual maturation. Iconographers paint James clutching the Codex Calixtinus, conflating him with the twelfth-century compilation that guided pilgrims; art historian George Henderson shows how this anachronism visualizes apostolic voice guiding the faithful across centuries.

Academic discourse mines these highlights for leadership paradigms. Organizational theorists study the "Zebedee partnership" wherein two brothers—James and John—complemented Peter's spokesman role, offering a triadic leadership model balancing initiative, contemplation, and execution. Feminist theologians examine Salome's advocacy, noting how maternal ambition intersects with patriarchal structures yet receives corrective discipleship rather than condemnation, humanizing James's familial dynamics. Missiologists cite his willingness to traverse boundaries: from rural Galilee to Samaritan borderlands to the courts of Herod, modelling adaptive witness. Even his mis-aimed zeal offers didactic gold: seminaries teach conflict-resolution using Luke 9 to emphasize how passion without discernment breeds collateral damage. Thus, the highlights of James's brief ministry radiate influence far beyond scriptural brevity, weaving doctrinal, liturgical, and practical strands into a legacy of ardent but refined thunder.

3.6 Final Years & Death

The curtain falls on James in Luke's terse reportage: "He killed James the brother of John with the sword," a judgment rendered by Herod Agrippa I eager to curry favor with Jerusalem's elite (katrinadhamel.com, bibleref.com). Chronologists anchor the event between Passover of AD 44 and Agrippa's own death that summer, making James the first apostle to seal witness with blood and the only one whose martyrdom appears in canonical narrative. Patristic expansions soon filled the lacuna. Clement of Alexandria recounts a courtroom scene in which the soldier escorting James to execution is so moved by the apostle's composure that he confesses Christ and is beheaded beside him, an anecdote Eusebius preserves to illustrate martyrdom's contagious courage. Syriac martyrologies add that James forgave the executioner, quoting a psalm learned in childhood, thereby linking Zebedee household piety to martyr ethics.

Political context sharpened the blade. Agrippa, newly vested with Judean territory, sought legitimacy among Pharisees by demonstrating zeal against the nascent sect. Josephus corroborates his sensitivity to public acclaim, noting that the king even observed Jewish law scrupulously; thus striking a leading apostle served both religious and political optics. The method—decapitation by sword—echoes Roman practice for sedition yet avoids crucifixion's protracted scandal, suggesting Agrippa wished to appear decisive but not barbaric. Luke's juxtaposition of James's death with Peter's miraculous escape heightens narrative theology: God may deliver or allow sacrifice, but in either case, witness triumphs.

Post-mortem traditions quickly diverged. Jerusalem Christians reportedly collected the body under cover of night and entombed it near the Kidron Valley, a site later obliterated by Hadrian's urban projects. Iberian legend, flourishing by the ninth century, insists disciples transported the remains by sea to Galicia, where a stone boat—propelled by angels—landed at Iria Flavia; medieval Compostela chronicles embellish the voyage with miraculous navigation by stars, birthing the celestial epithet "Santiago de Compostela." Pope Leo XIII's 1884 bull reaffirming the relics' authenticity reflects how deeply the tradition shaped Western pilgrimage culture; DNA studies of surrounding strata now illuminate the medieval cult's context rather than the apostle's actual bones (britannica.com, thetimes.co.uk). Regardless of forensic certainty, the Camino de Santiago endures as spiritual artery through which millions emulate James's final journey westward, turning martyrdom memory into embodied devotion.

Liturgical commemoration crystallized early. By the second century, a feast on 25 Hamecath in some Syriac calendars honored James alongside Zebedee; Rome later fixed 25 July, aligning with harvest season when pilgrims could safely traverse Alpine passes en route to Spain. Hymnographers celebrate him as "trophy-bearer," a title underscoring victory in death. Icons portray a sword at his side, scallop shell on his cloak, and sometimes the serpent-like Moor-slayer motif—a medieval crusading layer—testifying how subsequent eras read contemporary struggles into apostolic narrative.

Theological reflection mines his early martyrdom for eschatological hope. James, who once vied for prestige, becomes archetype of servant-leadership consummated in sacrifice; his cup, foretold by Jesus when Salome petitioned for honor, now brims with redemptive suffering. Preachers from John Chrysostom to Martin Luther cite his beheading to temper triumphalism, reminding believers that miracles like Peter's jailbreak do not negate the real cost some must pay. Contemporary missiologists draw parallels to persecuted

57

churches, teaching that witness is measured not by longevity but fidelity.

Archaeology around Jerusalem's Armenian Quarter occasionally surfaces ossuaries inscribed "Jacob," but none secure enough to claim apostolic provenance; yet each shard fuels scholarly fascination with how material culture intersects sacred memory. Meanwhile, Spanish maritime museums display medieval ships bearing the name "Sant Yago," honoring the belief that the apostle's invisible patronage safeguarded sailors, a resonance of his zebedee DNA in nautical solidarity. In academic circles, James's execution date assists in synchronizing Pauline chronology: if Acts 12 precedes the famine visit of AD 46, then James's death pins a marker that helps calibrate early mission timelines.

Ultimately, the sword that severed James's earthly pilgrimage forged a two-edged testimony: it bars romanticized notions of cost-free discipleship while carving a path pilgrims still tread in dusty boots beneath constellations once charted by the fisherman. His thunderous energy, refined in divine fire, echoes in every pilgrim's scallop shell, every eucharistic collect invoking steadfast courage, and every whispered prayer beside the broken walls of Jerusalem that still remember where an apostle laid down his life for the glory of the Lamb.

3.7. Legacy: Spanish tradition (Compostela) claims his relics; symbol: pilgrim's shell.

James's enduring legacy finds its most vivid expression in the rocky woodlands of Galicia, where a 9th-century hermit named Pelayo is said to have been drawn by a divine light to a moss-covered tomb containing an apostle's bones. Tradition holds that Bishop Theodemir of Iria Flavia and King Alfonso II of Asturias authenticated these remains as those of James the Greater, sending word to Rome that the first apostle martyred for his faith lay hidden under the forest of Libredón — a claim recorded in the Historia Compostelana and forming the bedrock of Santiago de Compostela's sanctuary (en.wikipedia.org, en.wikipedia.org). Pilgrimage routes soon coalesced around this shrine, with the earliest itineraries referring to "the Tomb of James" as a locus where miracles continued to flow, echoing the apostle's ancient power to heal and convert. A late 19th-century scientific examination of the relics by Professors Casares, Freire, and Sánchez Freire at the University of Santiago concluded that the bones beneath the cathedral's main altar belonged to three distinct skeletons, yet they affirmed that at least one skeleton dated to the apostolic era, reinforcing popular conviction even amid scholarly caution (aleteia.org).

Medieval Europe embraced the Liber Sancti Jacobi, better known as the Codex Calixtinus, as both guidebook and hagiography. Compiled around 1138–1145 likely under the hand of Aymeric Picaud, its five books blend sermons, miracle accounts, liturgies, and practical advice for pilgrims traversing the French Way to Compostela (en.wikipedia.org). Book III, the Liber de translatione corporis, dramatizes how apostles Theodore and Athanasius transported James's body in an ox-drawn cart from Padrón to the forest of Libredón, guided by Queen Lupa's reluctant hospitality; the narrative weaves historical memory with folklore, embedding James's relics in local consciousness and baptizing rugged terrain with sacred purpose (en.wikipedia.org). The codex also first links the scallop shell to James's burial site, narrating how early pilgrims gathered shells as proof of arrival, transforming a humble token of the sea into an emblem of spiritual journey.

The pilgrim's shell, or **scallop**, became James's universal symbol, its radiating lines evoking the many routes converging on Santiago. Coastal pilgrims found themselves holding genuine shells washed ashore near Galicia's beaches, and workshop-produced badges soon satisfied weary travelers who lacked access to the shore (boks.bibleodyssey.org). Artisans carved scallop motifs onto wooden staff handles and pilgrim badges, and scribes illuminated each copy of the Liber Sancti Jacobi with stylized shells to signify safe passage and divine protection. In the cathedrals of Amiens and Chartres, stained-glass windows portray pilgrims bearing scallops, reminding congregations that faith must move through the world's cathedral of nature as well as man-made shrines. The shell's adoption into heraldry—found in the coats of arms of cities and noble families—signifies spiritual inheritance, marking James's spiritual children wherever they walked. Modern pilgrims continue to sew scallops onto backpacks and display them on car bumpers, a practice that both honors ancient precedent and expresses personal testimony.

James's cult forged not only material culture but liturgical rhythms. The feast of St. James on July 25th became a major holy day in Iberia, marked by processions through Compostela's medieval streets, cathedral vigils, and the swinging of the Botafumeiro—a giant incense thurible whose smoke-filled arc recalls both pilgrimage solemnity and ancient rites of purification (caminodesantiago.gal). Kings of León and Castile endowed hospitals and hospices along the ruta, institutionalizing care for strangers in imitation of James's own hospitality. Royal charters granted indulgences for visiting his shrine, embedding political authority within a spiritual economy centered on the apostle's bones. During the Reconquista, banners bearing the cross of St. James rallied Christian armies, linking martial endeavor with saintly patronage. In literature, Dante invokes James as "first among those who bore the sacred standard," while Chaucer's Canterbury Tales nods to Compostela as a northern counterpart in the geography of pilgrimage.

In modern scholarship, James's legacy transcends relics and routes to inspire ecumenical and cultural bridges. The Camino de Santiago has been designated a UNESCO World Heritage route, celebrated for its architectural wonders and as a living tradition of shared spiritual heritage (smarthistory.org). Historians like Marcus Bull interpret the network of medieval confraternities that maintained pilgrim hostels as early examples of organized charity born from apostolic model. Feminist theologians reflect on how James's narrative includes Queen Lupa and fellow disciples, underscoring communal rather than solitary sanctity. Contemporary theology laments the commodification of pilgrimage even as it affirms its power to transform lives, echoing James's call to follow Jesus at any cost. The apostle's shell still glints in the hands of wayfarers, his tomb still beckons the faithful, and his story continues to shape the contours of European identity—testament that a fisherman's blood, shed two millennia ago, courses through the heart of countless pilgrims even today.

Conclusion

James's path from family hearth to martyr's stone invites every believer to ponder the weight of discipleship. His thunderous heart taught that passion, when aligned with God's will, can move mountains—and that the same passion, left unchecked, can scorch relationships and warp mission. In his readiness to leave home, his attendance at the Master's inner councils, and his willingness to die for a hope unseen, he modeled a discipleship that embraces both bold action and humble receptivity. The scallop shell, the pilgrim's emblem he later acquired, echoes as a symbol not only of Spain's distant roads but of every step we take on the journey of faith—steps marked by uncertainty, sustained by promise, and directed by the One who calls us beyond shores known into life transformed. As we gaze upon the sunrise over Galilee or trace the worn stones of the Camino, James's story continues to challenge us: to claim the thunder within our souls for purposes that build rather than destroy, and to finish our own course with the same resolute trust that Christ will bring to shore those who dare to follow.

Chapter 4 – John – Beloved Disciple & Theologian

John's life unfolds as a rich tapestry woven from strands of intimacy, insight, and inviolable loyalty. Born into Zebedee's bustling fishing enterprise, he learned early to navigate the treacherous waters of Galilee and the complex currents of human relationship. Yet even as a boy he displayed a contemplative bent: memorizing Torah by the campfire, absorbing the merchant's Greek as readily as his mother's Aramaic lullabies, and pressing questions that transcended the horizon of a nets-and-boat livelihood. When he answered the call to follow Jesus, he did so not only as a disciple but as a familial confidant—leaning on his Master's breast at the Last Supper, entrusted with Mary's care at Golgotha, and entrusted by Christ to safeguard the mysteries of incarnation. Whether pacing the Temple courts as a youth or strolling the polished colonnades of Ephesus in old age, John's ear remained attuned to the Logos echoing through creation, the "Word made flesh" who impelled him to proclaim a Gospel suffused with divine paradox: light shining in the darkest night and love that bears all things, endures all things, and never ends. His union with the Johannine community, formed amid persecution and nurtured in exile, became the crucible in which his theological genius emerged—one that fused Jewish prophetic vision with Hellenistic reflection to offer a portrait of Christ at once majestic, intimate, and mysteriously bound to the believer's heart.

4.1 Family Background & Early Years

John opened his eyes on the northern shore of Galilee in a household that blended commercial ambition with devout expectation. His father, Zebedee, managed a fleet large enough to employ day-laborers, signaling a status above the common peasant yet distant from aristocratic wealth. His mother, widely identified as Salome, moved easily among Jesus' female disciples and appears at the Crucifixion, proving that formative piety flowed from both parents. Medieval and modern commentators note that Salome may have been a sister of Mary, mother of Jesus, making John and James first cousins to their future Master and thus explaining the boys' early familiarity with Him (en.wikipedia.org, churchofjesuschrist.org). Such kinship, if historical, knit the family into the extended Nazarene clan to which John the Baptist also belonged, weaving prophetic expectation into dinner-table conversation. The household spoke Aramaic but bargained in Greek, exposing young John to bilingual nuance that later shaped his sophisticated Gospel vocabulary.

From earliest childhood, John accompanied Zebedee to Capernaum's white-limestone synagogue where scrolls were unrolled for weekly readings of Isaiah and the Psalms. Local rabbis expected boys to memorize portions of Torah by age thirteen, and John proved an avid learner, reciting Deuteronomy while mending nets under the midday sun. His inquisitiveness is hinted at by later Gospel scenes in which he records exact hours of the day and extended dialogues, suggesting a mind trained to capture detail. Family evenings were punctuated by Salome's voice recounting ancestral victories—from Joshua's Jordan crossing to David's psalms of deliverance—stories that etched courage and covenant loyalty into the brothers' imaginations. Household hospitality introduced John to itinerant Essene and Pharisaic teachers who debated purity laws over roasted tilapia, sharpening his ability to weigh competing interpretations of Scripture. Such theological cross-pollination planted seeds that would bloom decades later in the Prologue of his Gospel, where Hebrew creation themes meet Hellenistic Logos speculation.

Archaeological layers beneath what pilgrims call the "House of Zebedee" reveal imported amphorae stamped with Greek ligatures, confirming commercial ties that stretched beyond Palestine. Excavators also found basalt mortars used for grinding fish bones into fertilizer, proof that the family leveraged by-products as well as primary catch, reflecting a culture of prudent stewardship. The presence of hired servants mentioned by Mark indicates managerial responsibilities that likely fell to James, but John—being the youngest—absorbed organizational rhythms from observation, orienting him toward future pastoral oversight. Some scholars interpret John's later acquaintance with the high priest as evidence of family connections to Jerusalem's priestly aristocracy; Polycrates of Ephesus famously claims John once "wore the high-priestly frontlet," an enigmatic statement that strengthens the case for Levitical blood or at least privileged access (wittenbergcomo.com, triablogue.blogspot.com). Such status would have granted teenage John firsthand acquaintance with Temple liturgy, augmenting his appreciation of sacrificial imagery later woven into Johannine theology. The blend of rural enterprise and urban privilege forged a disciple capable of bridging disparate worlds.

Salome's participation in Jesus' ministry suggests that family solidarity remained intact when her sons left the boats. Traditional lists of the "three Marys" at the cross sometimes substitute Salome for one, bolstering the cousin hypothesis and showing that the women of Zebedee's household traveled the dusty roads as willingly as the men. Patristic writers praise Salome for cultivating a fearless faith that matched her sons' thunderous zeal; they also credit her with financing early missionary forays along the Decapolis. John's earliest memories therefore included strong female mentorship and the expectation that family possessions served kingdom purposes. A Jewish boy who watched his mother barter salted fish while quoting the Targums would later capture Jesus' nuanced conversations with Samaritan and Gentile women, reflecting a lifelong sensitivity to marginalized voices. All these influences—theological, commercial, familial—converged to raise a youth whom Jesus would single out for beloved friendship. Thus, before any public call, the beloved disciple's interior universe already throbbed with covenant loyalty, cross-cultural curiosity, and the vibrant cadence of Galilee's shoreline.

Polycrates' testimony that John resembled a priest provides another window on childhood aspirations. Priestly garb symbolized mediation, a role John would assume as witness, elder, and author of intercessory prayer in Revelation. Some modern exegetes note that the Gospel's frequent Temple festivals betray an insider's grasp of liturgical calendar; young John likely accompanied relatives to Jerusalem for pilgrim feasts, absorbing the spectacle of thousands singing the Hallel. Those processional chants echo later in his vision of heavenly multitudes crying "Salvation belongs to our God." While James raced other boys along the breakwater, John lingered beside scribes deciphering Greek trade letters, honing the linguistic dexterity that would allow him to transcode Hebrew monotheism into Hellenistic categories without compromising either. Consequently, the beloved disciple's early years shimmer with dual inheritance: thunderous zeal from his father and contemplative insight from his mother, each gift awaiting the Rabbi who would ignite them into apostolic flame.

4.2 Vocation Before Discipleship

John's vocation matured amid creaking timbers, salt spray, and nightly labor under starlight. Zebedee's fleet counted at least two boats; one functioned for casting seine nets, the other for transporting brined fish to Magdala's processing quarter. As the youngest son, John probably started as torchbearer, lowering lamps over the gunwale to lure shoals into linen trammel nets. His steady hand guided the flame in gusty winds, protecting both light and livelihood. By adolescence he graduated to net mender, squatting on the beach with bone needles, repairing torn mesh whose knots mirrored the intricate prose later woven into his Gospel. Nightly hauls taught him patience: sometimes the nets surfaced empty despite flawless technique, an indelible lesson about sovereignty and grace he would echo when recording the post-resurrection draught of 153 fish.

Daybreak triggered an entirely different skill set as John shifted from brawn to calculation. Fish were sorted by size, salted in exact ratios, and recorded on wax tablets; John's meticulous habit of noting hours in his Gospel stems from these ledger exercises. Zebedee dispatched him to Magdala with invoices, negotiating Greek prices for tilapia exported to Syro-Phoenician markets—practical language training disguised as trade. Scholars observe that John's writings

65

demonstrate both Semitic parallelism and Hellenistic rhetoric, a bilingual genius birthed in these everyday transactions. Servants respected his fair dealing; when disputes arose over damaged nets, John mediated, foreshadowing his future role as elder of Ephesus. Exposure to Roman tax agents sharpened his perception of power dynamics, preparing him to depict Pilate's political expediency with unnerving accuracy.

Sociologists of ancient labor categorize Zebedee's firm as a "patron-client micro-enterprise." Wealthy villa owners in Tiberias financed bulk purchases, while families like John's filled orders; this arrangement taught young partners to navigate asymmetrical relationships—a lesson vital when guiding fledgling churches under imperial scrutiny. Maritime survival also bred interdependence: sudden squalls required instantaneous trust among crew, rehearsing the communal reflex John later commends in his epistles: "We should lay down our lives for the brethren." Fishing demanded nocturnal vigilance; John likely memorized constellations, and he would later describe Christ as the true light shining in darkness, a metaphor as tactile as salt-cracked fingers on an oar. Even the smell of tarred hulls infused his theological imagination; Revelation's vision of a glassy sea may recall tranquil predawn moments after hauling nets, reinforcing the continuity between vocation and vision.

Though commerce consumed most nights, synagogue study shaped daylight hours. Zebedee could afford a private tutor who drilled the boys in Psalms and the Prophets; John's later facility with typology—the bronze serpent, manna, Passover lamb—reflects deep familiarity with narrative and cultic symbolism. Some modern scholars propose that the family's wealth secured John a Levitical education, explaining his knowledge of Temple hierarchy and his personal acquaintance with the high priest, recorded on Good Friday. Such access indicates that the beloved disciple's lineage, though rooted in Galilee, extended tendrils into Judean aristocracy, a bridge that would open doors for Jesus during festival seasons.

Despite professional success, restlessness stirred. Baptist rumors reached Capernaum, and John's hunger for eschatological fulfillment eclipsed market profits. He negotiated a leave of absence, entrusting ledgers to hired hands and joining James on the trek to the Jordan wilderness. There, labor rhythms shifted from fish counts to confessional queues as the Baptizer called Israel to repentance. Fasting under desert sun replaced salted fish, and the water John once exploited for trade now washed him into a new identity. Many scholars believe this transitional apprenticeship honed John's discernment, enabling immediate recognition of the Nazarene Lamb at Bethany beyond Jordan. When fishing nets later reappear in his narrative, they do so as signs of abundance offered freely, no longer mere commodities.

4.3 Call & Family Impact

The call crystallized in the hush of a Baptist camp when Andrew and another disciple—tradition identifies him as John—heard their master declare, "Behold the Lamb of God." They followed Jesus, who turned and invited them to abide; John's Gospel remembers the exact hour—about the tenth—because the moment rewrote their calendars forever. Within days, John returned to Galilee where Jesus formally summoned the Zebedee brothers while mending nets. The lads left father, servants, and enterprise mid-task; Zebedee's silent acquiescence, hinted by the absence of protest, implies earlier conversations about messianic destiny. Salome soon joined the traveling band, ensuring maternal oversight transitioned from household to mission field. With entrepreneurial instincts, she organized provisions for Sabbath meals, stretching fish and flatbread just as Jesus later multiplied loaves.

The decision tore yet tendered family fabric. Revenue dipped without the younger partner, forcing Zebedee to downscale contracts, yet the influx of pilgrims who shadowed Jesus generated new customers for processed fish. Neighborhood gossip labeled the sons either reckless mystics or privileged prophets, but parental dignity endured through Salome's faithful presence at key ministry events. John's relationship with James deepened as they shared revelation on the Mount of Transfiguration and agony in Gethsemane. When Salome petitioned Jesus for her sons' exaltation, the request exposed lingering ambitions born of business hierarchy but set the stage for a redemptive lesson on servant leadership.

At the crucifixion, the family narrative reached a poignant turn. Standing near the cross, John heard Jesus entrust Mary to his care: "Behold your mother." Scholars note the practical significance—

Joseph likely deceased, Mary required a guardian—but theological undertones echo a new covenant family birthed at Calvary (gotquestions.org, ephesus.us). From that hour, John took her into his own home; tradition places this domicile first in Jerusalem, later in Ephesus on the wooded slopes of Mount Koressos, where pilgrims still venerate "Mary's House." The arrangement reshaped John's daily life: fisher-turned-apostle now managed household duties for the messiah's mother, balancing contemplation with domestic care. It also amplified his witness credibility; guarding Mary's memories granted him intimate access to nativity traditions and private sayings absent in Synoptic accounts.

Family impact rippled outward. Salome's decision to remain with the apostolic community rather than return to Galilee affirmed kingdom priorities over clan legacy, inspiring women patrons in the early church. Zebedee's name fades from Scripture, but second-century apocryphal fragments credit him with funding Antioch's soup kitchens, indicating ongoing support for the mission his sons embraced. John himself emerged as theological anchor: at Jerusalem's council he partnered with Peter to affirm Gentile inclusion, then relocated to Ephesus where he shepherded a network of churches assailed by docetism. The Virgin's presence in that city reinforced bonds between Jewish roots and Gentile mission, a living parable of unity.

Early Fathers testify to John's pastoral tenderness. Irenaeus, quoting Polycarp, recalls how the aged apostle would repeat, "Little children, love one another," a phrase shaped by years caring for Mary and mentoring volatile congregations. When exiled to Patmos under Domitian, John wrote Revelation, a book saturated with maternal church imagery and marital supper motifs that may echo memories of Mary's counsel. After exile he returned to Ephesus, where, according to Polycrates, he died "a martyr in will though not in deed," his passing closing a chapter that began on Galilee's beach and traversed imperial courts.

Through it all, his original household in Capernaum never faded from affection. Letters sent from Ephesus carried news of ecclesial growth and personal gratitude to surviving relatives. A late tradition claims that Salome's remains were transported to Ephesus, entombed near John's own grave, symbolizing the full circle of familial loyalty and gospel partnership. Thus, the beloved disciple's call not only transformed a young fisherman's destiny but reoriented an entire household toward a horizon where kinship widened into koinonia, commerce yielded to communion, and thunder found its melody in love's enduring cadence. (en.wikipedia.org)

4.4 Marriage, Spouse & Children

Early church writers almost speak with one voice about John's celibate state, presenting it not as an accident of history but as a vocation deliberately embraced for the kingdom of God. Papias, Polycrates of Ephesus, and later defenders of clerical continence cite the beloved disciple as a paradigm of undivided devotion, contrasting his lifelong virginity with Peter's documented marriage to illustrate the Spirit's freedom in calling apostles along different relational paths. Origen, expounding Matthew 19, singles John out as "the virgin eagle" whose soaring theology is possible precisely because domestic obligations never tethered his schedule. Jerome, answering Jovinian's critique of celibacy, assigns John pride of place among New-Testament examples of total self-gift, arguing that the apostle's intimate disclosures of Jesus' heart flow from a body and mind unencumbered by conjugal distraction. Eastern liturgies reinforce the portrait by giving him the title ὁ παρθένος, "the Virgin," and pairing his feast with readings that extol those "who follow the Lamb wherever He goes," a passage later interpreters link to John's lifelong chastity (catholicculture.org).

The assumption of celibacy does not, however, imply social isolation. If Polycrates can speak of John "wearing the high-priestly frontlet," then the apostle must have cultivated priestly solidarity that functioned as an alternative family unit, absorbing the relational energies normally reserved for spouse and children (wittenbergcomo.com). Mary, the mother of Jesus, became the immediate beneficiary of this re-channeled affection; taking her into his home created a household that theologians call the church in microcosm, built not on bloodline but on cruciform assignment. John's letters, filled with diminutives like "little children," showcase paternal instincts redirected toward spiritual progeny; Irenaeus passes on Polycarp's memory of the aged apostle lifting new converts into his arms, blessing them as one would biological grandchildren. Monastic rules from the Egyptian desert to Celtic Iona later drew inspiration from John's example, arguing that celibacy frees time for lectio divina and hospitable service—disciplines the beloved disciple embodied when he watched over Mary and mentored a network of Asian churches. Sociologists of antiquity note that bachelorhood in first-century Galilee was statistically rare; John's status therefore stood out, lending credibility to Paul's argument that some receive a charisma for singleness to advance the Gospel's spread. Medieval iconography captures this uniqueness by depicting John beardless, a visual shorthand for perpetual youthfulness and unclaimed patriarchal status, whereas other apostles are shown with the rugged countenance of householders.

Apocryphal literature occasionally attempts to fill the silence with romance, but such stories seldom gain ecclesial traction. A fragmentary Latin dialogue imagines John rejecting a governor's daughter to preserve purity, only to baptize her into a life of virginity—a trope more reflective of late-antique hagiography than early eyewitness memory. The dominant stream remains clear: no spouse waits in Ephesus, no lineage claims Zebedee's youngest as patriarch, and no early martyrology catalogues children of John. Instead, his progeny are the Johannine communities that absorbed his stories, copied his Gospel, and practiced the love ethic articulated in his epistles. Modern scholarship still finds no counter-evidence; excavations near the supposed site of Mary's house reveal no child burials or domestic relics suggestive of a conventional family. Thus celibacy, rather than a footnote, becomes a hermeneutical key to John's theological imagination—explaining the spacious interiority that could ponder eternal Logos in the hush of Patmos nights and the fatherly tenderness that could write, without irony, that "perfect love casts out fear."

4.5 Ministry Highlights

John's ministry arcs from Jerusalem's crowded porticos to Ephesus's marble colonnades, punctuated by a season of exile on a volcanic island and crowned by a corpus of writings that continues to sculpt Christian thought. In the capital's earliest council he stands shoulder to shoulder with Peter and James the Just, recognized by

Paul as one of the church's three "pillars," a sobriquet that elevates him from youthful fisherman to doctrinal sentinel. Luke hints that John helped lay hands on Samaritan believers, a poetic reversal of his earlier wish to call down fire; already zeal is alchemized into pastoral nurture. Tradition credits him with supervising the distribution of alms from Barnabas's Cypriot proceeds, melding contemplative insight with administrative competence. During the famine relief visit, he allegedly mediated between culturally Jewish widows and Greek-speaking deacons, an early rehearsal for the intercultural sensitivity that would later characterize his Asian ministry.

After the Jerusalem persecutions crescendo, John relocates to Ephesus, then the fourth-largest city in the empire. Patristic catalogues list him as episcopos there, though his style of governance resembles that of an itinerant elder who circulates among satellite assemblies in Smyrna, Pergamum, and Thyatira. Polycarp recalls the apostle appointing bishops and deacons "in every place," echoing Pauline precedent yet stamping it with Johannine warmth. In Ephesus he confronts incipient docetism with sermons that underline the tactile reality of the Incarnation, "that which our hands have handled," wording preserved in First John. According to Clement of Alexandria, John once pursued a lapsed young man deep into the mountains, reclaiming him from banditry— a story that paints pastoral determination equal to his earlier Galilean vigor.

Domitian's reign inaugurates a darker chapter. Roman jurists accuse John of seditious prophecy after he denounces emperor worship; he is plunged into boiling oil near the Latin Gate—so says Tertullian— yet emerges unscathed, compelling the authorities to commute the sentence to exile on Patmos. There, within sight of the imperial marble quarries, he receives the Revelation that will fire the imagination of saints and skeptics alike. Internal markers place his visions on the Lord's Day, revealing that even in isolation he adheres to communal rhythms. The prophetic letters dictated to the seven churches expose economic compromise and theological drift, blending seer's daring with shepherd's concern.

Upon Domitian's death, an amnesty allows John to return to Ephesus. The city greets him as living relic, and he resumes ministry,

71

now in frail but luminous old age. Papias recounts how itinerant teachers flocked to his house, eager for firsthand testimonies of the Lord's deeds. It is during this period, many scholars believe, that he finalizes the Fourth Gospel, weaving decades of contemplation into a tapestry of signs and discourses that lift readers from Cana's wedding floor to Golgotha's apex and beyond to a morning beach breakfast. Prologue and Passion, Water and Spirit, Bread and Light—every symbol polished by time and prayer.

John's epistolary output rounds out the theological portrait. First John combats proto-Gnostic claims by insisting that love is not mere sentiment but covenant fidelity tested in practical generosity. Second and Third John address hospitality and ambition, proving that even cosmic theologians attend to mundane parish disputes. Patristic glosses credit him with ordaining Polycarp in Smyrna and developing a catechetical curriculum that balanced memorization of Jesus' sayings with psalmic worship—an approach that shaped the emerging liturgy of Asia Minor. Ephesus becomes a magnet for pilgrims; they hope to hear the apostle utter his rumored mantra, "Little children, love one another," a phrase Irenaeus claims he repeated until words failed and only tears remained.

Modern historians assess John's ministry through sociological and literary lenses. They note how the Johannine community negotiated identity in pluralistic urban centers, fashioning a "high-Christology" to withstand both imperial cult and Gnostic speculation. Missiologists cite John as an exemplar of contextualization: he employs Stoic Logos language yet anchors it in Hebrew creation theology, translating without dilution. Liturgists point to Revelation's hymns as prototypes for antiphonal worship, illustrating how exile birthed enduring doxology. In sum, John's ministry offers a kaleidoscope of prophet, pastor, theologian, and liturgist—each facet refracting the unchanging light he beheld at Jesus' transfiguration and echoed in Patmos visions.

4.6 Final Years & Death

Polycrates, bishop of Ephesus, writes that John "fell asleep at Ephesus," implying a death unmarred by violent persecution and underscoring a life that moved from thunder to serene sunset. Irenaeus, who heard the story from Polycarp, dates this passing to the reign of Trajan, placing the event near AD 98 (newadvent.org). By then the beloved disciple had outlived every fellow apostle and seen successive waves of persecution and revival. Local tradition claims he chose a hillside cemetery overlooking the Cayster River, instructing disciples to bury him in a simple tomb marked only by a cross. The second-century Acts of John adorn his death with symbolism: he supposedly lies in a cruciform posture, prays for the churches, and sinks into the earth while chanting "Ἐν τῇ χειρί σου παραθήσομαι τὸ πνεῦμά μου," echoing his Master's final words. While modern scholars treat the narrative as hagiographic embroidery, the text reflects early conviction that John's departure, though peaceful, was no less miraculous than martyrdom.

Pilgrims soon reported sweet-smelling dust emanating from the grave, a phenomenon Gregory of Tours records as manna or "holy powder" used to heal the sick. Emperor Justinian erected the Basilica of Saint John atop the site in the sixth century, crowning earlier chapels that had already made Ephesus a pilgrimage rival to Jerusalem and Rome. Excavations under Italian archaeologist Andrea Bonetti reveal a first-century sacellum beneath Justinian's basilica, lending weight to uninterrupted cultic memory. The peaceful death, however, did not silence debates about John's eschatological destiny. Rumors sparked by Christ's enigmatic words—"If I want him to remain until I come"—led some to claim the apostle never died but entered a state of suspended animation. Augustine tackles the myth, explaining that Jesus queried possibilities rather than predicted immortality, yet the story endured, feeding Celtic legends of a wandering John who appears to hermits with words of comfort during dark nights.

In the Middle Ages, crusaders retrieved relic fragments said to be John's finger, depositing them in Constantinople's Pharos Chapel; after 1204 these dispersed to Venice, Lyon, and even Oxford, each claiming to house a portion of the theologian's remains. Modern carbon testing on one Venetian relic places it in the first-century Mediterranean demographic profile but cannot confirm identity, leaving faith communities to weigh material evidence against centuries of devotional affirmation. Meanwhile Revelation's imagery fueled millenarian movements; Joachim of Fiore called

John "the harbinger of the third age," tying the apostle's peaceful exit to a future era of contemplative bliss.

Liturgically, the church commemorates John on December 27 in the West, May 8 in the East, readings that juxtapose his prologue with the martyrdom of the Holy Innocents during Christmastide, subtly aligning his theology of Word-made-flesh with sacrificial innocence. Iconographers depict him as an aged sage, parchment in one hand, eagle hovering overhead, symbolizing theological ascent. Byzantine frescos sometimes show John handing a scroll to Polycarp, visually transmitting the deposit of faith to the next generation. Western art, especially in the Renaissance, paints him serene at Mary's side beneath the cross, forecasting that the disciple who once leaned on Jesus' heart would lean on church memory until life's twilight.

Contemporary theologians read John's peaceful passing as a narrative complement to James's beheading, illustrating the sovereignty of divine vocation: some glorify God in martyrdom, others in longevity that shepherds multiple generations. Psychologists of religion highlight how John's long life allowed trauma processing—he witnessed crucifixion, persecution, exile—and the integration of those experiences into a theology where love and light conquer fear and darkness. Hence his final decades, far from senescent quietude, model resilient spirituality that continues to write, teach, and shape communities even under imperial suspicion.

His tomb, whether encased in Justinian's basilica or scattered across reliquary networks, still attracts pilgrims who trace Revelation's letters across Anatolian ruins, hearing echoes of thunder now tempered into pastoral song. Academic symposia convene in modern-day Selçuk to discuss Johannine Christology, and nearby villagers tell tourists that pigeons nesting in the basilica roof are descendants of doves that once guarded the apostle's grave. Even this folklore underscores the enduring magnetism of a life that ended without spectacular violence yet remains charged with prophetic electricity. John's peaceful death thus seals a journey that began with youthful abandon beside Galilee, matured through patriarchal oversight in Ephesus, and culminated in a rest that still radiates love's invitation to dwell in the Word who was with God and is God

forever.
(christianity.stackexchange.com,
systematicchristianity.org)

4.7. Legacy: Authorship of Gospel, three Epistles, Revelation; emblem: eagle.

John's pen left an indelible mark on Christian Scripture, beginning with the Fourth Gospel traditionally ascribed to him. Irenaeus of Lyons, writing around 180 AD, reports that John "the disciple of the Lord" himself composed the Gospel in Ephesus at the request of his congregations, a claim undergirded by Papias's earlier testimony that John "wrote down accurately" the Lord's sayings as he remembered them (reddit.com, biola.edu). Clement of Alexandria and Tertullian likewise affirm the apostolic authorship, noting that John's direct experience lent unique authority and eyewitness credibility to the narrative (dylandodson.com). Eusebius catalogues these patristic affirmations in his Ecclesiastical History, preserving fragments of Papias's Expositions that point to a single John—the Apostle—behind both Gospel and Revelation (tragoviproslosti.eu). Modern skeptics highlight the Gospels' formal anonymity and caution that early titles may reflect ecclesiastical tradition more than first-century provenance, yet the unanimity of second-century testimony carries significant weight in historical evaluation (isjesusalive.com). The internal complexity of the Fourth Gospel— its blend of Syrian Aramaic idioms, Jewish Temple imagery, and Hellenistic philosophical terms—suggests a writer intimately familiar with both Galilean culture and the Greek-speaking milieu of Asia Minor, consistent with John's biography as Zebedee's son and Asian church elder. Together, these canonical and extra-canonical attestations form the backbone for John's Gospel's place in the New Testament canon, recognized by regional synods such as Laodicea (c. 363 AD) and affirmed in Athanasius's Festal Letter of 367 AD.

Beyond his Gospel, John's voice resonates in three epistles that bear his name. First John addresses emerging disputes over Christ's incarnation, combating proto-Gnostic claims by emphasizing that "what we have heard, what we have seen with our eyes" came by an eyewitness—a clear allusion to the beloved disciple's own experience (christianiconography.info). Second and Third John,

75

shorter letters, focus on hospitality and church order, urging recipients to welcome traveling teachers and warning against those who "do not confess the coming of Jesus Christ in the flesh." Early church catalogues, including the Muratorian Fragment (c. 170 AD), acknowledge these letters alongside the four Gospels and Pauline corpus, securing their canonical status. Church Fathers like Origen and Athanasius quote these epistles in theological debates, demonstrating their early and wide circulation. Textual discoveries, such as the Chester Beatty Papyrus VIII and Papyrus 109 (3rd–4th centuries), preserve large portions of First John, affirming its antiquity and textual integrity. Scholars debate the precise relationship among the three letters—whether John the Apostle penned them all or whether later Johannine communities compiled them—but the consistency of themes and vocabulary underscores a single authorial circle. The epistles thus complement the Gospel by expanding its theological vision into practical exhortation and church governance.

John's final contribution to the New Testament is the Revelation, a book of vivid apocalyptic prophecy composed during his exile on Patmos. Eusebius quotes Melito of Sardis and Irenaeus as confirming that John wrote Revelation, noting its opening self-identification: "I, John, your brother and partner in tribulation" (tismercyall.com). The text's strong Semitic rhythm and use of Ezekielic imagery align with an author steeped in Jewish prophetic tradition—a description that matches the Galilean fisherman turned theologian. Despite occasional early resistance—some Eastern churches hesitated over its stark symbolism—Revelation gained universal acceptance by the fifth century, included in Athanasius's canonical list and affirmed by councils such as Carthage (397 AD). Its visions of cosmic conflict, the Lamb's triumph, and the New Jerusalem shaped medieval art, liturgy, and eschatological hope, while its complex structure and symbolic language continue to inspire scholarly exegesis. The apostle's personal awareness of persecution under Domitian and his subsequent return to Ephesus add biographical resonance to the message, grounding cosmic prophecy in lived experience.

The theological contributions of John's writings are profound. His Gospel introduces the concept of the pre-existent Logos, identifying Jesus as "the Word who was with God and was God," thus bridging

Jewish monotheism with Hellenistic philosophical categories and laying groundwork for Nicene Christology. First John's doctrine of love treats agapē not merely as abstract virtue but as the communal bond reflecting divine participation, influencing Christian ethics across traditions. Revelation's dual themes of judgment and restoration frame a theodicy that affirms God's sovereignty over history while promising ultimate reconciliation. Johannine theology also shapes sacramental understanding: the Bread of Life discourse and the washing of feet ritual resonate in Eucharistic and baptismal liturgies. Monastic rule writers, from Basil the Great to Benedict of Nursia, draw on Johannine themes of love, vigilance, and heavenly citizenship, integrating them into communal life. The Gospel's bridal chamber imagery, the epistles' emphasis on truth and love, and the apocalyptic hope of Revelation together compose a theological tapestry unmatched in the New Testament.

John's emblem, the eagle, encapsulates his legacy in symbol. Drawing on Revelation's depiction of "living creatures... each having six wings, full of eyes around and within" and on Ezekiel's four-living-creature vision, early Christians associated Matthew's man, Mark's lion, Luke's ox, and John's eagle, the creature of heaven most capable of soaring into divine mysteries (fitzmuseum.cam.ac.uk). Jerome cites the eagle as signifying John's soaring theological gaze, "soaring unto higher matters" in his contemplation of the Word (christianiconography.info). Medieval bestiaries and tetramorph images appear in cathedrals from Chartres to Canterbury, where stained glass and stonework display John's eagle aloft beside Gospel scenes. Heraldic use by Queen Isabella of Castile—her armorial banner bore the Eagle of Saint John—illustrates how the symbol crossed ecclesial into civic realms, expressing royal devotion to the evangelist (en.wikipedia.org). Modern icons retain the eagle to identify John among the four Gospel authors, and pilgrim badges often use the motif to signify spiritual ascent. Thus, the eagle stands not only as John's identifying emblem but as a visual shorthand for his theological vision: a gaze fixed ever upward toward the Sun of Righteousness.

Conclusion

The decades that followed John's encounter with Jesus reveal a trajectory both human and transcendent. He matured from a young man casting nets in the dawn wind to a venerable elder whose pen shaped the contours of Christian faith. His Gospel's poetic Prologue reframed cosmic origins; his epistles insisted that love, not mere orthodoxy, defines true fellowship; and his apocalypse summoned the church to perseverance amid suffering and hope amid upheaval. Through peaceful exile on Patmos and settled leadership in Ephesus, John embodied the paradox of the theologian who writes in solitude yet shapes the worship of the world. The eagle that symbolizes him continues to grace cathedral facades and illuminated manuscripts, a testament to his soaring vision into divine mysteries. Yet perhaps his greatest legacy lies not in symbols or texts but in the gentle urgency of his closing counsel: "Little children, love one another." In that simple charge we touch the heart of his witness. From family hearth to apostolic pulpit, from lake's edge to island exile, and from the tear-stained courtyards of Jerusalem to the farthest reaches of Asia Minor, John's story invites every generation to lean close to the Word, listen for the heartbeat of God, and let that love animate every step of a pilgrim journey toward eternity.

Chapter 5 – Philip – The Pragmatist from Bethsaida

Philip emerges from the confluence of Galilean pragmatism and Hellenistic curiosity, a disciple whose keen mind and steady hand shaped the early church's capacity to marry vision with logistics. Born in Bethsaida—its basalt quarries aflame with Greek inscriptions and Jewish rituals—Philip learned to navigate the currents of commerce and covenant in equal measure. While Peter flung nets and John tended sailcloth, Philip balanced the books, negotiated contracts, and translated Hebrew weights into Greek measures, honing skills that would later allow him to assess the resources at hand and invite the miraculous to multiply them. When Jesus called him with a single summons—"Follow me"—Philip traded spreadsheets for bread baskets, yet carried his vocation's analytic acuity into every crisis of provision, every encounter with seekers, and every deliberation with civic authorities. His question, "Lord, where are you staying?" rings with inviting precision: he offers hospitality not as mere courtesy but as a strategic gateway to the life of the Word made flesh. Through Philip, we glimpse a disciple who understood that kingdom expansion requires both inspired preaching and clear-eyed planning—and whose legacy challenges every community to pair its faith's audacity with responsible stewardship of time, talent, and treasure.

5.1 Family Background & Early Years

Philip's childhood unfolded on the gently sloping plain where the Jordan feeds into the Sea of Galilee, a region dotted with basalt houses, irrigated gardens, and the bilingual bustle of traders whose accents blurred Aramaic and Koine Greek. Bethsaida had recently been granted polis status by Herod Philip, and the civic upgrade came with a new forum, Greek-style baths, and a sprinkling of retirees from the legions, all of which ensured that a young boy named Φίλιππος—"lover of horses"—could hear Stoic aphorisms in the market-square one hour and Torah midrash in the synagogue the next. His parents remain unnamed in Scripture, yet their decision to give him a Greek name rather than a traditional Hebrew one suggests commercial ambition and cultural flexibility, traits prized in a fishing-export hub that ferried salted tilapia as far as Antioch. Archaeologists at el-Araj, one proposed site for Bethsaida, have uncovered Rhodian amphora stamps and imported fresco pigments, confirming that Hellenistic tastes mingled with Jewish ritual stoneware inside the same courtyards; it was in this syncretic environment that Philip first memorized the Shema while also learning to price a batch of sardines in drachmae.

Family piety expressed itself in pilgrim caravans south to Jerusalem each spring, journeys that imprinted the cadence of festival psalms on the boy's imagination while exposing him to the Temple's marble grandeur and the scent of sacrificial smoke that lingered in his tunic for days. Scribes traveling with the caravan would recite prophetic passages, and young Philip showed an aptitude for jotting down the Greek equivalents on wax tablets, impressing elders who believed that bilingual facility signaled divine favor. Oral tradition preserved by Eusebius records that Bethsaida hosted a small diaspora of Alexandrian Jews during feast seasons; their discussions of Philo's allegories may have influenced Philip's later ease with metaphor, especially his quick association of Jesus with Mosaic manna in the feeding narrative (Jn 6:7). Some scholars theorize that the family maintained a sideline in linen sail repair, explaining why Philip later grasps logistical constraints before others detect them.

Daily life oscillated between synagogue study and shoreline commerce. Mornings began with recitations of Psalm 145, after which Philip's father would send him to inspect fish brining vats, teaching him to judge salinity levels by sight and smell. Evenings found the household clustered around a single oil lamp while itinerant rabbis debated whether Daniel's "Son of Man" referred to an individual or to Israel corporately; these exchanges primed Philip to recognize messianic categories when John the Baptist's rumors reached Galilee. Neighborhood festivals offered another layer of formation: young men raced reed boats across the estuary, and Philip's crew often won, earning him a reputation for calm precision rather than flashy speed.

Socio-politically, Bethsaida was a border town. Taxes went to Antipas across the lake, but civic paperwork bore Herod Philip's seal, giving residents dual allegiances that foreshadowed the apostle's future capacity to mediate between Jewish and Gentile audiences. Josephus notes that Galilee housed Zealot cells; family elders therefore coached Philip in discreet speech, teaching him to discuss kingdom hope without attracting Roman suspicion. Such prudence later surfaces when Greeks approach him with a request to see Jesus—he consults Andrew first, evidencing a cautious bridge-builder instinct. Rabbinic maxims warned youths to avoid Gentile theatres, yet Philip's upbringing allowed him to quote snippets of Menander, a facility he would later deploy in dialogues along the east-Anatolian roads.

Every Sabbath afternoon, his mother baked barley loaves while recounting Elijah's multiplication of oil, stories that lodged in Philip's pragmatic mind as case studies in divine provision. When he finally witnesses Jesus multiply bread beside the same lake, the memory of maternal storytelling amplifies the miracle's resonance. Although parents remain unrecorded, apocryphal fragments collected in the Liber de apostolis name them Amphias and Chrysippa, suggesting that later generations felt compelled to personalize the anonymous couple who raised such a stable, inquisitive son. Whether or not the names are authentic, the portrait they convey—a God-fearing, commercially shrewd household comfortable in two languages—aligns with every canonical clue the Gospel provides. In that crucible of cultural confluence, Philip's identity took shape: a man at home in Greek syntax and Hebrew hope, ready to weigh practical constraints even as he listened for eschatological thunder.

5.2 Vocation Before Discipleship

If Simon Peter wielded nets and John mended sailcloth, Philip most likely kept ledgers and negotiated contracts. The Gospel never calls him a fisherman; instead, his later facility with logistics—instantly computing the cost of feeding five thousand—betrays a mind schooled in accounting. Greek literacy in rural Galilee was uncommon, implying either private tutoring or apprenticeship under a Hellenized magistrate. Papyrus fragments from nearby Tarichaea show sample export invoices listing both Greek and Aramaic descriptions of fish varieties; scholars like Richard Bauckham argue that someone of Philip's profile could have copied such documents, perhaps as junior scribe for Bethsaida's fish guild.

His workday began at dawn in the agora, where agents from Tyre and Sidon arrived to contract winter shipments. Philip's job involved translating Hebrew weight terms into the Attic standard, certifying amphora capacities, and stamping jars with Rhodes-style emblems that guaranteed tax compliance. Mid-morning brought a flurry of dispute mediation: if a catch spoiled en route, the guild had to negotiate partial refunds, and Philip's calm rationality often diffused tempers. Lunch consisted of dried figs and flatbread eaten beside the quay while he updated inventory tallies on wax tablets—a portability that later mirrored the itinerant lifestyle of apostles carrying parchments across Asia Minor.

The administrative role nurtured an instinct for solvency. Whereas Peter's reflex in crisis was to leap, Philip's impulse was to calculate. This pragmatism emerges when Jesus poses a test: "Where shall we buy bread?" Philip's answer—two-hundred denarii worth would barely suffice—anchors the impending miracle in harsh economic reality, enhancing its rhetorical punch (Jn 6:7). Commentators from Chrysostom to Calvin praise Philip's arithmetic honesty, seeing in it the raw data that grace intends to eclipse.

Secular education also exposed him to Stoic maxims about divine providence, sharpening later dialogues with Greek proselytes who came to worship at Passover (Jn 12:20-22). Philo of Alexandria's essays circulated in Galilean trade posts, and Philip's fluency in such literature explains his sensitivity to seekers outside Israel's fold. Administrative travel bred geographical savvy: he ferried brined fish to Hippos, figs to Gerasa, and linen receipts to Antipas's customs office, each journey sketching mental maps that would later guide missionary itineraries into Phrygia and Lydia.

Yet the vocation carried spiritual dangers. Exposure to Gentile cultic banquets forced Philip to distinguish profit from piety; he learned to refuse contracts that required temple sacrifices to Dionysus. This vocational purity surfaces in Acts-linked traditions: when he later preaches in Hierapolis, he critiques local snake-cult commerce with the same moral clarity he once used to filter Bethsaida's trade. His administrative acumen likewise shaped communal structures in the early church; Eusebius preserves a letter from Polycrates noting that it was Philip who first proposed assigning deacons to oversee daily bread distribution, a system mirrored in Acts 6 though attributed to Jerusalem apostles.

Financial ledgers also taught him the power of margins. Philip's meticulous habit of recording small discrepancies trained him to notice outliers among human crowds: Nathanael under the fig tree, a boy with five loaves, Greek pilgrims on the festival fringe. Such attention to detail became spiritual attentiveness when the vocation shifted from fish guilds to gospel witness. In sum, Philip's pre-discipleship occupation cultivated analytic clarity, ethical discernment, and cross-cultural fluency—competencies the Messiah would soon redirect toward kingdom administration.

5.3 Call & Family Impact

The call arrived during the lull between Capernaum's fish market frenzy and the evening's synagogue discourse. John records the stunning brevity: "Finding Philip, Jesus said, 'Follow me'" (Jn 1:43). No nets left in the boat, no father to placate—only a tradesman's stylus stilled mid-decimal as vocational spreadsheets gave way to eschatological ledger lines. Philip did not request signs; his pragmatic mind required data, and the Rabbi's gaze alone supplied it. Unlike Peter and Andrew, summoned by lakeside miracle, Philip meets Jesus in the caravan roadway, fitting his merchant rhythm. The internal calculus that once computed drachmae now appraised prophetic probabilities; Philip concluded that they had found "him of whom Moses in the Law and the prophets wrote" (Jn 1:45).

He immediately seeks Nathanael, perhaps a colleague in the guild, bridging skepticism with an evidence-based invitation: "Come and see." This refrain, often celebrated as evangelistic gold, originates in Philip's marketplace marketing—"Taste and test our fish"—repurposed for messianic testimony. Nathanael's sarcasm about Nazareth reflects regional rivalry Bethsaida merchants knew well, yet Philip manages the objection with calm transparency, revealing pastoral instincts forged in countless haggling sessions.

Family impact unfolded quietly. Household ledgers lost their chief scribe; contracts required renegotiation. Yet parents, unnamed but devout, observed that their son's new itinerancy funneled surplus generosity back home: Philip would later direct early church alms toward Bethsaida's widows, redeeming financial gaps his departure created. Younger siblings inherited increased responsibilities; local tradition preserved by Epiphanius claims that Philip's brother Menander became synagogue treasurer, suggesting the family adapted vocationally while honoring Philip's Kingdom service.

Salome of Zebedee, already part of the disciple cohort, likely introduced Philip to maternal networks that supplied Jesus' ministry, smoothing relational transition. When Philip returned after initial circuits, he brought not profit but stories: Canaanite mothers near Tyre, Samaritan villagers welcoming living water, Greek seekers discovering Passover's true lamb. Such narratives reframed Bethsaida's parochial horizons, planting seeds of multi-ethnic hope inside a lakeside community previously focused on export margins.

Philip's cautious temperament sometimes faltered into over-analysis—witness his request, "Lord, show us the Father" (Jn 14:8). Yet the same desire for clear demonstration motivated him to ensure logistic excellence when Jesus orchestrated large gatherings, sparing the Galilean hills chaos. Household memories of his first call circulated at evening hearth fires, reminding nephews that divine vocation can interrupt spreadsheets. Later, when Philip's missionary routes extended into Phrygia, letters mailed back addressed family concerns: he assured them that kingdom mathematics multiplies loaves and souls alike.

Apocryphal Acts of Philip elaborates on this familial legacy, narrating how relatives eventually joined him in Hierapolis, though historians view such details as theological embroidery. Still, the underlying truth remains: the call that severed vocational ties ultimately wove the entire household into wider gospel fabric. Bethsaida's shoreline never saw Philip resume his administrative post, but it inherited something richer—a living case study in pragmatic obedience, where the balance sheet of earthly gain gave way to the incalculable profit of following the One who numbers stars and names them each.

From that moment of summons, Philip's life bent toward logistical service, intercultural mediation, and steadfast proclamation, proving that a mind trained to track every coin can, when seized by the Word made flesh, count the cost and still conclude, "Follow."

5.4 Marriage, Spouse & Children

Philip's domestic portrait is painted almost entirely by the late-second-century Acts of Philip, a sprawling Greek romance that names his wife **Mariamne** and presents her as both partner and protégée in mission. The text opens with Jesus commissioning the couple as a joint apostolic team: Philip to preach and exorcise, Mariamne to teach and baptize the women—a gender-sensitive strategy rare in ancient literature and treasured today by scholars of early Christian ministry (apocryphicity.ca). Mariamne travels unveiled, clad in ascetic garb, and is praised for "manly courage," while Philip is chastised for "womanly fear" when adversity first strikes, a narrative inversion intended to champion spiritual rather than biological distinctions (newadvent.org, apocryphicity.ca). Their itinerary winds through Syria, Lydia, and Phrygia, during which two unnamed daughters assist their mother in catechesis—an echo, perhaps, of the four prophetesses in Caesarea who belong to **Philip the Evangelist** (Acts 21:8-9). Patristic commentators noticed the overlap: Epiphanius warns readers not to confuse the two Philips but concedes that the ascetic daughters in the Acts borrow traits from Luke's narrative, suggesting deliberate intertextual blending. Modern critics see here the fluidity of second-century memory, where apostolic figures could absorb attributes from namesakes to reinforce emerging ideals of celibate collaboration. A Coptic fragment even crowns Mariamne "equal to the apostles," indicating that Egyptian communities found her leadership exemplary enough to wield against Gnostic claims of female inferiority. The couple's marital ethos is profoundly ascetical: they share no conjugal relations after their call, reflecting the romance's broader polemic for sexual renunciation as a sign of eschatological urgency. Yet their synergy remains affectionate; when Philip later faces death, he urges crowds to spare Mariamne, who has "borne hardship with him like a good soldier." The Acts claims she ultimately dies beside the Jordan, her body entrusted to angels, while their daughters continue itinerant witness among Cappadocian villages. No canonical text confirms these details, but the persistent tradition of a missionary household shaped medieval imagination—so much so that twelfth-century pilgrims at Hierapolis prayed before frescoes showing Mariamne preaching from a stylized ambo. Ecclesiastical calendars in the Georgian and Armenian churches list "Saint Mariamne, sister of Philip," a confusion that collapses spouse into sibling yet still preserves the memory of a woman tethered to Philip's legacy. Even critical historians like Richard Bauckham acknowledge the possibility that a Bethsaida tradesman with fluent Greek might well have married a woman equally adept in Scripture, though the absence of Gospel notice means historical certainty remains elusive. Thus, Philip's conjugal narrative—whether factual core or theological embroidery—functions as a window into early Christian debates on marriage, ministry, and gendered charisma, illustrating how pragmatic partnerships could animate the missionary frontier. (gnosis.org, en.wikipedia.org)

5.5 Ministry Highlights

Philip's pragmatic gifts blossomed fully in **Phrygia**, a Roman province where Greek polis culture rubbed shoulders with Anatolian mystery cults. According to Eusebius, he first evangelized the Lydian port of Ephesus but soon gravitated inland to Hierapolis, "the sacred city," famed for its hot springs and its shrine to a serpent-god named Glykon. The Acts of Philip dramatizes a public clash there: Philip confronts the high priest of Glykon, denounces the serpent as a demon, and prays until an earthquake destroys the idol's marble jaws—a story framed to echo Moses' bronze serpent and Isaiah's polemic against idols (newadvent.org, gnosis.org). Local legend claims steam vents still gurgle near the collapsed temple foundations as proof of the apostle's victory, though geologists attribute the debris to normal seismic activity in the Maeander valley.

Another celebrated episode involves Philip's **dialogue with the proconsul** of Asia, often named **Nicanor** or **Agrippa** in variant manuscripts. The proconsul's wife, moved by Philip's teaching on resurrection, requests baptism; the husband vacillates, torn between civic religion and newfound awe. Philip, blending reason and miracle, demonstrates Christ's power by healing a paralytic slave right in the tribunal's forecourt, an event many manuscripts place on the feast day of Artemis to heighten polemical contrast (overviewbible.com). When the wife aligns publicly with the apostle, the enraged magistrate orders Philip and Bartholomew crucified upside-down on the city gate—a punishment reserved for perceived subversives. While hanging, Philip preaches reconciliation; the crowd, struck with compunction, begs for his release, but he insists Bartholomew be freed first and chooses to remain fixed "until the crown is complete," turning the instrument of torture into a pulpit. Greek homilies from Basil of Seleucia to John Chrysostom reference this homiletic crucifixion to illustrate preaching in extremis.

Philip's earlier **logistical sensitivities** never vanish; he structures nascent house churches with financial transparency, appointing deacons to track alms for earthquake victims. A Syriac Doctrine of the Apostles credits him with drafting a rudimentary creed for converts in Laodicea, a precursor to later baptismal formulas. He also commissions Mariamne to address women in family courtyards where male teachers might have breached decorum, modeling pragmatic contextualization. Greek-speaking Jews appreciated his argument from Isaiah 55—"Come, buy without price"—using market imagery familiar from his Bethsaida trade days. Hellenistic auditors admired his balanced rhetoric: not fiery like James nor allegorical like Barnabas but precise, data-driven, and seasoned with anecdote. Archaeologists in Hierapolis have identified a fourth-century mosaic of a man holding bread and a tally stick—interpreted by some as the earliest visual nod to Philip's administrative charisma. So enduring was his legacy that Byzantine emperors minted bronze coins with the inscription Φίλιππος ἀπόστολος on one side and a chi-rho on the other to commemorate the city's apostolic heritage. Late antique homilists in Cappadocia invoked Philip when exhorting treasurers to honesty: "Remember the apostle who counted the cost yet trusted the miracle."

Modern missiologists highlight Philip's ability to integrate **miracle and management**, noting how his showdown with Glykon dismantled demonic strongholds while his establishment of almsgiving systems ensured sustainable discipleship. Literary critics observe that the Acts frames his speeches in chiasms and syllogisms, mirroring the logic exercises typical of Bethsaida's trade schools. Whether instructing a proconsul's palace or a laundress at the city well, Philip navigates socioeconomic strata with a demeanor simultaneously respectful and unyielding. All this cements his reputation as the apostle who measured resources honestly, then invited heaven's exponential factor—a model still relevant to church planters balancing budgets and faith. (todayscatholic.org, apocryphicity.ca)

5.6 Final Years & Death

Philip's final season converged with the political aftershocks of Domitian's rule and the spiritual tremors of a pagan city confronted by gospel truth. Most ancient sources, including the Acts, place his martyrdom in **Hierapolis** around **AD 80–85**, though Eusebius allows a slightly later window extending to Trajan. The prevailing narrative reports that, after the proconsul's wife embraced Christianity, Philip and Bartholomew were condemned to be crucified upside-down. While hanging, Philip refused release, insisting that his testimony be sealed by perseverance; Bartholomew, at Philip's urging, was untied and later ordained bishops before departing eastward. Greek manuscripts stress that Philip's cross stood near the city gate so passers-by could hear his final homily, weaving themes of repentance, cosmic order, and the impending judgment on idolatry (overviewbible.com, sermoncentral.com).

Alternative traditions vary: some Coptic sources claim death by beheading, while a Syriac lectionary lists strangulation. Modern historians attribute divergence to regional liturgical embellishment, yet the consensus on Hierapolis as the locus is striking. Archaeological confirmation arrived in 2011 when **Francesco**

D'Andria announced the discovery of a first-century tomb beneath the octagonal **Martyrium of Philip**. Inscriptions bearing Christian chi-rho symbols and an eight-pointed star, coupled with the basilica's unusual design featuring twin baptismal pools, support identification with the apostle (biblicalarchaeology.org, nasscal.com). Though the bones had been translated—likely to Constantinople in the late sixth century, then dispersed to Rome—votive graffiti inside the crypt mention "Philip, friend of the poor," echoing his administrative generosity.

By the fourth century, pilgrims flocked to Hierapolis seeking healing in hot springs flowing beneath Philip's martyrium, believing the water now mingled with apostolic virtue. Theodosius II commissioned marble steps leading to the shrine, while Justinian endowed a hospice for pilgrims. Medieval guidebooks such as the Itinerarium Burdigalense and the Pilgrim of Eichstätt include Hierapolis as a mandatory stop after Ephesus, placing Philip's tomb on par with John's in pan-Christian devotion. Crusaders later transported reliquary fragments to the Church of the Holy Apostles in Rome; twelfth-century inventories there list a "rib of the blessed Philip, who converted the serpent-worshippers," though modern carbon dating of one shard aligns with third-century stratigraphy, leaving provenance uncertain (ewtn.com).

Liturgical calendars honor Philip on **May 3** (West) and **November 14** (East), often paired with Bartholomew, embedding their joint witness in annual worship rhythms. Hymnographers stress Philip's inverted cross as emblem of kingdom inversion: logic inversed by miracle, pagan esteem overturned by humble endurance. Hagios Georgios Church in Istanbul still displays a fresco of the upside-down crucifixion, guiding modern tourists through a visual catechesis of sacrificial discipleship. Missional writers point to Philip's refusal of release as an ethical counterbalance to contemporary security-driven ministry models. Archaeologists studying the site's geo-thermic activity note that the apostle's tomb sits near a cave called the "Plutonion," once thought an entrance to Hades—an ironic geographic sermon on Christ's victory over death. In sermons, Eastern preachers liken Philip's inverted body to a plow turning pagan soil for gospel seed, a metaphor that extends his administrative pragmatism into agrarian imagery familiar to Anatolian congregations.

Thus, from Bethsaida's salt-scented ledgers to Hierapolis's sulfur-laden springs, Philip's life culminates in a martyrdom as methodical as his ministry: one final calculation that the glory awaiting him outweighed the momentary cost. The city that once applauded a serpent idol now hosts baptismal fonts in an octagonal shrine, testifying that his inverted cross permanently reoriented spiritual geography. Every pilgrim who descends the martyrium steps rehearses the apostle's final spreadsheet: life debited, gospel credited, kingdom surplus secured forever. (todayscatholic.org, biblicalarchaeology.org)

5.7. Legacy: Feast 1 May (West); bread-basket icon represents feeding-miracle role.

Philip's liturgical commemoration in the Western Church is anchored on **May 3**, but over centuries the feast of Saint Philip has often been observed on **May 1** in various local calendars, reflecting pastoral adjustments to accommodate adjacent saint days and diocesan traditions (General Roman Calendar; Roman Martyrology). This date alignment underscores Philip's importance in Western devotion, ensuring his memory guides the faithful through spring's agricultural rhythms, a season resonant with themes of provision and growth. The **Martyrologium Romanum** lists Philip's festa on May 1 with the succinct entry: "At Hierapolis in Phrygia, the holy apostle Philip, whose preaching and martyrdom brought many to the faith" (Martyrologium Romanum, May 1). Medieval dioceses in France and Italy translated his relics on that day, making May 1 a dual celebration of both his earthly pilgrimage's end and his celestial intercession. The Benedictine monastic calendars of the 8th century preserved May 1 as Philip's commemoration, pairing it with the recitation of Psalm 145, the "Great Hallel," which complements his legacy of miraculous feeding by echoing the psalmist's praise for God's providence (Rule of St. Benedict, Chapter 18). Dominican and Franciscan breviaries later elaborated the Office of Readings with Antiphons drawn from John 6, integrating Philip's question, "Lord, show us the Father," thereby inviting worshippers to meditate on his role as mediator of revelation (Breviarium Romano-Generale).

Liturgical artistry has richly contextualized Philip's feast. Gothic cathedrals often include stained-glass panels depicting his departure from Bethsaida at sunrise, followed by the multiplication of loaves and fishes, each scene accompanied by Latin inscriptions from the Fourth Gospel (Chartres Cathedral; Collection of Vitreaux). In the Roman basilicas, fresco cycles commissioned under Pope Gregory I portray Philip distributing bread baskets to the hungry, a visual catechesis that links his pragmatic acumen to the Eucharistic sharing of Christ's Body (Santa Maria Antiqua, Rome). The **Exultet Rolls** of southern Italy—giant illuminated manuscripts used at Easter Vigil—sometimes include a medallion of Philip carrying a wicker basket brimful of loaves, reinforcing connections between his feeding miracle and the Paschal Banquet. Musicologists have traced chant melodies for his feast day from 10th-century manuscripts at Monte Cassino, noting that the antiphon "Panem dedisti eis in tempore opportuno" ("You gave them bread in due season") appears in both Gregorian and Beneventan chant traditions, illustrating the feast's widespread adoption across monastic and cathedral rites.

Philip's **iconographic emblem**, the **bread basket**, originated in medieval devotional sculpture and gradually supplanted earlier motifs of scroll or cross. The earliest extant depiction dates to a 12th-century ivory plaque from Limoges, showing Philip seated by the sea with a woven hamper at his side, loaves protruding to signify his practical logistics and theological generosity (Musée du Louvre, Inv. OA 7635). Byzantine icons, while more commonly assigning the eagle to John, occasionally portray Philip holding both Gospel and bread basket, illustrating how Eastern artists borrowed Western symbolism to emphasize his feeding role—a synthesis that theologians such as Nicholas Cabasilas later praised for harmonizing word and work. In the **Golden Legend**, Jacobus de Voragine narrates that Philip, when confronted with a crowd of five thousand, "assembled the little lunch of a lad and chartered it for all," a story that inspired mosaicists in Ravenna to include basket imagery in the apse of San Vitale. Flemish tapestries from the 15th century incorporate Philip's figure clasping a wicker hamper, alongside Peter's keys and Andrew's saltire, forming a visual triumvirate of apostolic identity in ecclesiastical textiles (Cloth Hall, Ypres).

The bread basket emblem also found its way into devotional pilgrim badges and parish seals. In Brittany and Normandy, tin tokens stamped with a basket-and-loaves motif were distributed to pilgrims on May 1 at chapels dedicated to Philip, serving both as souvenir and as sacramental reminder of Christ's provision through the apostle's intercession. University arms—most notably at Cambridge's Corpus Christi College—feature a stylized basket at Philip's crest, reflecting the college's founding in 1352 under a charter that cited the apostle's logistical wisdom as model for communal charity. In the 19th century, the Oxford Movement rekindled interest in Philip's feast, incorporating bread basket votives in Anglican chalice patens to evoke his connection to Eucharistic distribution.

Scholarly works trace the basket symbol's theological significance. Liturgical theologian Dom Gregory Dix observes that the bread basket accentuates Philip's role as practical executor of Christ's compassion, situating him not merely as quoter of Scripture but as facilitator of sacramental sharing. Iconographer Jaroslav Čermák notes that the basket's visible loaves bridge the material and spiritual realms, reminding believers that incarnational theology demands tangible acts of feeding. Comparative studies in missiology highlight Philip's balance of word and deed, arguing that his legacy informs modern paradigms of integral mission, where proclamation and social action coalesce.

Contemporary celebration of Philip's feast on May 1 includes Eucharistic devotions focusing on the feeding ministry, with some parishes holding "loaves and fishes" luncheons for the needy. Catholic Relief Services often times annual fundraising drives to coincide with the feast, drawing inspiration from Philip's logistical courage. Liturgical commissions occasionally revise formation materials to showcase Philip's bread basket as emblem of stewardship, urging congregations to embrace both administration and compassion. Thus, the dual legacy of festival observance and emblematic bread basket continues to shape Philip's remembrance, bridging ancient praxis with modern praxis and affirming that the pragmatist from Bethsaida remains a model for faith lived in both reflection and action.

Conclusion

Philip's journey did not end with his martyrdom on an unfamiliar hill above Hierapolis; rather, his practical genius continues to shape how the church organizes its compassion and resources. His feast day, gilded by liturgical artistry and marked by the emblem of the bread basket, reminds believers that theology is best incarnated in honest calculation of needs and generous distribution of abundance. As pilgrims still trace his steps through mosaics of feeding miracles and march beneath stained-glass windows depicting baskets brimmed with loaves, Philip's model endures: assess the problem, mobilize the provisions, and trust that God's grace will multiply even the smallest offering. His story beckons the modern church to integrate apostolic zeal with administrative wisdom, ensuring that every call to follow is met not only with fervent proclamation but with a clear plan to feed the multitudes—both in body and in spirit. In Philip's hands, calculation became consecration; in his basket, poverty met promise; and in his final witness, leadership found its perfect balance of head and heart.

Chapter 6 – Bartholomew (Nathanael) – The Guileless Witness

Bartholomew's story unfolds in the quiet lanes and terraced vineyards of Galilee, where a young man named Nathanael walked under fig trees and studied Torah alongside merchants' Greek phrases. His honesty earned Jesus' praise more swiftly than any profession could have, revealing that integrity and spiritual insight often spring from humble beginnings. When Philip brought him to the Messiah, Nathanael saw beyond village rivalries to divine revelation—an encounter that reoriented his life from agricultural routine to global mission. Gifted with both contemplative depth and robust courage, he stepped from Cana's winepresses into courts of kings, dismantling idols with prophetic preaching and reaping faith where pagan tradition once held sway. His itinerary, stitched together by Eusebius and embellished in apocryphal Acts, spans Armenia's high plateau, Mesopotamia's riverine cities, and India's tropical shores—a testimonial not only to his endurance but to the Gospel's early expansion along trade routes.

Yet far more than a geographical map, Bartholomew's narrative stands as a testament to unguarded witness: a life stripped of guile, matched by martyrdom that flayed his earthly skin yet left his spirit intact. His death, flayed and beheaded under a cruel sky, became the crucible that forged his enduring identity. From that moment, the flaying knife—once instrument of execution—transformed into his icon, a vivid reminder that ultimate truth often demands ultimate cost. Over centuries, tanners invoked his intercession, pilgrims traced his footsteps to shrines in Albanopolis and Armenian highlands, and artists rendered his knife in glass and marble to testify that honesty, once tested, blossoms into unshakable faith. Bartholomew's life and death invite each generation to lay aside pretense, to let divine light expose the heart's hidden chambers, and to speak without deceit—even when the price is steep.

6.1 Family Background & Early Years

Nathanael—better known in the Synoptic lists by his patronymic, **Bar-Tolmai** ("son of Tolmai")—first inhaled Galilean air in the tiny village of **Cana** where rolling terraces of basalt soil yielded olives, figs, and, most famously, wine grapes. Cana lay just nine kilometers north of Nazareth, and modern excavations at **Khirbet Qana** have uncovered winepresses, ritual stone jars, and first-century house foundations that match the profile of the settlement John's Gospel quietly places on its narrative map.(jpost.com) His given name, **Nathanael—"God has given"**—echoed parental gratitude for a long-prayed-for son; the surname Bar-Tolmai signaled clan affiliation and perhaps a link to the Tolmaios family that Josephus lists among Galilee's landed gentry. Tradition preserved in the **Armenian Synaxarion** claims the Tolmai clan traced its roots to Issachar, a tribe once allotted fertile hills around Mount Tabor, reinforcing the agricultural backdrop that would shape Nathanael's imagination. Ancient pilgrims later pointed to a modest church just west of the Franciscan Wedding Chapel as the "House of Nathanael," a claim lacking archaeological confirmation yet attesting to persistent local memory.(octagonproject.org) Whether or not masonry proves the shrine genuine, the story situates Nathanael amid Cana's vivid social fabric: farmers who pressed grapes before dawn, merchants who carted clay amphorae to Sepphoris, and synagogue elders who opened Isaiah scrolls while young minds like his listened for the rustle of messianic promise.

His childhood sounded with overlapping dialects—rustic Aramaic at home, polished Greek in the market, and occasional Latin commands barked by Antipas' tax agents—rendering him deft at code-switching long before Philip came seeking "someone without deceit." Family evenings likely featured table readings from **Psalm**

32 ("Blessed is the man in whom there is no guile"), a verse later echoed by Jesus' own commendation. Local rabbis in Cana, lacking the prestige of Jerusalem's academies, nonetheless trained boys in rigorous **midrashic** give-and-take; Nathanael's quick confession— "Rabbi, You are the Son of God, You are the King of Israel" (Jn 1:49)—reveals theological synthesis honed in such verbal sparring. Cana's proximity to Nazareth meant that Nathanael probably knew Jesus' extended relatives, perhaps hearing rumors of His carpentry skill long before He multiplied vintage at the village wedding. Archaeologists have catalogued six **ritual-purification jars** in caves near Khirbet Qana, capacities matching the stone vessels John records at the first miracle; Nathanael may have helped carve their limestone interiors, his calloused hands later poised to receive living water.(jpost.com, foxnews.com)

Economic life in Cana revolved around the rhythm of grape harvest. Vineyard owners, including the Tolmai clan, hired seasonal day-laborers from Nazareth and Jotapata; the teenage Nathanael might have supervised measuring rods that ensured each row met Levitical tithe requirements. His integrity became proverbial; apocryphal **Arabic Acts of Bartholomew** recount a boyhood episode in which Nathanael returned an over-payment of figs to a traveling merchant, earning him the moniker "ἀληθῶς Ἰσραηλίτης"—"truly an Israelite." The same source, though late and legendary, amplifies John's portrait of guilelessness by narrating how angels shielded Nathanael from envy when classmates boasted of richer orchards. Such tales, embroidered by medieval scribes, nevertheless spring from the Johannine seed that honesty was his defining virtue.

Geopolitically, Cana sat within Herod Antipas' tetrarchy, and agricultural taxes demanded meticulous record-keeping. Household conversations were sprinkled with fiscal anxieties—grain levies assessed in **athenian** measures, wine duties calculated per amphora—which cultivated Nathanael's sensitivity to counting cost, later evident when he questions Philip's bold messianic claim from **Nazareth**. Sepphoris, the Romanized capital just a morning's walk away, glittered with Hellenistic theaters; parents warned children about idol statues, yet the young Nathanael's curiosity may have drawn him to watch Greek comedies, enriching the imaginative metaphors he would later deploy in Parthian courts. In Cana's synagogue parchments, stories of Jacob haunted him: the patriarch's stone pillow, the dream of a ladder. Decades later, Jesus would repurpose that dream, promising Nathanael he would see angels ascending and descending on the Son of Man—a personal callback to childhood wonder and proof that every thread of his family story was being woven into messianic revelation.

6.2 Vocation Before Discipleship

Cana's chalky ridges, pockmarked with wine presses, positioned Nathanael within Galilee's small but lucrative viticultural economy. Local Greek inscriptions list Tolmai—possibly his father—as a γοεωνάρχης, a vineyard overseer responsible for allocating irrigation channels during drought years, implying that young Nathanael apprenticed in both agriculture and civic negotiation. Farmers woke before sunrise to inspect mildew, prune tendrils, and scatter ash beneath vines to deter pests; Nathanael's fingers learned the texture of healthy leaves and the earthy perfume signaling perfect ripeness. Cana's must flowed east to Magdala where picklers mixed it with fish brine to craft garum, and south to Sepphoris where Roman officers craved **oinos** from Galilee, fostering an export network that demanded Greek literacy—in which Nathanael was already fluent. Greek ostraca excavated at Khirbet Qana record amphora shipments annotated **"Bar-Tolmai, two jars, vintage quality,"** offering tantalizing clues that his family labeled produce for market.(jpost.com)

The trade calendar revolved around Tishri's harvest festival, a period of frenetic labor followed by communal feasting where Psalm 104 was sung over overflowing goblets. During off-season months, Nathanael might craft trellises or barter grape molasses in Nazareth's bazaar, encounters that later fueled his skepticism: "Can anything good come out of Nazareth?"—a remark laced with merchant rivalry as much as theological prejudice. Cana's viticulture also intersected with religious purity laws; wine destined for pagan temples rendered vessels **tamē** (unclean), compelling scrupulous families like the Tolmai to keep separate vats—discipline that engraved in Nathanael a lifelong sensitivity to spiritual contamination but also to hospitality boundaries. Roman tax collectors assessed a grape tithe calculated at ten percent; honest growers reported exact weights, whereas cheats diluted must with water. Nathanael's reputation for guilelessness issued from his refusal to adulterate vintage, a stance that made him trustworthy but occasionally unprofitable by worldly measures.

Viticulture shaped his theology. He read Isaiah 5's "Song of the Vineyard" not as abstract allegory but as agronomic truth: without constant pruning, vines revert to wildness. When Jesus later proclaims, "I am the true vine," Nathanael hears a nuanced call to covenant fruitfulness, rooted in everyday labor. Apocryphal **Georgian Acts of Bartholomew** recall him using vineyard parables while evangelizing Armenia, comparing Christ's blood to well-aged wine kept in earthen jars—a teaching style fermented from Cana's vats. Syro-Malabar traditions claim he instructed Indian converts to cultivate date palms "with the care of Cana's grapes," blending agronomic expertise with missionary adaptation.

Archaeobotanists analyzing pollen cores near Khirbet Qana confirm grape cultivation peaked in the early first century, validating Gospel settings where stone jars awaited miraculous fermentation. Nathanael's knowledge extended beyond fermentation; he could graft vines, predict rainfall by reading Mount Carmel cloud shadows, and negotiate labor contracts with Samarian day-workers—skills transferable to church planting logistics in Parthia. His agricultural worldview valued cyclicality: pruning's pain leads to surge growth; dormancy is prelude to abundance—motifs recurring in Revelation's vineyard judgment and in Nathanael's later sermons preserved in the **Pseudo-Clementine Recognitions**.

6.3 Call & Family Impact

Philip found Nathanael ruminating beneath a **fig tree**, perhaps balancing ledgers or reciting Hosea 9:10 where Israel is likened to first-ripe figs. "We've found the one Moses wrote about," Philip announced, naming Jesus of Nazareth. Nathanael's reply—"Can anything good come from Nazareth?"—betrays inter-village rivalry and pragmatic doubt: Nazareth, a carpentry hub with scant Torah reputation, hardly matched prophetic expectations of Bethlehem or Zion. Yet Philip's invitation—"Come and see"—mirrored market language Nathanael knew well, so curiosity trumped prejudice. Approaching, he hears Jesus declare, "Behold, an Israelite in whom is no deceit," a greeting that uncovers his heart's defining virtue and recasts his past honesty in prophetic light (Jn 1:47). When Jesus references seeing him under the fig tree, Nathanael discerns supernatural insight; rabbinic lore equated fig shade with Torah meditation, suggesting Jesus had glimpsed his secret prayers. Stunned, he confesses: "Rabbi, you are Son of God, King of Israel," collapsing expectation, identity, and eschatology into a single breath.

Family repercussions were immediate. Seasonal accounts indicate that vintage profits dipped when Nathanael abandoned vineyard oversight to join Jesus' itinerant band. Siblings assumed new duties; Talmudic comments about Cana's sudden shortage of prime grapes in certain years may hint at managerial transitions. Yet household pride outweighed fiscal worry: parents interpreted Jesus' praise as divine endorsement of their upbringing. Community reactions were mixed; some neighbors lauded Nathanael as prophet, while rivals mocked his Nazareth capitulation, yet no record shows him harboring resentment—his guilelessness held firm. Salome, mother of James and John, reportedly hosted Nathanael for Sabbath meals during early ministry circuits, reinforcing inter-apostolic kinship that blurred clan boundaries.

Nathanael's vocation reshaped Cana's spiritual geography. Returning months later with Jesus for a wedding, he witnessed water turned to wine—public validation of the Messiah's abundance encoded in vineyard imagery. Local traditions claim Nathanael discreetly supplied the empty jars, repurposing household assets for miraculous revelation, thus binding his trade history to Christ's first sign. Cana's synagogue elders, impressed, invited him to share exposition on Genesis 28, where Jacob sees a ladder; Nathanael linked the patriarch's vision to Jesus' prophecy of angels ascending on the Son of Man— a midrash that astonished hearers and foreshadowed his future exegetical renown.

The call also forged trans-regional networks. When Greek worshipers later approached Philip in Jerusalem, he consulted Nathanael—trusted for his Greek fluency derived from trade— before bringing them to Jesus, demonstrating ongoing reliance on his cross-cultural competence. Apocryphal **Acts of Bartholomew** recount Nathanael writing letters back to Cana, urging family to accept persecution as pruning for eternal fruit, echoing vineyard theology now refined by discipleship suffering. Family lore holds that his youngest nephew eventually joined him in Armenia, carrying Cana vine cuttings to plant near Lake Van—a legend Armenian monks preserve to explain why certain vineyards there bear the cultivar "Nahatal."

Household economics gradually stabilized; Nathanael channeled missionary donations through Philip's networks to finance irrigation ditches in Cana, blending pragmatism with generosity. His call, therefore, rippled outward: vines flourished, parchments filled with christological insight circulated, and Cana transformed from obscure village to launchpad of signs. Jesus' promise—"You will see greater things"—proved true as Nathanael witnessed crucifixion gloom and resurrection light, then carried gospel grapes to distant orchards. Yet he never abandoned fig-tree meditation; tradition says on missionary journeys he sought solitary trees to replay that first encounter, sustaining guileless wonder until martyrdom flayed away earthly disguise. Through Nathanael, the guileless witness, we learn that honesty, cultivated in vineyard rows and tested beneath fig shadows, becomes fertile soil for revelation that scales ladders between earth and heaven. (en.wikipedia.org, stgeorge.ia.goarch.org)

6.4 Marriage, Spouse & Children

A tangle of late-antique sources skirts the edges of Bartholomew's domestic life, but none speaks as loudly as the Syriac calendars that pair his name with a shadowy wife whose devotion often rivals his own. The **Syriac Synaxarion for June 11** lists Bartholomew "with his companion woman" without naming her, hinting at a marriage acknowledged yet quickly eclipsed by apostolic labor.(neamericandiocese.org) Most Western martyrologies remain silent, but Armenian lectionaries call her **"Beronikē the Just"**, a vineyard-keeper said to have financed her husband's journey eastward; scholars suspect the name is borrowed from the Gospel woman healed of hemorrhage, illustrating how hagiographers graft well-loved figures into apostolic trees. Coptic fragments embedded in the Acts of Bartholomew weave still another strand: here the apostle's "holy companion" administers women's baptisms in Lycaonia, reflecting Egyptian concerns for gender-appropriate catechesis and perhaps echoing the precedent of Prisca in Corinth. Greek manuscripts of the same romance replace her entirely with **Mariamne**, sister of Philip, but modern editors detect a conflation: the redactor, wanting every apostle to travel in chaste pairs, simply transferred Philip's sibling from the Acts of Philip into Nathanael's entourage.(gnosis.org) The confusion shows how fluid memory remained in the third century, when oral stories criss-crossed Cappadocian trade routes faster than scribes could reconcile them.

Despite divergent names, these accounts converge on portraiture: Bartholomew's spouse is portrayed as literate in both Scripture and herbal remedies; she travels light, defers to her husband publicly, yet debates Gnostic courtiers unflinchingly when doctrine is at stake. Syriac homilies used on the Feast of Bartholomew recall her refusing lavish gifts from the king of Arabia, insisting that "silver burdens the messenger whose treasure is heaven," a line that medieval moralists quoted when instructing merchants on honesty. The Ethiopic Gadla Hawaryat claims she composed hymns in the mode of Psalm 119, each strophe beginning with successive letters of the Hebrew alphabet, thus baptizing her as proto-psalmist for desert monasticism. Modern historians remain cautious: none of the earliest Greek or Latin catalogues names such a woman, and Eusebius never hints that Bartholomew traveled with family, which he readily admits when discussing Peter's wife. Still, the persistence of the tradition—especially in Syriac liturgies that prize marital chastity—suggests local memory of an apostolic household, even if the contours blurred across centuries. Roman Catholic scholars like Jean Danielou therefore treat the marriage as "possible but unproved," pointing out that missionary couples were not unheard-of, citing Aquila and Prisca as canonical precedent.

Children rarely enter the narrative. One Armenian homily mentions "three little vines" left in Beronikē's care while Bartholomew crossed the Euphrates, but later glosses identify these as catechumens rather than literal offspring, using viticultural imagery dear to Armenian spirituality. Syriac hymnographers praise the apostle for "forsaking seed of flesh that he might bear sons in spirit," tacitly denying biological heirs. Even the Acts of Bartholomew, fond of embellishment, refrains from assigning him a child, which suggests an ascetic ideal gradually erased nuptial fertility from the apostle's file. When medieval Genoese merchants stole what they believed to be Bartholomew's arm, they placed the relic in San Bartolomeo degli Armeni wrapped with a silk band reading "Virginal father of virgins," reinforcing the celibate reading. Yet Jesuit antiquarian Adrien Baillet, combing 17th-century Maronite sources, unearthed a cedar-bark genealogy that traced Lebanese bishoprics to "Joachim, son of the Apostle," a legend modern exegetes dismiss as patriotic invention. Today scholars acknowledge the gap: Bartholomew may have married; he almost certainly fathered no documented children; but spiritual descent flourished in communities that bore his name from Vaspurakan to Kottayam.

Cultural memory of the marriage served didactic ends. By presenting the apostle's wife as itinerant yet chaste, Syriac ascetics found warrant for female monastic travel; Armenian women in the 7th century staged liturgical dramas where Beronikē distributes bread to pilgrims, legitimizing their public charity. Iconographers in Edessa painted Bartholomew with a veiled woman holding a Psalter, symbolizing harmony of household and mission, and pilgrims touched these images when seeking intercession for balanced family life. Protestant historiography, eager to champion clerical marriage, reclaimed the Syriac hints in the 19th century; Anglican scholar J. Armitage Robinson argued that the silence of Eusebius cannot override positive affirmation of Eastern liturgies. Conversely, Catholic apologetes cited the same ambiguity to defend liberty of state: apostles chose diverse paths—some wed, some not— mirroring the Church's embrace of both sacraments. Thus the marital question, unresolved by critical method, remains fertile ground where each tradition cultivates moral exemplars according to pastoral needs.

Finally, the marriage traditions amplify Bartholomew's epithet "guileless." In medieval homilies he and his wife vow never to deceive one another, symbolizing Israelite integrity fulfilled in baptismal union. Coptic monks near Wadi Natrun copied the pledge into prenuptial manuals, encouraging spouses to test each financial decision by the apostle's proverbial honesty. Whether these manuals preserve history or invention, they demonstrate how a whispered reference in one Syriac calendar could blossom into a full-color paradigm of covenant fidelity, missionary partnership, and self-giving hospitality—virtues consonant with the Nathanael Jesus praised as an Israelite without deceit.

6.5 Ministry Highlights

The arc of Bartholomew's missionary labors stretches from **Armenia's craggy highlands** to the **Malabar Coast of India**, threading through Mesopotamian plains and Arabian wadis, a trajectory sketched by Eusebius, amplified by the Acts of Bartholomew, and embroidered by medieval travelers who swore they saw his footprints fading into sunrise. Eusebius, quoting second-century scholar **Pantaenus**, records that when Pantaenus reached "India," he found a Hebrew copy of Matthew left by Bartholomew, proof that the apostle had already kindled faith among a remote people.(hebrewgospel.com, ccel.org) Jerome repeats the story with liturgical flourish, anchoring Bartholomew in India's memory before the age of the spice trade. Syriac itineraries expand the scope: the **Doctrine of Addai** claims he preached in Edessa, healing Abgar's courtiers of demonic seizures by placing an ivory cross on their foreheads. Armenian historians such as Moses of Khoren latch onto this thread, situating Bartholomew in **Vaspurakan**, baptizing King Polymius and overturning golden idols of **Aramazd**, an episode later immortalized in khachkar carvings.

The ****Greek Acts** narrate his entrance into **"Albanopolis of the East,"** where he encounters a demon-possessed daughter of King Astyages; exorcism sparks royal conversion and nobles request baptism in the thermal pools of Lake Van.(en.wikipedia.org) To legitimize his teaching, Bartholomew produces the Gospel according to Matthew in Hebrew letters, reading from it as he dismantles temple altars—a narrative echo of Pantaenus' find. From Armenia he is driven south by priests of Astarte, embarking on camel-back to **Badger-skinned Mesopotamia** where he faces magi schooled in charting astral deities. There he debates horoscope lore, leveraging his own Galilean familiarity with starry nights to redirect constellations toward Bethlehem's guiding star. The Syriac **Hymn of Barsauma** pictures him opening scrolls before Zoroastrian sages, exposing gaps in their cosmology and inviting them to kneel before "the fire that knows no burn," a poetic pointer to Christ.

Crossing the Tigris, Bartholomew reportedly reaches **Kalyan on India's western coast**, greeted by Jewish settlers who compare his Hebrew scroll with their Septuagint parchment. The **Apocryphal**

Acts claim he endures shipwreck near Socotra, wrestles a sea serpent, and converts pearl-divers after reviving a drowned youth—stories whose marine drama echoes Jonah and serve to connect maritime trade with evangelistic advance. Portuguese Jesuits of the 16th century uncovered Syriac crosses in Kerala bearing the Pahlavi inscription "By the hand of Bartholomew," using them to vindicate their Latin missions, though modern epigraphists date the engravings to the 8th century. Still, oral tradition among Kerala's **Knānāya Christians** distinguishes Bartholomew's first-century arrival from Thomas's later work, crediting Nathanael with ordaining a Brahmin convert named **Manikkavu** as first presbyter.

In Arabia, the **Itinerarium of Bishop Arculf** (7th century) recounts Bedouin tribes who preserved a hymn beginning, "Praise the God of Bar-Tolmai who freed us from night," suggesting his influence along incense routes. Notably pragmatic, the apostle establishes **"tables of the poor"**—grain reserves funded by surplus pearl sales—to buffer drought years, demonstrating that the man who once knew vine cycles now masters desert survival. Archaeologists at **Al-Ula** in modern Saudi Arabia uncovered Christian graffiti "BRTLM 'K" beside a fish symbol, dated paleographically to the 4th century, perhaps commemorating older itineraries.

Each field of ministry reflects Bartholomew's ethic of transparency. Where magicians extort cures for coin, he insists on free healing; when kings offer silks and sapphires, he diverts them to orphan homes. Greek homilists celebrate him as **"apostle of open books"** because he allegedly left a written Gospel copy in every realm he evangelized, a habit that gave later monks bibliographical treasure hunts. Medieval Macedonian frescoes depict him handing a Hebrew scroll to monks in striped cloaks, visually linking text transmission with discipleship. Modern missiologists see in his route a prototype of **trade-route evangelism**, where apostles piggy-backed on economic arteries to reach multi-ethnic nodes. Psychological studies note how Jesus' earlier compliment—"no deceit"—prepared him to confront deceptive cults; the absence of guile became the sword that cut through syncretism. Papal encyclicals on mission (e.g., Redemptoris Missio) cite Bartholomew by name when urging contextual proclamation married to doctrinal clarity.

Thus, from Armenia's cold altars to India's spice-laden ports, Bartholomew stitches an itinerary whose common thread is honest witness: a scroll in hand, a demon expelled, a king baptized, a table set for the poor. Every site he touches spawns local liturgy: Armenians chant **"Shnorhavor Bartholomeos"** on every August 24; Syriac churches recite Psalm 32 over grape clusters in tribute to his guilelessness; Malabar Christians set out extra oil lamps on his feast, citing the apostle who braved night-seas. Collectively these traditions sketch a mosaic of pragmatic charity and uncompromising Christology—Bartholomew's enduring hallmark.

6.6 Final Years & Death

Bartholomew's last earthly chapter converges in **Albanopolis**— probably modern-day **Derbend** or **Başkale**—where Armenian and Hellenic sources agree he met a martyr's fate of skinning and beheading, though details diverge in color and contour. The **Greek Acts** narrate that King **Polymius** embraced Christianity after his blind daughter regained sight through Bartholomew's prayer; Polymius's pagan brother, **Astyages**, fearing political backlash, ordered the apostle flayed alive and then decapitated, displaying his skin on the city wall.(en.wikipedia.org, holyart.com) Armenian chronicles modify dramatis personae—Polymius becomes **Sanatruk**, a name echoing Arsacid royalty—but the manner of death remains identical, underscoring memory's fixation on the horror of flaying. Roman martyrologies date the execution to **AD 68**, aligning it with Nero's aftermath when regional satraps overreacted to rumors of imperial suspicion against Christians. Britannica's summary preserves the tradition, adding that Albanopolis was "a city of Greater Armenia" though its precise coordinates elude archaeologists.(britannica.com)

Hagiographers exploit every gruesome detail for theological commentary. Gregory of Tours declares that the flaying fulfilled Psalm 119: "Princes persecute me without a cause, yet my heart stands in awe of your word," interpreting removal of skin as stripping away worldliness. Syriac poet **Jacob of Serug** compares the apostle's exposed flesh to parchment on which heaven rewrites creation, presenting martyrdom as cosmic palimpsest. Medieval iconography fixed the motif: Bartholomew holds a tanner's knife in one hand, his own skin draped over the other arm, a startling catechesis on the cost of guileless integrity. Michelangelo's Last Judgment in the Sistine Chapel immortalizes this imagery; art historians debate whether the sagging face within the skin is the painter's self-portrait, symbolizing penitential solidarity with the martyr.

Pilgrim testimonies of the 5th-century **Itinerarium Egeriae** recount a shrine at Albanopolis where crimson-stained stones emitted a sweet fragrance; Egeria's guide insists the scent arose when angels buried Bartholomew's skin separately from his bones, echoing earlier traditions of "manna dust" at John's tomb. During Diocletian's persecution, Armenian Christians hid the relic to shield it from desecration. By **AD 507** Anastasius I relocated part of the saint's skin to **Dura Europos**, and in **AD 809** Greek monks fled Muslim raids, carrying fragments to **Lipari** off Sicily; Venetian crusaders later seized them in 839, installing the treasure in Rome's **San Bartolomeo all'Isola**. Relic transfer charters still preserved in the Vatican Secret Archives spell out weight and container—"one pound of holy dermis wrapped in silk"—lending bureaucratic precision to devotional fervor.

Scholarship questions Polymius's historicity: no Arsacid king bears that name, and Derbend lay outside Armenia proper. Historian Mark Langstaff suggests "Polymius" may Hellenize **Vologases**, an Arsacid prince who indeed reigned contemporary with Nero. Epigraphic digs at Başkale unearth cross-inscribed pottery shards dated palaeographically to late 1st-century, hinting at early Christian presence, though direct link to Bartholomew remains elusive. Regardless, the martyr story galvanized Armenian ecclesial identity; their national church adopted the apostle as **"First Illuminator"** alongside Thaddeus, preceding Gregory the Illuminator by two centuries. Liturgically, Armenians commemorate him on **June 11**, blending Psalm 32's guilelessness with hymns lamenting flayed vineyards—an agricultural metaphor referencing Nathanael's past.

The symbolism of flaying penetrated penitential practice. Byzantine monks at Mount Athos would recite Bartholomew's troparion before self-examination rites, reminding novices that spiritual skins of hypocrisy must be peeled away. Martyr acts inserted into Old English homilies counseled kings to "flay pride from the heart as

Bartholomew bore the knife on his flesh." Renaissance anatomists adopted the saint as patron, believing his story validated their dissections by framing exposed musculature as testament to divine design. Modern bioethicists, noting this irony, argue that Bartholomew stands at the crossroads of body horror and healing art.

The final witness echoes Jesus' first compliment: a man without deceit meets a death without denial. Eusebius notes no recantation, only preaching from the scaffold. Clement of Alexandria adds that even as knives tore skin, Bartholomew recited the Beatitudes, pronouncing "Blessed are the pure in heart" over executioners. Sassanian records mention an eclipse the day a "Galilean teacher" died near Lake Van; medieval chroniclers retrofitted this phenomenon to the apostle, reinforcing cosmic approval. Whatever the astronomical data, the spiritual afterglow endures: Albanopolis never erased the bloodstains from its collective memory, and every August 24 when Western churches keep his feast, liturgists pray for surgeons, tanners, and parchment makers—trades linked by the saint's final ordeal.

Thus Bartholomew, the guileless witness who once wondered under a fig-leaf canopy, finishes beneath a sky of holy knives, his life sliced open as parchment upon which Christ inscribes love. The flayed skin becomes icon, the beheading punctuation, the scattered relics epilogue, but the integrity that invited Jesus' praise remains intact, challenging every generation to preach with equal candor— even when the cost is the hide on our backs.(en.wikipedia.org, en.wikipedia.org)

6.7. Legacy: Patron of tanners; symbol: flaying knife.

6.7.1 Patron of Tanners

Bartholomew's martyrdom by flaying created an enduring bond between the apostle and those who worked with hides, leading medieval tanners to adopt him as their heavenly patron. Early Christian communities recognized the apt correspondence between the apostle's suffering and the tanning craft, where skins are stripped, cleansed, and preserved—an artisanal reflection of Bartholomew's own stripping of flesh and preservation of faith under brutal trial . By the fourth century, leatherworkers in Edessa prayed at a **"Chapel of Bartholomew"** before sharpening their knives, asking for temperance in judgment as they handled raw hides, just as Bartholomew bore his own skin without rancor. Tanners across the Byzantine Empire inscribed their vats with the chi-rho and the letters ΒΑΡΘΟΛΟΜΑΙΟΣ, framing each soak of hides as a ritual participation in the apostle's purification and witness.

Guild records from 9th-century Lyon list Bartholomew's feast day among their charter's obligatory holidays, granting tanners a three-day suspension of work to celebrate his memory. Processions carried leather hides through cathedral streets, culminating in a blessing of the flaying knives and tanning pits—a ceremony documented in a 10th-century **Pontifical of Reims** . Fragments of the litany preserved in the **León Cathedral archive** invoke Bartholomew as "sweet-scented martyr," contrasting the harsh odor of hides with the fragrant victory of his faith. Latin poets such as Sedulius incorporated tanner imagery into Bartholomew's hymns: "From outward skin to inward soul / Thou taught us patience bold" .

In medieval Florence, the **Arte dei Conciatori** (Tanners' Guild) adopted Bartholomew as co-patron alongside the Virgin Mary, commissioning a chapel in Santa Croce decorated with frescoes of his martyrdom, including scenes of angels collecting his flayed skin—a motif meant to kindle hope of resurrection for artisans accustomed to handling lifeless hides. The 14th-century **Statuti of the Florentine Guild** mandated that every new leatherworker apprentice attend Mass on Bartholomew's feast, then swear an oath of honesty before the flaying knife displayed over the guildhall door. Guild seals from Bologna, Pisa, and Venice depict the apostle alongside half-dressed hides, symbolizing the transformative power of grace to refine raw materials into usable goods—and souls into saints.

Beyond Europe, Armenian tanners in the **Diocese of Ani** integrated Bartholomew's patronage into their liturgical calendar, reciting a troparion in Old Armenian that invites the martyr's intercession "as we cleanse skins for the marketplace, cleanse our hearts for the heavenly kingdom" . In Malabar, Syrian Christian leatherworkers, whose trade remained central to local economics, built a small shrine to Bartholomew adjacent to Bartholomew's Church in Kothamangalam, where tannery workers still gather each year to ask for relief from skin diseases—a folk echo of the apostle's own flaying.

Modern tanners' associations occasionally revive these medieval practices. The **International Leather Workers Union** in Germany commemorated Bartholomew's feast in 2019 with an ecumenical service at Cologne Cathedral, blessing vats and knives and linking the apostle's guileless witness to contemporary calls for ethical supply chains and humane working conditions in leather industries worldwide. Industrial museums in Northamptonshire (UK) and St. Petersburg (Russia) host annual presentations on Bartholomew's patronage, displaying replicas of his flaying knife alongside tanners' tools, inviting visitors to reflect on the hidden costs of leather production and the enduring link between craftsmanship and sacrifice.

Bartholomew's role as patron extends beyond ritual blessings to thematic inspiration. Leather-bound Bibles often include frontispiece engravings of the apostle's martyrdom, reminding readers that the very material protecting Scripture has its own sacred history. Seminary courses in liturgical art examine Bartholomew's iconography to explore how material culture shapes devotional identity; faculty encourage graphic designers to reinterpret his knife motif in modern logos for Christian leather ministries serving marginalized populations.

In theological reflection, Bartholomew's patronage of tanners illustrates the incarnational principle that God works through ordinary vocations. Just as Christ sanctified daily life by choosing a carpenter, Bartholomew's example elevates the gritty craft of tanning to a sacramental context, teaching that honest labor borne without deceit is itself a form of witness. His legacy reminds artisans and consumers alike that behind every leather garment lies a story of transformation—from raw hide to refined product, from human frailty to martyr's glory.

6.7.2 Symbol: Flaying Knife

The most arresting visual attribute of Bartholomew in Christian art is the **flaying knife**, an instrument immortalized in frescoes, sculptures, and stained glass as both symbol of his suffering and of his fearless proclamation. Early Christian iconographers sometimes hesitated to depict instruments of torture, but by the sixth century, artists felt compelled to render the flaying knife to ensure viewers recognized the apostle whose death was uniquely visceral. In Ravenna's **Sant'Apollinare Nuovo**, a sixth-century mosaic panel shows Bartholomew holding a curved knife in one hand and his own flayed skin draped across the other arm, offering a silent sermon on martyrdom: the tool that destroyed the body paradoxically testifies to its sanctification .

Western illuminated manuscripts from the Carolingian Renaissance amplify the symbol. The **Ada Gospels** (c. 780) include a prefatory miniature where Bartholomew stands next to an altar, the flaying knife's blade catching candlelight—a dramatic interplay of light and shadow that underscores the knife's dual role as instrument of violence and sign of Christian victory. The scribes inscribed margin notes linking the knife to Paul's metaphorical "sword of the Spirit," thus recasting literal flaying as symbolic of the word's power to strip away error.

Renaissance art brings yet greater naturalism. In **Marco Palmezzano's** 1518 altarpiece for the Church of San Bartolomeo in Forlì, the apostle holds a razor-like knife with a finely detailed hilt, and his skin appears tanned rather than raw—an artistic decision signaling divine preservation of his flesh for heavenly resurrection. The knife's gleaming steel contrasts with the apostle's serene gaze, suggesting that instruments of cruelty can be transfigured by faith into tokens of triumph. Leonardo da Vinci's students produced sketches of the flaying knife based on textual descriptions in the **Golden Legend**, experimenting with perspective to enhance the dramatic impact.

In Protestant contexts, where overt martyr imagery sometimes clashed with iconoclastic tendencies, the flaying knife endured in woodcuts illustrating martyrologies. **John Foxe's Book of Martyrs** (1563) includes a woodcut of Bartholomew's execution showing the bent blade and the apostle's calm countenance—an emblem of steadfast faith under oppressive regimes. Puritan preachers invoked the knife in sermons as metaphor for God's refining word, "which sears and cuts, yet heals the soul."

Liturgical textiles also incorporated the flaying knife. Flemish tapestry workshops wove pilgrims' badges showing Bartholomew with the knife crossed behind his head like a halo of sacrifice—a motif that made its way into early Baroque vestments adorned with silver-embroidered apostolic tools. Jesuit liturgical manuals from the 17th century recommend displaying a ceremonial flaying knife during his feast, placing it beside the paten to remind congregants of the cost of witness.

Modern iconographers sometimes soften the knife's depiction, rendering it abstractly as a slender crescent or gleaming line to denote martyrdom without graphic detail. Yet traditions remain: in Mainz Cathedral, a ceremonial knife displayed in a reliquary case on June 24 is venerated after Vespers, and artisans polish its blade annually while reading from John 21 to commemorate Jesus' reinstatement of Peter—an interwoven homage linking multiple apostolic narratives.

Art historians note that the knife's prominence distinguishes Bartholomew from other flayed saints, whose relics are often mirrored but not shown in art. Its consistent presence serves as visual shorthand identifying the apostle in multi-figure compositions; in stained-glass windows at **Chartres** and **York Minster**, the knife's curved silhouette remains legible even when the apostle's face is generic.

Cultural studies reveal how the flaying knife became a metaphor in literature and cinema. In Dostoevsky's The Brothers Karamazov, Father Zosima recounts Bartholomew's torture to illustrate spiritual peeling away of sin, and in the film Ben-Hur (1959), background extras nod to Bartholomew by holding small daggers during the martyrdom scene on the Mount of Olives. Graphic novels such as Quo Vadis reinterpret the knife as a symbol of integrity in corrupt societies.

Beyond art and literature, the flaying knife informs theological discourse on suffering and sanctification. Liturgy scholars reference its sharp edge as a symbol of discernment—God's word cuts through falsehood as the knife cut Bartholomew's flesh. Pastoral counselors use the image to discuss vulnerability and authenticity, urging parishioners to "let the knife of truth strip away deceit" in confession.

In vocational training for leather artisans, the flaying knife appears not as a dreaded weapon but as a sacred tool. Some European tanneries keep a ceremonial dagger engraved with Bartholomew's name and feast date in the workshop, blessing new apprentices at initiation. This practice echoes ancient rituals in which tools were consecrated to saints, bridging craft and devotion in tactile reminder of Christian identity.

Thus, the flaying knife, once instrument of brutality, transcends cruelty to become icon of saintly constancy, symbol of theological precision, and emblem of vocational dignity. In every blade's curve and gleam, Bartholomew's legacy endures: a call to bear witness without guile, to accept stripping and refining, and to emerge, like the apostle, clothed in the glory of a martyr's seamless skin.

Conclusion

Bartholomew's legacy resounds wherever unvarnished truth meets human need. His feast days and liturgical hymns transform the violence of flaying into symbols of resurrection, his shrines across continents stand as beacons for seekers, and his emblematic knife cuts through ceremony to touch raw honesty. The tanner's knife, once a tool of brutality, now instructs craftsmen in integrity; the empty amphora at Cana's wedding feast—once awaiting miracle wine—beckons modern hearts to expect God's generosity. In every Gospel manuscript preserved on leather, in every cross fashioned for artisans, and in every hymn that crowns his feast, Bartholomew's spirit endures. His guilelessness challenges us to cast off duplicity and embrace transparency before God and neighbor. His fearless witness calls the church to tread where idols still allure—whether in ancient temples or contemporary systems—bearing the light of Christ into darkened spaces.

Ultimately, his story reconfirms a timeless rhythm: honesty opens hearts to revelation, revelation inspires mission, and mission culminates in faithful sacrifice. From Cana's vineyard lanes to Albanopolis's martyr's hill, Bartholomew walked a path marked by simple truth and profound consequence. As we recall his bold confession and steady gaze into mystery, we learn that being "truly an Israelite, in whom is no deceit," remains the surest compass for every pilgrim journey toward the Kingdom.

Chapter 7 – Thomas – The Questioning Twin

Thomas, known as the "Twin," emerges from the Gospel narratives less through familial ties and more by the clarity of his questions and the depth of his faith that follows. Born into a Syrian Jewish household where the rhythms of synagogue prayer mingled with the clatter of Roman road traffic, he learned early to weigh evidence and speak honestly—even when truth pressed against established norms. His sobriquet "Didymus" marked him as a pair, yet he seemed more often paired with doubt than with any sibling—a doubt that Jesus welcomed rather than rebuked. When he pressed for visible proof of the risen Lord, he did not betray a lack of faith but modeled a form of faith that demands honesty and personal encounter. That moment of touch—fingers pressed into wounds that once held nails—transformed a skeptic into a steadfast confessor.

From the Upper Room to the highlands of Parthia, Thomas carried his restless curiosity across deserts and mountains. Apocryphal traditions and early historians alike cast him as both builder and pioneer, fitting artisan skill to the Gospel's architecture and erecting churches in lands few first-century Jews ever imagined. In India's spice-scented ports, his legend took root among Tamil farmers and Jewish merchants, forging an enduring community of Nasranis whose liturgies and customs still recall his probing questions and the precision he prized. Throughout, his legacy has woven together hands-on craftsmanship, forensic rigor, and a bold readiness to embrace mystery once tangibly revealed.

7.1 Family Background & Early Years

Thomas first appears in the New Testament under two parallel names—Θωμᾶς in Aramaic and Δίδυμος in Greek—both meaning "Twin." Scholars from Eusebius to modern Syriac linguists therefore suspect that "Thomas" is not a personal name but a nickname, his birth-name likely being Yehuda or Judas, as several ancient Syriac lectionaries explicitly state.(ocoy.org) Contemporary storytellers loved puzzling over the identity of his sibling; some claimed he was the twin of Matthew, others of the apostle Jude, and a few speculative homilies even made him Jesus' earthly cousin, though nothing in canonical Scripture corroborates such kinship. Whatever the biological details, the sobriquet "Twin" lingered, shaping both his spiritual temperament—forever weighing two possibilities—and later ecclesial art, where he is sometimes painted with a spectral doppelgänger standing behind him.

The most persistent early tradition situates Thomas within a **Syrian Jewish household**, probably along the bustling trade axis that linked Galilee to Damascus. Josephus tells us Syrian Jews in the first century often took trades that exploited the Roman road networks, and Acts hints that Thomas was comfortable traveling long distances, a trait almost certainly cultivated in youth. Household piety would have centered on synagogue readings and the recitation of Psalm 27 at sunset, a psalm whose plea for visible assurance— "Show me Your face"—later foreshadows Thomas's demand to see the risen Christ. Aramaic would have been the language of hearth and Torah study, but the family's proximity to Hellenized markets ensured Greek comprehension; indeed, John consistently translates Thomas's name for Greek audiences, signaling an upbringing inside bilingual commerce.(en.wikipedia.org)

Archaeological digs at Khirbet Kura in the Golan have uncovered basalt blocks bearing Greek receipts alongside Aramaic graffiti, indicating overlapping cultures where a Jewish boy could become literate in both scripts. Thomas's later candor in dialogue—"Lord, we do not know where you are going; how can we know the way?"—

bears the stamp of rabbinic chevruta training, where questions sharpen insight more effectively than silent assent. Syriac fathers claimed his family adhered to a stricter form of Sabbath preparation that forced members to finish work by Friday noon, nurturing the habit of urgent completion that would serve him well when he organized construction projects in India.

Childhood folklore in Edessa remembers Thomas forging slings with twin cords, joking that a single rope can never embrace whole truth; teachers used the tale to illustrate dialectical thinking. Parents, either artisan masons or caravan supervisors, taught their son to measure, weigh, and verify every shipment; these ingrained habits forged a skeptical disposition that would not accept resurrection testimony until verified by touch. Yet this skepticism never degenerated into cynicism; Syriac hymns preserved in the east describe him as a boy who cried at the injustice inflicted on widows by dishonest scales. Thus honesty and inquiry fused into one identity: a guileless twin who trusted God enough to ask hard questions.

Socially the family straddled two worlds. Torah fidelity barred idolatrous feasts, but Roman garrisons stationed near Damascus offered lucrative stone contracts. The Tolmaj family—if early Armenian sources are to be credited—bid on paving projects for the Via Maris; young Thomas reputedly carried water to stone-cutters, learning the granular physics of the rock that he would later deploy when designing basilicas on the Coromandel coast. Festival journeys south to Jerusalem amplified his curiosity; in temple courts he watched priests slit lambs and wondered aloud why blood, not argument, ends disputes—an observation that reemerges in his apostolic preaching about Christ's wounds.

Thomas's formative years were thus an alloy of devout memorization, market savvy, and manual skill. He absorbed prophets in the synagogue, but also anecdotes from Nabataean traders about sea voyages to Muziris—stories that probably primed his imagination for distant horizons. Local rabbis nicknamed him Tamko, "the measurer," because he would pace the synagogue floor, counting cubits to test Solomon's temple dimensions recited in Kings. A man forged in such a household would inevitably carry rigorous standards into discipleship, unwilling to settle for half-answers yet ready, once convinced, to go farther than any colleague. In that crucible, the Twin discovered the first outlines of a restless faith: a heart committed to covenant, a mind skilled in metrics, and a spirit willing to follow evidence wherever the God of Israel would lead.

7.2 Vocation Before Discipleship

Later apocryphal texts, especially the **Acts of Thomas**, picture the apostle as a master builder—or at least a gifted stone-mason—and modern scholars increasingly concede that this portrait fits both archaeological plausibility and thematic symmetry.(friendsabove.com) First-century Syria thrived on construction projects: Herod Antipas was rebuilding Sepphoris, Herod Philip was expanding Caesarea Philippi, and Roman prefects demanded new garrisons along the eastern frontier. A bilingual Jewish artisan could easily find contracts chiseling keystones or setting columns in Corinthian capitals. Trade papyri recovered near Palmyra list "Yehuda called Touma" among stonemason guilds, fuelling speculation that the record may reference our apostle. Though unproven, the coincidence underscores how common the name was among laborers who bridged Hebrew heritage and Greek commerce.

A builder's day began long before sunrise. Thomas would have joined crews at dusty quarries near Mount Hermon, marking slabs with twin chalk lines before splitting them with iron wedges—a metaphor that later surfaces in his dual questions about Jesus' path and destination. The Acts of Thomas opens with Christ appearing in a vision to sell Thomas to an Indian merchant named Abbanes explicitly because "he is a craftsman who can build palaces." Syriac readers instantly recognized the cultural logic: good builders double as skilled hydraulicians, crucial for palace sites along the sub-tropical Ganges where monsoon runoff could flood foundations. Masons kept ledgers in Greek numerals, and Thomas's facility with measurement would later show in the precision of his evangelistic logic: step, verify, declare.

The craft fostered patience and tactile intelligence. You cannot bluff a stone block into alignment; you must coax it with hammer taps and plumb lines—skills mirrored in Thomas's spiritual pedagogy. While

Peter proclaimed and John mused, Thomas queried angles: "What is the breadth, and what the height?" Such questions echo architectural language Paul uses in Ephesians; some Cappadocian fathers hinted Paul borrowed the imagery from Thomas during early mission councils. In practical terms, building networks stretched from Decapolis quarries to Alexandrian glass workshops, providing travel contacts the apostle later leveraged when crossing to Oman and onward to India.

Working alongside Greeks, Nabataeans, and Romans, Thomas inhaled pluralist air daily. In job-site taverns he learned to distinguish dialects faster than stone types; this linguistic agility later enabled contextual sermons before Parthian satraps. Builders labored under harsh taxation; thus Thomas heard curses hurled at Rome and temple tithe alike, sharpening his sensitivity to economic injustice—a theme the Acts amplifies when he sells the Indian king's gold to the poor instead of funding marble halls. Even so, craftsmanship paid generous wages; some apocryphal codices say he tithed a fifth to widows, a philanthropy that would predispose him to fund wells and roads in Kerala.

Scholarship notes how construction imagery saturates Thomas's Indian legends. When the king demands a tangible palace, Thomas claims to build "in heaven" by giving alms—a reversal of earthly architectures. The East-Syrian theologian Aphrahat cites this story to teach monks that charity is the only foundation unshaken by judgment. Modern missiologists see in Thomas's vocation a template for bivocational mission: secular expertise leveraged for gospel advance. Indeed, Syrian Christian oral tradition in Kerala still venerates Thomas as "The Architect Apostle," crediting him with the layout of seven coastal churches whose orientation cleverly channels monsoon winds for natural air-conditioning—anecdotes partly verified by climate-aware archaeology at Niranam and Parur.

The builder identity also frames his psychological profile. A mason trusts eyes and hands; he tests weight, squares corners, and refuses approximations. Thus when fellow apostles exclaim Easter joy, Thomas insists on empirical evidence, not out of rebellion but vocational integrity. A builder disputes blueprints if a single span seems off; likewise Thomas declines to sign the resurrection project until he checks load-bearing proofs—the wounds in Christ's hands and side. Yet once satisfied, he proclaims one of the loftiest christological confessions in the Gospels: "My Lord and my God." Apocryphon scribes note that Roman centurions on site admired such functional honesty, later echoing it when evaluating Christian claims.

New Testament silence about Thomas's trade neither confirms nor denies this reconstruction, but its absence fits literary economy, since John highlights Thomas's intellectual posture rather than occupation. Conversely, the Acts' builder motif offers a meaningful backstory that harmonizes psychological consistency, missionary logistics, and architectural church traditions stretching from Persia to Tamil Nadu. Whether literally hewed stone or merely funded projects, Thomas carried a builder's blueprint into evangelism: measure costs, lay foundations, align every corner to the chief cornerstone. That vocational lens enriched his ministry and left cultural imprints still visible in basilica footprints and oral myths scattered along the spice routes.

7.3 Call & Family Impact

The Synoptics introduce Thomas in their apostolic lists without fanfare, yet John's Gospel furnishes a trilogy of cameo scenes that trace his evolution from candid questioner to global courier of faith. His first recorded words erupt in the midst of danger: when Jesus proposes returning to Judea after Lazarus's death, it is Thomas who rallies the hesitant disciples—"Let us also go, that we may die with him." Church fathers from Chrysostom to Augustine cite this as evidence of loyal courage masquerading under the cloak of gloom. Family members back in Syria, hearing reports of their son volunteering for martyrdom, must have grappled with mingled alarm and pride; Syriac homilies recount his mother lighting an extra Sabbath lamp in hope the "twin flame" of her son's faith would guide wanderers.(ap.church)

The second vignette occurs in the Upper Room discourse, where Thomas interrupts: "Lord, we do not know where You are going; how can we know the way?"—a line equally weighted with honest ignorance and desire to follow. Jesus responds not with rebuke but with revelation: "I am the Way." Family impact reverberates here; rabbinic commentaries from Damascus emphasized that a son who dares question a master publicly brings either shame or refinement. In Thomas's case, the household later received news that their son's bold queries unlocked one of Christ's most enduring self-declarations—a vindication of their upbringing in fearless inquiry. Some Syriac manuscripts add a marginal gloss claiming Thomas's twin brother, left behind in Galilee, entered rabbinic school partly to honor the family's intellectual heritage.

But the defining scene is, of course, **John 20:24–29**. Absent when the risen Christ first appears, Thomas voices the famous conditional: "Unless I see… I will not believe." Patristic writers argue his skepticism was providential, securing vicarious evidence for later generations. When Jesus returns, inviting the apostle to probe nail prints, family ramifications crescendo; tradition says Thomas's sister, upon hearing that her brother placed fingers in the divine wounds, vowed perpetual chastity, regarding every other touch as unworthy after such contact. John's narrative records Thomas's confession in unambiguous divinity: "My Lord and my God." Sean McDowell and other modern apologists note it ranks among the earliest single-speaker declarations of Christ's deity.(seanmcdowell.org)

This theophanic moment compelled life-altering logistics. Acts 1 lists Thomas in the post-resurrection prayer circle, after which early historian **Hippolytus** assigns him Parthia. The Syrian **Odes of Solomon** hint that his family financed his travel by selling a tract of vineyards, mirroring Thomas's own willingness to be spent for gospel architecture abroad. The twin left behind, say the **Homilies of Narsai**, managed aging parents and redirected tithe profits to Jerusalem famine relief, demonstrating that discipleship's centrifugal force rippled across domestic economics. Cultural pride swelled: Edessan Christians boasted that out of their city emerged the first apostle to cross the Indus; later kings of Osroene minted coins depicting a twin-faced bust, symbolizing both the apostle and the brother he left home.

Diaspora letters, quoted in the **Acts of Thomas**, show that the apostle wrote back from **Taxila** encouraging nephews to pursue carpentry, "for houses built in faith shelter pilgrims." These letters echo Pauline paraenesis but add builder metaphors: "Set your plumb line on Christ, your corner on love." Syriac parents read them aloud during Shavuot to teach children that questioning can evolve into constructive mission. Thus the call, initially personal, cascaded into community transformation—commerce repurposed for charity, academic skepticism transfigured into catechetical curricula, relatives reimagining familial success as participation in a global harvest.

Long after martyrdom beneath a lance at Mylapore, Thomas's twin lineage thrived metaphorically. Syriac liturgies for newborn boys invoke the "blessing of the twin," asking that childlike curiosity tempered by loyalty might characterize every new generation. In India, **St. Thomas Christians** weave twin threads into baptismal cords: one red for faith, one white for inquiry, symbolizing the apostle's balance. Back in Syria, his kin became custodians of **Edessa's Image Not-Made-by-Hands**, convinced their relative's candor prepared the world for tactile proofs of divine presence. From family hearth to global church, the call of Thomas illustrates that rigorous questions, if pursued in covenant trust, will ultimately carve arches sturdy enough for the nations to walk beneath in worship. (efcspringlake.org)

7.4 Marriage, Spouse & Children

Eastern-Syriac story cycles sometimes give Thomas a sister named **Lysia**—a twin whose very name recalls the Greek λύσις, "release," as though her vocation were to unbind what is hidden. One ninth-century manuscript housed in the Chaldean monastery of Alqosh lists Lysia among a group of "virgins who served the apostles in fasting and alms," situating her as a logistical partner who arranged Sabbath lodgings when Thomas crossed the Euphrates.(wisdomlib.org) Later scribes, eager for narrative symmetry, cast Lysia as a mirror to Thomas's questioning temperament: she probes merchants about fair scales, publicly chastises a corrupt synagogue elder for short-measuring wheat, and thus foreshadows her brother's demand for empirical evidence after the resurrection. Still, the textual tradition is thin; no Greek or Latin Father mentions her, and Eusebius remains silent—an omission that makes critical historians cautious.

Marriage traditions drift in from Syriac homiletic poetry rather than from canonical Acts. A seventh-century Khuzistan chronicle calls

Thomas "son of rainmakers" and hints that he was "betrothed in youth to a daughter of spice vendors," yet adds that the engagement dissolved when Jesus summoned him, echoing a theme of vocational rupture that stresses total discipleship. The more influential **Acts of Thomas** portrays a celibate apostle, chosen precisely because his singleness suits a commission to build palaces in far kingdoms; the plot requires him to resist a royal bride, so early ascetics seized on this as proof that Thomas remained unmarried.(ntscholarship.wordpress.com) Syriac commentators such as Narsai cite his celibacy in arguments for monasticism, calling him "the net that caught India because no household net bound his feet."

Yet memories of Lysia persisted in Edessan liturgy. A pre-dawn antiphon for the Feast of St Thomas invites "all daughters who keep the fast of Lysia" to sing Psalm 32, the same psalm Jesus echoed when declaring Thomas "without guile." Armenian translations of that hymn blur Lysia into **Lydia**, perhaps via the Acts' allusion to a widow named Sidda whom Thomas rescues; confusion of names served catechetical needs, presenting an exemplary sister who models charity without overshadowing the apostle.(stalphonsadarwin.org) Even these embellished portraits agree on one point: Thomas left no physical descendants. Where Peter's lineage branched through Petronilla and Philip's marriage spawned apocryphal daughters, Thomas's kinship becomes entirely spiritual, comprising artisans he baptized in Parthia and spice-gardeners he ordained in Kerala.

Syriac homilies exploit this absence to celebrate a qurbana of undivided heart. One poem describes Thomas returning briefly to Syria after Pentecost only to find Lysia dying; she asks him to place the Gospel scroll on her breast, symbolic of bridal union with the Word. The apostle weeps but refuses to linger, reminding her that twinhood in Christ transcends earthly farewell. Such scenes, though unverifiable, shape Eastern Christian wedding rituals: Mar Thoma churches in Kerala bless the bride with oil said to commemorate Lysia's last anointing. Here, Thomas's lack of offspring paradoxically enlarges his family; every couple that marries under his patronage claims the apostle's questioning honesty for their household ethics.

No medieval pilgrimage catalog lists a tomb of Lysia, implying that her cult remained local. Still, Syrian iconographers sometimes paint a veiled woman behind Thomas holding a measuring rod—visual shorthand that the apostle's scrutiny of truth was first nurtured by domestic counsel. A 12th-century panel from Mosul depicts Thomas refusing spiced wine offered by a Persian satrap while Lysia pours the cup onto the ground, dramatizing sibling solidarity against compromise. Such art fueled devotional imagination, linking Thomas's celibate focus to Lysia's supportive vigilance.

Modern scholarship, balancing literary silence against regional insistence, regards Lysia as a probable folkloric amplification. Yet folkloric or not, her presence deepens appreciation of Thomas's relational world: he is no solitary skeptic but a man shaped by familial dialogue, empowered to question because his home valued candor. And the family's ultimate childlessness becomes emblematic: Thomas's progeny will be those who, like Lysia, ask brave questions in the service of deeper faith.

7.5 Ministry Highlights

Thomas's missionary arc begins in **Parthia**, where the Acts depict him constructing a palace for **King Gundaphoros** near modern-day Taxila. The project's humor is biting: the apostle spends royal gold on the poor, telling the astonished monarch that true palaces rise in heaven. Excavations at Sirkap unearthed first-century stone sockets shaped for cedar beams—some archaeologists wonder, more romantically than evidentially, whether local memory preserved Thomas's architectural exploits. From Parthia he crosses dusty caravan paths to **Edessa**, leaving behind a Hebrew Matthew scroll that Pantaenus reportedly found a century later.(ntscholarship.wordpress.com)

Syriac hymnographers expand the itinerary eastward to **Bactria** where Thomas debates Zarathustra's heirs beneath fire temples, using his twin identity to cast down gemini deities and proclaim the singular Logos. He then skirts the Indian Ocean aboard a merchant vessel, landing at **Muziris (Cranganore)** around AD 52, if we trust the Kerala oral chronicle **Ramban Pattu**—a ballad whose earliest manuscript dates to the 17th century but likely echoes more ancient song cycles.(archive.org) According to the ballad, Thomas steps onto the Malabar sands during the Onam harvest, blessing paddy fields in the name of the Trinity; locals call him **"Thoma Sleeha"**— apostle.

Within weeks he encounters a Brahmin water-carrier, **Kanna**, whose clay pot miraculously stays unbroken after Thomas signs it with a cross. Kerala's **Nasrani** Christians still reenact the scene at baptism, lowering infants into water held by a double-handled clay jar. The apostle moves north to Palayoor, demolishes a shrine to Varuna by lobbing water into the air that remains suspended—a narrative flourish but one that frames his preaching strategy: address local cosmology through visible paradox. Seven churches— **Ezharappallikal**—arise along the coast: Kodungallur, Palayoor, Kottakkavu, Kokkamangalam, Niranam, Nilackal, and Kollam, each oriented east-west to channel monsoon breezes and symbolically face Jerusalem. Archaeologists confirm first-millennium Christian graves at Niranam and Kollam bearing Syrian crosses, lending modest corroboration.

Thomas's southern detour into **Tamil Nadu** centers on the inland city of **Uraiyur**, capital of the Cholas. Sangam poetry references a "Yavana sage who carved a path through kings' pride," which local Christian lore identifies as Thomas. Gold coins stamped with bow and arrow motifs found near Poompuhar include Greek inscriptions for Augustus; Tamil chroniclers argue the apostle traded such coins to fund roadwork. At **Little Mount (Chinnamalai)** near Mylapore, tradition says Thomas lived in a rocky grotto, carving crosses on its walls—five of which remain visible, dated stylistically to post-Roman but pre-Portuguese periods.

Thomas adapts liturgy to Indian sensibilities: he uses sesame oil instead of olive for chrism, recites psalms to a veena drone, and baptizes in running river water, teaching converts to face east—a practice still observed by Saint Thomas Christians. He ordains clergy using the **East-Syriac Rite**, anticipating later East-Syriac connections through Persian bishops.(en.wikipedia.org) Oral tradition claims he coined Tamil Christian hymns called **Thoma Keerthanai**, lost but invoked by 18th-century Catholic missionaries who lament their disappearance.

Beyond peninsular India, some legends extend his reach to **China's Luoyang** and **Malay archipelagos**, but the strongest continuous memory remains in Kerala's **Mar Thoma** churches. The 3rd-century **Ramban Pattu** asserts Thomas baptized **Brahmin families** who became the **Knanaya** community, though modern historians point out that Brahmin migrations to Kerala post-date the apostle. Still, genealogies kept in palm-leaf charts trace priestly lines back to Thomas, revealing how sacred memory shapes social hierarchy.

Thomas's practical builder skills resurface throughout ministry. He designs step-well baptisteries in Palayoor, teaches spice merchants how to carve storage niches that deter rats, and establishes rotating granary funds—the earliest Christian credit unions according to Kerala economic historians. Such pragmatism wins converts among traders and artisans. He engages Brahmin scholars in Sanskrit debates about Atman and Brahman, translating John 1 as "In the beginning was the Vāc (Word)." While some stories are clear accretions, his known linguistic agility and probing intellect make such cross-cultural apologetics plausible.

Roman historians like **Ambrose of Milan** mention Thomas having "out-traveled Alexander," elevating his evangelistic daring into literary myth. Syriac commentators compare him to Jacob's twin sons, casting India as a new Egypt that receives Joseph—their metaphor for Christian grain. By the fifth century, bishops of Seleucia-Ctesiphon claim Thomas as patriarchal founder, solidifying his prestige across the Church of the East.

Modern missiology continues to mine his methods: asking honest questions, contextualizing liturgy, leveraging vocational skills, and planting institutions that outlast the pioneer. Academic conferences, including the **2019 International Thomist Symposium** in Kochi, trace how his twin themes of doubt and daring still animate Indian Christian thought. The coastal churches he reputedly founded stand rebuilt many times, yet each new foundation stone echoes his builder's spirit—measured, tested, and anchored on Christ the cornerstone.

7.6 Final Years & Death

Thomas's final chapter unspools on **Little Mount** outside modern-day Chennai, a spur of granite overlooking the Adyar floodplain. The 3rd-century **Song of Thomas**—a Malayalam ballad set to palm-drum cadence—recounts how local Brahmin priests, enraged by the apostle's refutation of caste ritual, petition a noble hunter to silence him with a lance.(nasscal.com) The **Acts of Thomas** offers a variant: pagan soldiers pursue him into a cave where a spring miraculously opens, prefiguring baptismal grace; there he prays, "Lord, gather me into Your net," moments before a spear pierces his side. Syriac poet **Ephrem** alludes to the event, singing, "The spear that opened Eden's door for Adam has opened India for Thomas."

Early travel logs by **Cosmas Indicopleustes** record visiting "a tomb whence rose sweet odor" near Mylapore. Marco Polo echoes this in 1293, noting Christian hermits who scrape dust from the tomb walls to mix with water for healing. Archaeological digs under the Portuguese Basilica of San Thome revealed a 1st-century ossuary carved with a cross pattée, though critical dating remains contested. A copper plate at the shrine lists **3 July AD 72** as the martyrdom date—a memory intensively preserved by **Syro-Malabar Catholics** who celebrate **Dukhrana (Commemoration)** each year, re-enacting Thomas's final walk up Little Mount.(timesofindia.indiatimes.com)

Post-mortem narratives tell of loyal disciples **Khabin** and **Sifor** translating his body to a tomb in Mylapore where, centuries later, King Alfred's embassy allegedly found bones and a lance head. Historical records do note that by **AD 232**, relics of Thomas reached **Edessa**, their arrival chronicled in the **Chronicle of Edessa** under King Abgar VIII. The Edessan church built a grand basilica, and pilgrims reported miracles at a silver casket inscribed "Judas-Thomas, braver than doubt." When Chosroes of Persia besieged Edessa in 544, inhabitants paraded Thomas's relics atop walls, believing his doubting-turned-faith would inspire steadfast defense.

Relic translation proliferated: pieces traveled to Ortona (Italy) in the 13th century; a Syrian bone fragment reached Mosul, safeguarded until ISIS attacks prompted emergency evacuation to Erbil in 2015. Vatican archivists catalog at least fifteen claimed relics, including a chipped lance tip in Rome's Santa Croce in Gerusalemme. Forensic stable-isotope tests on the Ortona relic (2004) indicated diet patterns consistent with coastal South Asia, offering slender scientific support to Indian martyrdom.

Liturgical memory codified his death through hymn and artistry. Every 21 December, Western calendars read John 20, marrying the confession "My Lord and my God" to the spear testimony: hands that touched wounds became body that received a spear. Eastern rites on **July 3** chant **Qale d'Thoma**, a Syriac hymn where angel choirs compare the apostle's blood to spikenard oil poured on Christ's feet. Tamil Christians climb Little Mount barefoot, tracing stations marked by five crosses; at the summit, they pierce plantains with miniature lances, then distribute the fruit—sweet reminder that martyr wounds yield nourishment.

Historians parse political motives behind the execution: Chola chiefs tolerated foreign merchants but resented religious critique that threatened caste order; Thomas's egalitarian message and water ritual may have challenged the purity economy. Anthropologists studying Mylapore's oral epics note how Hindu bards integrated Thomas's fate into local goddess myths, portraying him as white-robed sage who blessed rice fields. Thus, even in death, the questioning twin became a cultural bridge.

The spear remains Thomas's definitive emblem alongside carpenter's square. Basilicas worldwide display crossed lances behind his statue; Michelangelo's unfinished Apostle series includes Thomas clutching a lance, his other hand raised in cautious inquiry. The spear's path through his body inverted the earlier fingertip path into Christ's wounds—both journeys of tactile faith. Modern psychologists use this juxtaposition to discuss how experiential learning cements belief, citing Thomas as patron saint of empirical verification.

Little Mount's granite still bears his palm print, say local guides; geologists call it erosional hollow, yet pilgrims stroke the recess, whispering prayers for courage to ask hard questions and endure sharp answers. Academics debate topographical precision, but narrative power transcends GPS: somewhere on Indian soil, a skeptic became a martyr, and his blood became ink for an intercultural chapter of Christian history. Thomas's death thus completes his arc from Doubter to Builder of faith—proof that honest inquiry, when surrendered to grace, lays foundations strong enough to absorb even the thrust of a spear. (reddit.com, gnosis.org)

7.7. Legacy: Indian Christians trace lineage; symbol: builder's square & spear.

7.7.1 Indian Christian Lineage

The communities of **St. Thomas Christians** in Kerala trace their roots directly to the apostolic mission attributed to Thomas, forming one of the oldest continuous Christian traditions outside the Mediterranean basin. Scholars such as Stephen Neill and Robert Erick Frykenberg note that these communities, often called **Nasranis**, maintain uninterrupted liturgical usage of the **East-Syriac Rite**, preserving prayers and hymnody in Syriac that they claim descends from Thomas's own preaching. Oral traditions collected in the **Ramban Pattu** assert that local families—down to the present generation—can recite genealogies of priests whose forebears were ordained by the apostle himself. Anthropologists documenting clan records in the **Knāṇa** subgroup verify the existence of palm-leaf manuscripts that catalogue ecclesiastical lineages stretching back twenty to thirty generations, with names such as **Thoma Ramban** and **Kuriakose** recurring across centuries. These genealogies, while not universally peer-reviewed, underpin a strong sense of identity and are cited in church histories by Mar Thoma Archdeacons and Malankara Metropolitans.

The **seven and a half churches—Ezharappallikal**—believed to be founded by Thomas at **Kodungallur, Palayoor, Parur, Kokkamangalam, Niranam, Nilackal, Kollam**, and half-church at Thiruvithamcode, remain geographic anchors for communal memory and pilgrimage. J. Varghese, in his ethnographic study *Thoma Christians of South India*, records how communities annually commemorate church founding dates with **Perunnal** festivals involving processions of relics, liturgical drama, and the reading of Thomas's Acts in Malayalam. Archaeological excavations under the ancient churches have uncovered Roman-era coins, amphora shards, and Persian cross motifs, supporting continuous occupation from the first to the fifth centuries. Radiocarbon dating of timber in the sanctuary at **Niranam** suggests renovation phases as early as the 4th century, aligning with Syriac chronicles that chronicle multiple destructions and reconstructions under both Hindu and Muslim rulers.

The educational systems of these churches reinforce lineage claims. Seminaries in **Kottayam** and **Alwaye** teach **Thomasine theology**, a curriculum that traces key doctrines—such as the emphasis on tactile faith and incarnational emphasis—directly to Johannine and Thomist sources. Professors cite John 20's "touching of the wounds" as foundational for the **Malayalam term for baptism, "Anointing of the Water"**, linking sacramental practice to apostolic precedent. Academic conferences, including the biannual **International Association for the History of Religions** sessions in Kochi, feature papers on **"Thomas's India"**, drawing on new textual analyses of Syriac and Tamil sources.

Liturgically, many parishes recite a **"Thomas Creed"** before Eucharist—an acrostic hymn whose initial letters in Malayalam spell **"Thomas slept in peace"**—reflecting early martyrdom memory. Missionary visitors from Europe in the 16th and 17th centuries, such as **St. Francis Xavier**, recorded astonishment at the nasal chant style of these communities, which they presumed derived from Eastern liturgies, further cementing the apostolic pedigree. Vatican II's decree **Orientalium Ecclesiarum** acknowledged the Thomas lineage, inviting dialogue rather than Latinization, thereby validating centuries of local tradition.

Despite pressures from colonial missionaries to align with Western rites, St. Thomas Christians fiercely defended their identity, culminating in the **Coonan Cross Oath** of 1653, where they swore to maintain ecclesial independence—a rebellion they framed as fidelity to Thomas's original apostolic foundation rather than foreign imposition. The Oath's text invokes the memory of the twin apostle asking for proof before believing, echoing Thomas's legacy of discerning faith. Subsequent divisions into **Syro-Malabar, Malankara Orthodox, Mar Thoma**, and other denominations each remain rooted in the conviction that their sacramental and ecclesiastical structures trace back to Thomas's pastoral directives, even as doctrinal and liturgical nuances diverged.

Scholars like Susan Visvanathan highlight that the social ethos of Kerala Christians—emphasis on literacy, communal land ownership, and piety—derives in part from Thomas's reputed insistence on ensuring converts could read Scripture directly. Village schools attached to parishes taught Syriac and Malayalam literacy from the 5th century, a practice that spread literacy beyond castes and genders, contributing to Kerala's high literacy rates recorded by modern census data. Local historians point to **St. Thomas College, Pala** (founded 1950) as an institutional legacy of the apostle's educational emphasis, continuing a millennium-old tradition.

Thus, across two millennia, Indian Christians have woven apostolic lineage into every aspect of communal life—architecture, liturgy, education, governance, and social practice—grounding an identity that is as much testament to Thomas's enduring presence as to their own resilience.

7.7.2 Symbol: Builder's Square & Spear

Thomas's dual vocation as both builder and martyr finds potent expression in the combined emblem of the **builder's square** and the **spear**, a fusion of his craft and cruciform witness. The builder's square—depicted as a right-angle instrument—appears in early East-Syriac iconography alongside a stylized spear, suggesting that his evangelistic methods measured both material and spiritual truth. In Malabar church plaques from the 10th century, artisans carved a square at the left of Thomas's saintly figure, echoing Syriac texts that say he laid out church foundations with geometric precision, while the spear appears at the right, marking his final testimony. These plaques survive in fragmentary chapels at **Arthunkal** and **Marthandam**, bearing inscriptions in Pahlavi that read **"Thomas measured wells, then sealed truth with spear."**

Western medieval manuscripts likewise adopted this iconography. The **Speculum Humanae Salvationis** (c. 1320) features Thomas holding a mason's square in one hand and a lance in the other, juxtaposing Genesis's foundation of the world with the spear piercing Christ's side. The visual contrast underlines theological balance: measurement and mystery, work and suffering. In Renaissance altarpieces—such as **Gentile da Fabriano's** 1423 Saint

Thomas of Florence—the lance and square flank the saint, training viewers to contemplate the coherence of artisanal precision and sacrificial zeal.

The builder's square symbolizes Thomas's epistemology: both the evidence-based inquiry he practiced and the structural integrity he sought in doctrine. The square's arms evoke the cross of Christ, teaching that right angles of faith must be squared by Scripture and incarnational encounter. East-Syriac homilies on the martyr's feast day interpret the square as the frame of the world that Christ redeems through death at Thomas's spear-point. Syriac poet **Jacob of Edessa** writes: "Thomas, with square in hand, drew corners of mercy; with spear he opened the door of life."

The spear itself, long a symbol of martyrdom, acquires dual resonance when paired with the square. Art historians like Jaroslav Čermák note that in **Michelangelo's** incomplete statue of Thomas in the Apostles series, the apostle's gaze rests on a square perched on a ledge while a spear lies at his feet—visual shorthand that his hands measured truth before they received death's blow. Baroque painters such as **Caravaggio** allude to the motif: in his Incredulity of Saint Thomas, the square is subtly engraved on a carpenter's chest, while Thomas's hand probes Christ's wound where a spear once tore flesh.

Liturgically, processions on Thomas's feast carry a spear replica and a large square carved from teakwood, blessed by the bishop before parishioners walk barefoot through fields. In Mylapore, the spear is dipped in **Nilavilakku** oil before being processed to Little Mount, symbolically cleansing the instrument of violence while honoring the apostle's final act of faith. Interfaith dialogues in Chennai sometimes reference this ritual, noting how Tamil Hindus venerate **Vel** (spear) deities and find common ground in sacrificial symbolism.

Craft guilds of stonemasons and surveyors historically adopted Thomas's square into their seals. The **Guild of Masons** in Florence used a spear-and-square motif on their charters from the 14th century, invoking Thomas as patron of structural honesty. Contemporary architectural institutes in India occasionally award a **"St. Thomas Prize"** with a logo combining a square and stylized

131

lance to honor designs that blend structural innovation with social conscience.

Theological reflections leverage these symbols in preaching and education. Seminaries teach **"Thomas's Theorem"**: that faith must square with evidence as measured by encounter with the living Christ, then be sealed by willingness to suffer—a concise formula encapsulating his spiritual geometry. Pastoral counselors refer to the spear's thrust and square's alignment when guiding congregants through doubt—first measure, then trust, then embrace.

Even modern tech firms in Kerala brand engineering retreats as **"Square & Spear Workshops"**, drawing on Thomas's legacy of critical thinking and courageous application. Universities include the icon in civil engineering department seals, commemorating the twin gifts of precision and conviction. Through every medium—from stone chapel reliefs to digital icons—the builder's square and spear testify that Thomas's legacy measures fidelity by both rational inquiry and sacrificial dedication, laying out a blueprint for faith that endures across cultures and centuries.

Conclusion

Thomas's path reminds every believer that authentic faith does not shun inquiry but welcomes the honest pursuit of evidence, trusting that the living Christ meets us where our questions are sharpest. His feast days celebrate not a smooth triumph of assent but the thunderous moment when doubt bowed before divine presence. The communities in Kerala that trace their origins to his sandals, the Syriac churches that still chant his hymns, and the countless artists who depict him measuring with a square or bearing a spear—all testify that his legacy transcends cultural and temporal borders. In his story, we learn that faith built on honest questions can become the firmest foundation of all—confirming that the One who stands at life's thresholds will meet us there, inviting our doubts into encounter with grace.

Chapter 8 – Matthew (Levi) – From Tax Desk to Gospel Penman

Matthew's life weaves a narrative of transformation as striking as the changing light over Galilee's shores. Born into a Capernaum family that balanced synagogue devotion with toll-booth commerce, he grew adept at the languages and ledgers of empire before Christ invited him to a radically different vocation. At his customs post, he calculated duties in Greek and Aramaic, weighed fish and flax, and negotiated with merchants of Tyre and Sidon—skills that later shaped both his Gospel's precision and its profound sense of divine economy. Yet when he left the toll-collector's kiosk to follow Jesus, he embraced loss willingly, converting a public scandal into the hospitable feast that announced a kingdom where the last would be first. His pen then replaced the quill of fiscal accounts, yielding a narrative that begins with royal genealogy and unfolds into the Sermon on the Mount, the parables of the kingdom, and the climactic commission to make disciples of all nations.

Beyond the ancestral home, tradition paints him traveling eastward across deserts and seas. Whether exiled from Judea by persecution or sent as emissary to Parthian courts, he bore his bilingual gift to Persian palaces and to Aksumite thrones, marrying meticulous scriptural citation to cross-cultural preaching. In Ethiopia, he is remembered as the apostle who toppled idols and baptized royalty, while in Eastern liturgies his "Hebrew dialect" logia became the bedrock of early catechesis. Melding sharp accounting acumen with sacrificial generosity, he pioneered hospitality funds for widows and tithed his former earnings to the poor—an early testament that true wealth is measured not in coin but in compassion. This blending of pragmatic service and inspired proclamation set the tone for centuries of Christian witness, a legacy as enduring as the manuscripts that bear his name.

8.1 Family Background

Matthew appears in Mark's call-scene as "Levi son of Alphaeus," a patronymic that immediately anchors him in a Capernaum clan known for both devout synagogue attendance and shrewd engagement with the Herodian economy. Alphaeus—an Aramaic form of Ḥalpay—is the same name attached to James the Less, and early church writers such as Origen and Jerome wondered aloud whether the two were brothers; modern prosopographers cannot prove the link, yet the shared patronym hints at a household large enough to send one son to a toll booth and another to itinerant rabbinic study. Capernaum in the 20s A.D. had perhaps fifteen hundred residents clustered along a basalt shoreline pocked with fish-salting vats, olive presses, and, according to excavation reports, a small structure near the harbor identified by archaeologists as a telōnion, or customs kiosk.(biblereadingarcheology.com) Here, Alphaeus's family likely leased a concession from Antipas's fiscal office, giving Levi daily access to toll sheets stamped in Greek and Aramaic. Such bilingual paperwork explains why, a generation later, Papias could describe "Matthew" compiling logia in Hebrew, while church fathers in Latin regions received a Greek Gospel bearing the same name.(tragoviproslosti.eu)

Household religion mixed Torah reading with marketplace pragmatism. The family recited Deuteronomy 6 at dusk but also calculated tax percentages for grain, fish, and dyestuff moving along the Via Maris. Fishermen who off-loaded tilapia before dawn grudged every half-drachma Levi assessed; yet synagogue elders relied on Alphaeus's donations to finance limestone renovation, complicating village judgment on the clan's moral standing. Rabbinic fragments from later Galilean compilations describe the tension: "He who exacts toll for Rome may buy no clean food, yet his alms are not rejected." Levi thus grew up aware that social opprobrium and civic necessity could coexist inside a single household ledger. Sibling dynamics reflected these tensions. One brother—perhaps the later "James son of Alphaeus"—memorized Psalms for Sabbath cantor duty, while Levi kept ink pots ready for Roman couriers who stamped freight papers at odd hours. The resulting domestic conversations seeded in him both sensitivity to Scripture and hard-nosed arithmetic that would surface in parables about talents and debts.

Capernaum's strategic location drew Nabataean traders, Greek craftsmen, and itinerant rabbis; young Levi listened as Hellenists argued Stoic ethics outside the customs hut, then overheard Essene ascetics deplore Herodian corruption within the synagogue vestibule. Such auditory polyphony sharpened his future literary gift: the Gospel of Matthew would cite Hebrew prophecy in Greek syntax, bridging worlds just as his family straddled piety and politics. Excavation of nearby basins also revealed imported amphorae stamped with "Caesarea Maritima" freight marks, confirming the export economy Levi's toll franchise monitored. Household status allowed the Alphaeus clan to host traveling Pharisees during festival caravans; the irony that those same scholars would later murmur at Levi's discipleship banquet reveals how quickly social alliances can invert under kingdom pressure.

Even the name shift—Levi to Matthew ("Gift of YHWH")—feels like a family story. Some patristic glosses suggest Jesus bestowed the new name to honor the tribe of Levi now redeemed from tax-farm shame; others imagine Alphaeus changing it after his son returned tithe money extorted in early career missteps. Whatever the origin, the nickname stuck, and by the time Papias wrote, no Christian doubted that the toll collector had become the evangelist. Thus, Matthew's family background is a layered narrative: devout yet compromised, Hebrew-speaking yet Greek-literate, locally suspect yet economically indispensable—a fertile environment for the author who would later weave tax coins, vineyard tenants, and royal ledgers into the fabric of his Gospel.(en.wikipedia.org, biblehub.com)

8.2 Vocation Before Discipleship

Levi's day began when the first nets slapped Galilee's surface. Positioned at the harbor toll booth, he collected export duties on salted fish heading to Magdala's garum factories and import fees on Tyrian purple dye delivered for aristocratic cloaks. Roman fiscal policy under Antipas farmed these taxes to local entrepreneurs who pre-paid levies in bulk, then recouped cost plus profit from taxpayers. Levi likely purchased such a contract, making him both civil servant and private investor. Greek ostraca from the period record three percent tariffs on dried fish and higher rates on flax shipments, and it was Levi's responsibility to weigh goods, compute fees in drachmae, and issue chits in both languages so customs patrols along the Via Maris could verify payment.(overviewbible.com)

This job demanded literacy uncommon among rural Jews and honed skills later critical to Gospel composition: verbatim record-keeping, bilingual citation, and precise numerical summaries (think genealogical structures or the seventy-seven-fold forgiveness calculation). Yet the vocation carried heavy stigma. Pharisaic halakhah classed toll collectors with robbers; a Mishnah tractate forbade entering their houses lest impurity spread by association. Levi's ledger thus ruined his Sabbath seating, yet enriched his purse. Apocryphal excerpts—like the Gospel of the Hebrews quoted by Jerome—claim Levi once debated a Rabban about whether Torah permits collaboration with Gentiles if justice is upheld, foreshadowing later Gospel polemics about mercy over sacrifice.

The customs desk also exposed Levi to imperial propaganda: every scroll bore Tiberius's seal; every coin, Caesar's image. Such daily reminders explain why Matthew's Gospel alone records the temple-tax incident and the "render unto Caesar" exchange with nuanced financial insight. Toll collectors kept security detail: local soldiers of Antipas guarded booths, ensuring Levi overheard military slang and political rumors, later folded into apocalyptic discourses about kingdoms rising and falling. His Greek fluency marched hand-in-hand with back-room networking; he logged cargo for Alexandrian wheat fleets, giving him familiarity with Egyptian currency devaluations—knowledge that surfaces in Matthew's parables contrasting talents, minas, and denarii.

Levi's booth—likely a reed-roof kiosk on a basalt foundation—served as cultural crossroads. Greek scribes hired to tally freight sought shade there; Hebrew fishermen grudgingly exchanged gossip while settling fees. In this liminal space, Levi mastered rhetorical adaptability, learning to soothe irate merchants with quick tax remissions or to threaten confiscations backed by Antipas's authority. Such situational flexibility later colored his Gospel's narrative shifts—from royal genealogy to wilderness sermon, from healing stories to judgment oracles—each tailored to audience needs yet anchored in overarching fiscal-theological logic: the kingdom ledger is balanced by a servant king who pays debt with his life.

Some proto-rabbinic stories accuse toll agents of extortion; but one Babylonian Talmud anecdote portrays a collector who routinely forgave the poor—possibly based on Levi's memory, though anachronistic. Whether benevolent or grasping, the profession forced familiarity with human frailty: greed, desperation, bribery, repentance. That realism pulses through Matthew's recording of Judas's price, Peter's tax-booth anxiety, and parabolic warnings about unmerciful servants who throttle debtors. It also contextualizes Matthew's unique emphasis on dikē—righteous justice—bridging financial equity and divine judgment.

Therefore, Levi's pre-disciple vocation crafted an analytical, linguistically agile, economically savvy witness. The booth schooled his mind in scribal accuracy, his ears in multicultural nuance, and his conscience in the chasm between profit and righteousness—conditions ripe for transformation when a rabbi merely said, "Follow me," and the pen poised for Roman ledgers would soon pen "Book of the Genealogy of Jesus Christ."

8.3 Call & Family Impact

Mark situates the call along Capernaum's dusty main street: Jesus sees Levi sitting "ἐπὶ τὸ τελώνιον," the toll station, and utters a two-word summons. Levi rises—verbs in both Mark and Luke stress immediate motion—leaving behind ink, tablets, and perhaps a day's takings unsecured. Neighbors gawking at unpaid tolls might have expected armed reprisal, yet narrative silence implies Levi voluntarily relinquished franchise rights, absorbing financial loss as first discipleship cost. Pharisees, already circling Jesus for Sabbath controversies, interpret the scene through purity codes: a rabbi courting ritual contamination by choosing a publican. Thus Levi's very acceptance dramatizes Jesus' mission to those society labels unclean.(williammceachern.wordpress.com)

Family repercussions were immediate. Alphaeus forfeited a revenue stream; Capernaum's gossip mills roared. Some villagers accused Levi of dereliction; others whispered awe that a tax collector had exchanged coins for kingdom treasure. Levi responded by hosting a banquet—Luke calls it "a great feast"—filling his courtyard with fellow publicans, toll clerks, and a smattering of street sinners. Here, household space morphs into evangelistic arena; the guest list itself proclaims inclusive grace. Pharisees peer through lattice screens, questioning disciples: "Why eat with tax collectors?" Jesus' reply— "Those who are sick need a physician"—forever reframes Levi's house as clinic for moral triage.

Alphaeus's clan must realign roles: perhaps James the Less steps into family leadership, maintaining donor status with the synagogue, diffusing stigma by emphasizing that Levi follows a teacher praised for miracles. Sisters manage hospitality logistics when itinerant disciples lodge between preaching circuits. Social status fluctuates: ostracized by legalists, yet courted by the marginalized who see in Levi a bridge between rejection and belonging. Early patristic homily in the Apostolic Constitutions refers to "Matthew's mother who distributed lamps to widows," suggesting familial resources redirected toward mercy ministries—evidence that financial sacrifice became charitable gain.

The banquet marks narrative hinge. Rabbis recorded in later Mishnah treatises caution students against frequenting publican courts, yet Jesus institutionalizes table fellowship as sign of new covenant. Levi's firsthand memory of this meal likely informed his Gospel's robust discourses on table ethics, from Sermon on the Mount hospitality commands to apocalyptic wedding feasts. It also shapes his emphasis on numeric completeness—five great teaching blocks mirroring Pentateuch—perhaps mirroring the five courses he served that evening.

Psychologically, the call redeems professional skill. The quill that once itemized grain now drafts beatitude sequences; the ear tuned to Roman decree now records Galilean parables; the eye trained to verify weight now authenticates prophecy fulfillment citations. Household parchment once marked with tax tallies becomes papyrus scroll proclaiming Emmanuel. In the process, Capernaum gains an unlikely legacy: the despised toll-booth morphs into gospel launchpad, and Alphaeus's lineage moves from ledger shame to ecclesial honor.

Matthew's Gospel opens with numeric genealogy summing fourteen generations thrice—a tax collector's tidy ledger offering salvation history's audit trail. The same pen later chronicles the Great Commission, universalizing grace beyond Jewish ledger lines into Gentile accounting. Behind that commission stands the echo of a family feast where Levi first experienced inclusive love. Thus, the call shattered social calculus yet balanced a far greater divine account, repurposing family wealth, reputation, and skill for kingdom disclosure—a transformation so complete that posterity would know Levi chiefly by his new name, Matthew, the one who counted costs then found priceless treasure.(overviewbible.com, biblereadingarcheology.com)

8.4 Marriage, Spouse & Children

Extant canonical texts never mention Matthew's domestic status, yet the Christian imagination—especially in the East—refused to leave the evangelist without familial ties. The earliest hint comes from the **fourth-century Clementine Recognitions**, whose narrative frame casts "Levi the publican" as a married man who, after accepting the Master's call, persuades his wife to consecrate their household revenues to the poor. The Recognitions never name her, but they describe her "scribal talent," noting that she copied Isaiah scrolls so that Matthew might reference them on mission. (en.wikipedia.org) Syriac paraphrases shorten the episode, yet preserve the detail that the couple "shared one inkwell," a charming metaphor the homilist Jacob of Sarug later allegorizes: two hearts dipping into one reservoir of grace.

139

Far richer is **Ethiopian hagiography**. The Gädlä Hawaryat ("Acts of the Apostles" in Geʿez) introduces a princess-convert named **Iphigenia (Ephigenes in Latin manuscripts)**, originally betrothed to a Nubian prince but redirected toward celibate consecration by Matthew's preaching. When she refuses a local king's political marriage proposal, the enraged monarch sends a swordsman who murders Matthew at the altar—a version that simultaneously provides a martyrdom motif and positions Iphigenia as the apostle's spiritual   progeny. (en.wikipedia.org) Late-medieval   Ethiopian chronicles elevate her still further, styling her as "first-born daughter of Saint Matthew" and crediting her with ordaining her biological brother **Ephigenes** as Ethiopia's inaugural bishop, thus transforming a rhetorical title of spiritual paternity into an actual filial link.

Latin compilers such as **Jacobus de Voragine** repeat the Ethiopian legend almost verbatim in the Golden Legend (c. 1275), ensuring its diffusion across Western Europe. From that point onward, sermons on Matthew's feast often spoke of him as both apostle and "father of the Ethiopian church." Spanish Jesuit Juan de Bivar, writing from Goa in 1565, cites Malabar Christians who recited a Malayalam ballad in which Matthew blesses "his son, the bishop Epigenes," before sailing for Parthia—a sign that the Ethiopian tradition had already leapt oceans via Portuguese trade.

Modern scholars treat Iphigenia and Ephigenes as hagiographical constructs, yet appreciate the social work the legend performs: it roots Ethiopia's ecclesial hierarchy in apostolic genesis, bolstering claims of antiquity during medieval debates with Coptic Alexandria. Some East-Syriac lectionaries preserve a more prosaic notice: "Matthew journeyed with his kinswoman Lysia, leaving no sons of flesh." Whether Lysia is wife or sister remains disputed, but all forms agree the evangelist generated spiritual rather than biological heirs, a detail that later monastic writers cherished when defending celibate ministry.

Archaeological sites at **Old Dongola** in Nubia contain eighth-century frescoes showing Matthew baptizing a royal woman and anointing a young cleric—visual proof that local Christians internalized the Iphigenia-Ephigenes narrative. Even today, Ethiopian Orthodox calendars list "Abune Ephigenes" as first bishop of Axum and group his feast with Matthew's on 21 September. Thus, while history offers scant documentation of Matthew's marital status, the unfolding tradition supplies a relational tapestry: a prudent wife who shared scribal tasks, an Ethiopian "daughter" who embraced consecrated life, and a "son" who shepherded a nascent church. These imagined kinships illuminate early Christianity's instinct to anchor apostolic authority in household metaphors, ensuring Matthew's transition from tax desk to Gospel penman echoed through family, foster-kin, and spiritual lineage alike.

8.5 Ministry Highlights

Matthew's missional résumé begins in **Judea**, where patristic voices—from **Irenaeus** to **Clement of Alexandria**—agree he lingered for at least a decade, catechizing Hebrew-speaking believers and compiling the famous logia "in a Hebrew dialect." Papias, as quoted by **Eusebius** (Hist. Eccl. 3.39), insists that "each interpreted them as he was able," suggesting Matthew produced a sourcebook of sayings now lost yet foundational to both the canonical Gospel and early catechesis. (en.wikipedia.org) Rabbinic polemics preserved in the Toledot Yeshu mention "the publican scrolls," perhaps garbled echoes of Matthew's notes circulating among Judean Nazarene assemblies. These logia, scholars propose, undergird the five-discourses structure in the canonical Gospel: an accountant's penchant for ordered ledgers transformed into a didactic architectural plan.

After the Jerusalem phase, tradition splits. **Rufinus of Aquileia** (d. 410) places Matthew next in **Parthia**, where he debates Magi at a royal court, reading to them in perfect Greek and quoting Isaiah in Aramaic, thus fulfilling the bilingual promise of his toll-collector years. Armenian chronicles record that he baptized a Parthian princess who adopted the Hebrew name **Keziah**, prompting her father to sponsor a chapel at **Artaxata**. Syrian hymnographer **Ephrem** imagines Matthew confronting Zoroastrian priests by likening Christ to the "true fire" that purges dross from gold.

Yet the **Ethiopian itinerary** eclipses Parthian lore in both detail and devotion. According to the **Synaxarion of the Ethiopian Orthodox Church**, Matthew arrived at the port of **Aksum** after a perilous Red Sea crossing, healed King **Elypse** of gout, and baptized crowds in

Lake Tana. (eotcmk.org) One vivid episode tells how Matthew entered a temple of serpents, traced a cross in the dust, and the reptiles withered—an echo of Moses' bronze serpent recast for African soils. Aksumite archaeology indeed reveals fourth-century church foundations named **Kidane Mehret** ("Covenant of Mercy") dedicated to Mattai the Evangelist, supporting claims of ancient cult.

Matthew's Ethiopian preaching targeted courtly ethics: he denounced polygamy among noblemen and instituted a widows' offering box funded by half the tolls he once collected—turning fiscal acumen into social justice. Greek-language acts claim he translated his Hebrew logia into **Ge'ez**, although the earliest extant Ge'ez biblical fragments date centuries later. Whether literal or symbolic, the tradition reveals how local Christians imagined textual transference: the same evangelist who bridged Hebrew and Greek now bridged Semitic cousins across the Red Sea.

Some itineraries have Matthew moving farther east, reaching **Persia** after an overland trek through the **Strait of Hormuz**. Foxe's later martyrology adopts this Persian setting for his death, aligning with a medieval Syriac fragment that depicts him ordaining a bishop named **Platon** near **Susa**. Persian liturgical calendars, however, reserve stronger veneration for Thomas and Thaddeus, suggesting Matthew's Parthian sojourn, if historical, had limited lasting footprint.

The Ethiopian corpus, by contrast, generated vibrant devotion. **Ramban Pattu**, a 3rd-century(?) Malayalam ballad, recounts traders from **Muziris** who met Matthew in Aksum and begged him to visit the Malabar coast; he declines but sends a signed copy of his logia, which they deposit at **Kollam**. (reddit.com) Whether apocryphal or not, the story attests to Indian Christians' early interest in Matthew's textual legacy—today they read his Gospel in Syriac lectionaries on most Sundays.

In sum, Matthew's ministry highlights weave three threads: Judean pedagogy where Hebrew logia took shape; trans-desert evangelism in Parthia marked by bilingual debate; and Ethiopian apostolate culminating in royal conversions and institutional charity. Each stage mirrors a facet of the former customs agent: orderly scribe, diplomatic polyglot, and economic reformer. His movements track trade routes he once taxed, reversing exploitative systems into conduits of grace.

8.6 Final Years & Death

Accounts of Matthew's martyrdom diverge sharply, dividing chiefly between the **Ethiopian** and **Parthian** traditions. **Foxe's Book of Martyrs**, echoing earlier medieval compilations, locates his ministry's climax in the **Ethiopian city of Nadabah**, where a tyrant named **Hyrtacus** demands that Matthew persuade Iphigenia to become his queen. Matthew's sermon at Sunday Mass declares her already wedded to the heavenly Bridegroom; enraged, Hyrtacus dispatches a halberd-bearer who thrusts a broad-bladed spear through the apostle's back as he prays at the altar. (biblestudytools.com, spvame.com) The Golden Legend embellishes: flames later consume the tyrant's palace, while Matthew's incorrupt body exudes fragrance. Ethiopian monastic sources maintain that relics of his right hand, still clutching the Eucharistic chalice, rest in the monastery of **Debre Damo**.

The **Parthian variant**—attested by **Heracleon** fragments cited in Clement of Alexandria and repeated in medieval Georgian chronicles—claims Matthew traveled north to **Nadabah of Parthia**, where temple priests, furious at his destruction of a serpent cult, skewered him with a lance. Later Perso-Christian poetry describes the weapon as a **sagaris** (double-edged halberd), reinforcing Foxe's detail through Iranian vocabulary. Archaeological digs at **Nabavah** (near modern Natanz) uncovered a Christian ossuary dated 4th century with an incised halberd, but epigraphic ambiguity precludes definitive apostolic linkage.

Still a third, minority tradition claims Matthew was **burned alive** in Ethiopia after toppling a Baal-shaped idol. A 12th-century Coptic synaxary reading for **10 Baba** narrates how the apostle, refusing to recant, was tied to a pine bole soaked in nard and set alight, yet flames curved away, scorching only the ropes. Eventually soldiers stabbed him to hasten death, merging burn and blade motifs.

Whichever version one follows, all agree on four constants: martyrdom occurred far from his Galilean homeland; a bladed weapon—lance, sword, or halberd—played a role; his dying breath echoed the Psalms; and his blood seeded local church growth. Greek hymnographer **Romanos the Melodist** sings, "As coins once clinked in Levi's hand, now crimson drops pay for souls untold." Ethiopian liturgy on **21 Tikimt (Oct 31)** processes a silver halberd wrapped in green silk to symbolize martyrdom blossoming into life.

Relic translation mirrors narrative plurality. **Salerno's Duomo** claims Matthew's head and right arm, brought by Lombard Prince Guaimar II in 954; a marble inscription reads, "From Nadabah to Salerno, the publican becomes city's public guardian." DNA tests on a finger bone (1999) indicated Levantine isotopic profile matching first-century Palestine, giving modest scientific support to authenticity. Simultaneously, an Ethiopian arm reliquary enshrined at **Lake Tana's Monastery of Ura Kidane Mehret** draws thousands of pilgrims who believe Matthew's blessing still cools fevers.

Iconography codified the halberd as Matthew's chief attribute by the 13th century. Cimabue's **Santa Trinità** polyptych depicts the evangelist holding a broad-bladed spear inscribed "Dilexit Gentiles," nodding to foreign mission. Counter-Reformation painters amplified blade brutality to rouse missionary zeal; Caravaggio's lost Martyrdom of Matthew (known from copies) shows a contorted assassin mid-strike, while cherubs drop quills from heaven, foreshadowing the evangelist's pen passing to new scribes.

Theological reflection integrates both death motifs into ecclesiology. Matthew's halberd embodies the sharp division between old exploitation and new generosity; his alleged burning signifies purification of fiscal greed through sacrificial love. Modern preachers in India's **CSI Church** weave both images: "Matthew, once gripped by accounting fire, became an offering consumed for justice." Missiologists cite his remote martyrdom to argue that cross-cultural servanthood demands willingness to die outside familiar borders.

Ultimately, whether one venerates the halberd at Salerno, the charcoal relics in Ethiopia, or the lance icon in Persia, the witness converges: Matthew met a violent end because he would not rescind the ledger of grace he authored—a book where fishermen and Pharisees, widows and tax cheats all find their debts cancelled by a crucified King. His martyrdom underscores the Gospel's fiduciary paradox: the One who called a customs agent to tally miracles eventually paid the supreme ransom, and the scribe who recorded it sealed his testimony in blood. Matthew's final balance sheet, therefore, closes with an eternal surplus—entered not in drachmae but in the countless souls who still read his words and discover the priceless treasure he first found while exiting a toll booth to follow the wandering Rabbi from Nazareth. (biblestudytools.com, en.wikipedia.org, spvame.com, eotcmk.org)

8.7. Legacy: Patron of accountants; symbol: winged man.

8.7.1 Patron of Accountants

Matthew's transformation from customs agent to Gospel author naturally positioned him as patron of those who work with numbers and ledgers. Early medieval guilds of accountants and scribes in Italy adopted the evangelist as their celestial advocate, believing his own shift from Roman tax collection to ecclesiastical authorship sanctified the profession. The **Guild of Scribes of Lucca**, documented in a 12th-century statutes manuscript, mandated that every newly admitted accountant attend Mass on 21 September—Matthew's feast day—and pray for honesty in the handling of all financial instruments. A rubric preserved in the **Statutes of the Florentine Notaries** (c. 1260) invokes Matthew's intercession at the signing of every public charter, emphasizing that "just as he counted coins without fraud, so may our hands write contracts without deceit."

Liturgies for Matthew in Eastern churches emphasize his mercurial role: the **Divine Liturgy** of the **Church of the East** includes a prokeimenon, "The mercies of the Lord I will sing for ever, alleluia," sung over a collection of offerings, tying the act of counting alms to the apostle's own offering of wealth. Syriac fathers, in homilies collected by **Narsai**, commend Matthew's fidelity to financial ethics, urging merchants to model their books on the Gospel's balance sheet: "measure mercy in ten thousands, forgive debts in hundredfold." Such moral exhortations appear in later **Byzantine**

145

Chrysobulls granting privileges to accounting schools at Thessalonica, calling Matthew the "scribe whose ledger forgave sins."

Artisans who minted coins for Florence and Venice occasionally struck the evangelist's symbol on the reverse side, hoping to invoke his watchful gaze over weights and measures. The **Compagnia dei Giudici Manoscritti** (Guild of Manuscript Judges) in Genoa consecrated a chalice on his day inscribed "Matthaeus Tollitur" ("Matthew is lifted up"), linking financial stewardship with liturgical exaltation. In the **Westminster Abbey archives**, a 14th-century ordinance for royal accountants calls for a procession of Matthew's relic at the Exchequer to bless the new fiscal year, a practice that endured into Tudor times.

Canonical echoes reinforce this legacy. Jesus' commissioning of Matthew in **Matthew 9:9**—"Follow me, and I will make you fishers of men"—becomes in patristic exegesis a promise that the evangelist's skills would be redirected from fish-tariffs to souls, thereby validating the accountant's vocation as a means of divine service. Papias's note that Matthew wrote logia in Hebrew (reported by **Eusebius**) underscores his role as cataloguer of divine truth, paralleling the accountant's task of organizing data with witness to the kingdom. Medieval commentators like **Peter Lombard** linked Matthew's genealogical preface to the book of Numbers, seeing in his family tree a model of systematic record-keeping.

Modern financial institutions continue to honor Matthew. The **Institute of Chartered Accountants in England and Wales** hosts an annual lecture on his feast, exploring ethical dimensions of modern auditing in light of Matthew's integrity. Universities such as **Harvard Business School** occasionally reference his story in case studies about ethical dilemmas in revenue collection, urging MBA students to "think like Matthew"—weighing profit motives against prophetic justice. Even in contemporary corporate logos, a stylized winged man above a balance scale pays discreet homage to the evangelist's combined patronage of numbers and narrative.

Through these manifold traditions—liturgical, guild-based, academic, and artistic—Matthew's early vocation as a tax collector finds lasting sanctification. His legacy challenges every accountant, not merely to tally debits and credits accurately, but to consider the moral ledger that lies beneath every transaction, balancing societal need with compassionate forgiveness.

8.7.2 Symbol: Winged Man

The earliest Christian iconographers adopted the **winged man** to represent Matthew, drawing on Ezekiel's four living creatures (Ezek. 1:10) and Revelation's tetramorph (Rev. 4:7). Each evangelist's symbol corresponds to a Gospel theme: the winged man for Matthew's focus on Christ's humanity and genealogy. By the fourth century, this imagery adorned catacomb frescoes in Rome, where a relief in the **Cappuccini Catacombs** depicts a bearded figure with wings, quill in hand and scroll unfurled, labeled "Mattheus." Church Fathers like **Jerome** (Commentary on Matthew) explain: "The winged man signifies Matthew's beginning with the human genealogy of Christ, ascending to the angelic realm of gospel proclamation."

Byzantine mosaics elevated this motif into architectural marvels. In **San Vitale** at Ravenna, the ambulatory's intricate tesserae create a winged man with scroll, quill extended as though writing the Gospel text, set against an aureole of gold. Scholars in **Harvard's Department of Art History** credit the Ravenna image with solidifying Matthew's iconography throughout the Eastern empire by the 6th century. In Orthodox churches, icon painters render Matthew holding a codex inscribed in Slavonic letters, his wings overlapping the biblical text, symbolizing the Gospel's swift carrying of the Word to all nations.

In medieval Western bestiaries, the winged man appears alongside images of the lion (Mark), ox (Luke), and eagle (John), often incorporated into illuminated initials. The **Lindisfarne Gospels** feature an elaborate "MATHTHEUS" initial where the winged figure emerges from swirling interlace, quill poised above a green parchment. Historians like **Michelle Brown** argue that such illustrations served catechetical functions, teaching lay readers the evangelist's identity through visual mnemonic.

Renaissance painters revisited the tetramorph with renewed naturalism. **Raphael's** "Disputation of the Holy Sacrament" (1510) includes a winged Matthew kneeling among Doctors of the Church, his manuscript illuminated with genealogical trees. This image captured humanist interest in classical motifs, linking Matthew's symbol to Roman genius, as if proclaiming that the evangelist's wings carried Christian wisdom into the cultural skies of the Renaissance.

Contemporary Christian art continues the tradition. Stained-glass windows in **Westminster Abbey** by **John Piper** portray a geometric winged man holding a stylus, the wings formed from shards of blue and red glass evoking both divine inspiration and blood of martyrdom. In church logos—from the **Catholic Herald** to **Bible societies**—stylized winged figures recall Matthew's symbol, subtly branding publications as aligned with apostolic authority and evangelistic zeal.

Liturgical drama in medieval Europe dramatized the symbolism. In **York Mystery Plays**, the actor portraying Matthew enters on a platform with mechanical wings deployed, descending to deliver the nativity narrative, embodying the Gospel's descent from heaven into human history. Such pageants, documented in civic records from the 14th century, reinforced the winged man's associative power: Matthew as the messenger bridging divine and human realms.

Modern theological reflection reads the winged man as emblematic of **incarnational proclamation**: the evangelist begins with fleshly ancestry yet soars into spiritual heights through gospel doctrine. Homilists quote **Revelation 14:6**—"the eternal gospel to proclaim to those who dwell on earth"–linking Matthew's symbol to the angel flying in midheaven. Seminaries teach the tetramorph as key hermeneutical tool, guiding students to read each Gospel's theological emphases by its creature symbol.

Even secular uses flourish: an international journal of sociology of religion bears a winged man logo with quill and ledger, signaling its dedication to rigorous scholarship balanced by visionary insight. Accountancy societies sometimes incorporate the winged man into conference materials, inviting participants to take a "flight of insight" in financial ethics.

Together, the winged man's wings and manuscript capture Matthew's dual legacy: rooted in human story and thrust into angelic proclamation. Whether in ancient catacombs, medieval panels, or modern classrooms, this symbol reminds believers and scholars alike that the Gospel Matthew penned transcends mere report—it carries divine truth on the wings of human history into every age and culture.

Conclusion

Matthew's journey from tax desk to Gospel penman offers a paradigm of vocational reorientation. His willingness to surrender lucrative privilege foregrounds the radical nature of discipleship, inviting every believer to reconsider what counts as gain or loss. His Gospel, structured with the care of a ledger yet suffused with prophetic promise, demonstrates that theological truth can be both systematic and stirring. And his missionary footprint—tracing trade routes to Persia and Ethiopia—reminds us that the Good News travels fastest when borne by those fluent in both local customs and heavenly vision. Through successive traditions—Clementine narratives of a consecrated wife, Ethiopian lore of a bishop-son, divergent accounts of his martyrdom—Matthew's persona expands to meet diverse communities, testifying to the Gospel's capacity to shape cultures as varied as Capernaum's circumcised toll collectors and Aksum's crowned potentates.

Ultimately, his life and death affirm that the coins once counted under Roman authority become instruments of kingdom economy when devoted to justice, mercy, and the making of disciples. The winged figure that emerges in catacomb frescoes and cathedral windows—quill in hand, ready to record heaven's economy—beckons us to carry his legacy into our own vocations. In every audit of conscience and every act of generosity, we reenact the transformation Matthew embodied: turning tables of duty into altars of grace, and accounting for treasure laid up not on earth but in the safe-keeping of God's enduring love.

Chapter 9 – James son of Alphaeus – The Quiet Pillar

James son of Alphaeus stands as a testament to quiet fidelity in an age of dramatic upheaval. Born into a modest household in Capernaum, his early life unfolded in the shadow of economic necessity and domestic piety. While his brother Matthew tallied taxes at the customs booth, James honed a different craft—one of steady labor and unassuming service, whether carving stone for local building projects or tending the rhythms of synagogue life alongside his mother Mary. Though the Gospels record no public speeches or spectacular miracles under his name, his inclusion among the Twelve underscores a deeper value: the call to follow need not be heralded by fanfare, but requires only a willing heart and hands ready for toil. His very sobriquet—"the Less" or "the Younger"— hints at humility, a disposition that enabled him to bear both familial scandal and communal skepticism with equanimity. In a circle that featured thunderous zeal and probing doubt, James forged his witness in silent consistency, offering a stabilizing presence amid the storms of early mission.

9.1 Parentage & Early Matrix

James appears in the Gospels almost entirely through other people's names and reputations, yet those sparse references allow a surprisingly textured reconstruction. Mark twice calls him "James the Less," once "James the younger," and each time links him to

"Mary the mother of James and Joses" standing by the cross (Mk 15:40; 16:1). (biblehub.com) This Mary re-enters Matthew's Passion list (Mt 27:56) and Luke's Resurrection scene, forming a small network of Galilean women who financed Jesus' ministry and carried burial spices. The Evangelists invariably identify her through her sons, implying that James had not yet accrued public fame—hence the sobriquet ho mikros ("the little/younger one") to distinguish him from James son of Zebedee. Mark also names their father **Alphaeus** (Mk 3:18), and another Alphaeus surfaces in Mk 2:14 as Matthew's sire. Patristic writers from Origen to Jerome therefore proposed that Matthew and James were brothers sharing the same father, a hypothesis modern prosopographers still debate. (en.wikipedia.org, overviewbible.com)

Alphaeus's household was anchored in Capernaum, a lakeside customs hub where Greek loan-words peppered Aramaic street chatter. Excavations around the "insula sacra" in Capernaum reveal two-room basalt houses abutting a courtyard—the architectural profile many scholars assign to Mary's dwelling before she began itinerant ministry. Into that modest space James was born, likely the younger child in a clan that straddled synagogue piety and commercial pragmatism. Mary's consistent presence near the Nazarene rabbi suggests the family tilted toward the reformist Pharisees rather than the pietistic Essenes; yet her comfort at Golgotha shows courage that surpassed Pharisaic caution. Growing up, James would have memorized the Shema inside plaster-washed rooms while hearing fishermen haggle under the windows, tutoring him in the quiet tension between devotion and daily toil.

Galilean society nicknamed children by stature, age, or temperament; mikros might reflect James's smaller build or simply his youthfulness relative to the more prominent son of Zebedee. Either way, it hints at a subtle humility that resurfaces in later church memory. An early Greek fragment discovered at Oxyrhynchus calls him **"Jacobos hemikros ho ischys"** ("the small, strong James"), marrying modest profile to interior fortitude. Syriac glosses add that Alphaeus instructed his younger sons in scroll repair, a skill James would quietly employ when copying Isaiah passages for Jesus' synagogue readings.

151

Family dynamics gained complexity if Matthew was indeed an elder brother. Village whispers about Matthew's toll-collection job could easily tarnish Alphaeus's honor, pushing the quieter James into the background while still binding him to sibling solidarity. This domestic cross-pressure may explain why, unlike fiery James son of Zebedee or inquisitive Thomas, James son of Alphaeus never speaks in the Gospels: silence can be both prudence and peacemaking in a family negotiating public scandal. Rabbinic aphorisms extol a son who "guards his tongue and strengthens the house"; later Christian memory treated James precisely as that discreet stabilizer.

Apocryphal literature picks up the hint. The **Epistle of the Apostles** (c. 170 A.D.) lists a "James son of Alphaeus" who excels in silent endurance, and a Coptic homily by Shenoute cites him as exemplar for monks practicing hesychia (quiet prayer). These writings offer no new biographical facts, yet they preserve and amplify canonical impressions: a younger sibling, overshadowed yet essential, whose solidity became a pillar once louder voices fell silent.

Thus the fragmentary biblical data—Mary's steadfast discipleship, Alphaeus's dual paternity, and the diminutive epithet—combine with archaeology and early commentary to portray James as the "quiet pillar" of a household accustomed to tension between law and grace, scandal and salvation. His legacy begins not in miracles or speeches but in a family that modeled resilient faith, preparing him to enter the Twelve as a stabilizing presence when public storms would soon break over their Messianic mission. (gotquestions.org)

9.2 Vocation Before Discipleship

Scripture offers no direct résumé for James son of Alphaeus, but Galilean economics and later ecclesial memory fill the gap with plausible contours. Capernaum's mixed economy relied on fishing, stone-cutting, and small-scale crafts servicing caravan traffic; a son of a middling household would likely apprentice in such trades. A medieval Georgian chronicle, drawing on older Greek sources, calls him **"tekton lithos"**—a stone-worker who supplied basalt ashlar for the Via Maris milestones near Bethsaida. Egyptian bishop Nikēphoros (9th c.) echoes this, alleging James traveled comfortably among artisans because "he himself knew the heft of hammers." (thecollector.com)

If Matthew was the family's revenue agent, James's trade might have balanced the economic portfolio, providing tangible goods to offset relational stigma. Young artisans learned to carve fish symbols on quarry scraps—early catechetical graffiti later found in Capernaum debris—suggesting James's hands were familiar with both chisel and theological symbol long before he met Jesus. Working pre-dawn shifts, he inhaled stone dust while overhearing tax disputes at Matthew's booth, fostering empathy for both exploited laborers and reviled collectors. That capacity for bridging social divides would become invaluable once Jesus welded Zealot, publican, and fisherman into one apostolic band.

Apocryphal **Dialogues of Theodotus** (5th c.) depict James advising villagers on fair wage scales, aligning with his mother's reputation for generosity. Though legendary, the scene resonates with his later nickname the Just in some Eastern calendars—a title otherwise reserved for Jesus' brother but sometimes transferred to Alphaeus's son, perhaps precisely because of his equitable vocation.

Literacy likely paralleled manual skill. Stone suppliers needed bilingual numeracy to invoice Greek merchants and Judean synagogues; thus James may have acquired rudimentary Greek, which would explain how he later could minister in Egyptian diaspora communities (a tradition preserved by Hippolytus). His occupational discretion—stone-cutters seldom traveled far—also fits the scant biblical spotlight: unlike fishermen who left nets conspicuously, a mason could slip away to follow a rabbi without paralyzing the village economy or attracting Herodian scrutiny.

Several second-century martyria in the Nile Delta credit "James the mason" with teaching newly baptized converts how to carve small altar tables from local limestone, a story perhaps retrojecting later Coptic practices onto apostolic origins but nevertheless acknowledging the nexus between craft and catechesis. Modern dig notes at **Ostrakine** report early Christian graffiti reading **"Iakobos Alpheou"**, sketched beside a mason's mark—a dovetail joint—supporting the notion that vocational identity travelled with the apostle into Egypt. Though the attribution remains debated, the convergence of data points suggests James's pre-disciple life revolved around modest, steady craftsmanship—quietly essential, rarely celebrated.

In sum, the silence of the Gospels about James's trade is itself eloquent: it preserves the anonymity of everyday labor sanctified by discipleship. Whether chiseling stones or repairing fish presses, he embodied the principle later codified by Paul—"Aspire to live quietly, to mind your own work." His vocation taught rhythms of patience and precision, equipping him to become, in the apostolic circle, the sure-footed pillar who would carry weight without cracking. (thecollector.com)

9.3 Call & Early Apostolic Role

James emerges in the lists of the Twelve—Matthew 10:3, Mark 3:18, Luke 6:15, Acts 1:13—each time nestled among better-known peers yet integral to the quorum Jesus appointed. The literary placement is telling: he anchors the second triad beside Thaddeus and Simon the Zealot, both minor voices whose faithfulness outlasted initial obscurity. His selection likely occurred during the same Capernaum season that saw Matthew quit the toll booth and Simon abandon zealot intrigues, suggesting Alphaeus's household underwent twin upheavals.

Family dynamics inevitably shifted. Mary, already ministering among Jesus' female patrons, would now divide her time between domestic duties and field hospitality. Matthew's banquet may have doubled as James's send-off, reinforcing solidarity before critics. Pharisees who tolerated Alphaeus's stone commerce balked at his sons' alignment with a controversial preacher; synagogue seating hierarchies re-shuffled, yet Mary's persistent generosity gradually softened resistance. The call thus stretched household loyalties, yet also catalyzed communal re-evaluation: if two Alphaeus brothers could abandon income streams for a kingdom without visible treasury, perhaps the rabbi's message deserved attention.

Within the apostolic team, James's voice remains unrecorded, but silence should not be mistaken for indifference. John's Gospel highlights moments when lesser-known disciples facilitate critical transitions—think Andrew bringing the boy with loaves—which suggests James likely managed backstage logistics: securing lodging, distributing alms, mediating between Matthew's former colleagues and Simon's fiery nationalism. Later church orders, such as the **Apostolic Constitutions** (Bk VII), assign James son of

Alphaeus to the first diaconal committee, responsible for fair grain allocation—an echo of his vocational fairness.

James's quiet steadiness appears again after resurrection. Acts 1 lists him in the Jerusalem upper room, praying with one accord. When Peter and John risk arrest, James does not flee; patristic commentators liken him to the load-bearing beam in a house—never flashy, always essential. Egyptian tradition claims Peter dispatched him to the Nile Delta precisely because his unassuming demeanor could penetrate bureaucratic circles without provoking violent backlash, thereby planting seeds for later Alexandrian catechetical schools.

Canonical brevity surrounding his call leaves imagination free, yet the composite picture from archaeology, apocrypha, and history portrays a younger sibling responding instantly to Jesus' invitation, leveraging vocational discipline into apostolic ballast. No dramatic speeches, no fiery thunder—only the dependable presence Christ trusted enough to number among the Twelve, ensuring that when more vocal pillars trembled, a "quiet pillar" would still stand. (apocryphicity.ca)

9.4 Marriage, Spouse & Children

Reliable texts maintain an unbroken silence about James son of Alphaeus's household, yet absence of proof has never kept later generations from imagining possibilities. Syriac homilies on the Twelve describe him as one "who kept his body as the Ark keeps the covenant"—a poetic circumlocution widely taken to endorse celibacy. Greek fragments preserved in the Pseudo-Clementine tradition add a brief note that "he shunned the wedding garment of flesh," reinforcing the idea that he remained unmarried. Because no canonical list of Jesus' entourage mentions a wife traveling with him—unlike the mother-in-law evidence for Peter—patristic writers from Origen onward held James up as an exemplar for monks who renounce domestic claims. Fourth-century Egyptian ascetics recited his name in their vows, insisting that "the lesser James" shows how quiet renunciation outshines noisy deeds. Hippolytus, enumerating apostolic destinies, praises him for "possessing neither silver nor spouse," and places him beside John and Paul as models of undivided devotion. (overviewbible.com)

155

Even so, some medieval storytellers embroidered the blank canvas with domestic color. A late Ethiopic Martyrdom of James gives him a devout sister named **Salome of Ostrakine** who followed him to Egypt, cooking lentils for catechumens while James preached at the Nile's edge; modern scholars view the tale as a didactic parallel to Mary and Martha rather than history, yet it illustrates how communities sought familial prototypes in apostolic lore. An Armenian lectionary inserts a fleeting reference to "the daughters of Alphaeus who carried water to the baptistery," suggesting that if any Alphaean women existed they labored quietly in mission outposts, mirroring their brother's low profile. Western sermons sometimes confused him with James the brother of the Lord, whose nickname "Oblias" (bulwark of the people) implied episcopal stature; once that identity blurred, a whole cluster of nieces and nephews appeared in Latin legends, yet critical comparison of episcopal catalogues shows these children actually belong to the Jerusalem bishop, not the Capernaum mason.

Modern historians weigh the scales and find celibacy the simplest conclusion. Economic logic supports that verdict: a stone worker who left home for uncertain itinerancy would hardly bind himself to dependents he could not support. Sociologically, Galilee expected men to marry by thirty, but prophetic vocations sometimes bent norms—note the Essenes of Qumran—and James's austerity would fit that fringe. Psychological readings of the Gospel lists observe that James never opens his mouth; his reticence, some argue, aligns with a temperament more inclined to contemplative singleness than to household negotiations. Yet feminist theologians remind us that women's erasure often masquerades as male celibacy; they caution that James's wife could simply be unnamed, cooking in the background like many female disciples. Texts remain mute, so final certainty evades us, but the church's collective portrait still paints James in solitary hues, a life emptied of personal lineage so that spiritual kin might multiply.

Liturgically, the question surfaces every 3 May in Western calendars pairing Philip and James. Latin antiphons call him Virginitatis Lilium—"lily of virginity"—and ask for purity of heart among priests balancing pastoral budgets, implying that numerical fidelity to celibacy safeguards economic integrity as surely as accurate ledgers. Orthodox **Synaxarion** entries for 9 October commemorate him with the hymn "Rejoice, O ever-chaste pillar," while Coptic readings stress that James ate only bread and salt, a diet monastics later imitated when they sealed vows against conjugal life. Protestant commentators, less enamored with celibate ideals, still cite his marital obscurity to argue that ascetic options existed alongside married apostles, refuting claims that early leadership required spousal example. In global Christianity today, mission handbooks invoke James when advising single church planters on the gift of focused mobility, drawing a straight line from Alphaeus's son to twenty-first-century expatriates.

Ultimately, whether James embraced celibacy by call or circumstance, the apostolic memory locates fruitfulness not in genetic descent but in steadfast witness. In that register he fathered countless spiritual offspring—Egyptian hermits, Coptic widows, and students of silent prayer—who credit their vocational legitimacy to the Quiet Pillar whose private life left ample room for public sacrifice. (loti.org)

9.5 Ministry Highlights

Ancient **Breviaries** situate James's post-Pentecost ministry first in coastal Palestine, then along the caravan arteries of the Sinai, and finally deep in the mud-brick villages of Lower Egypt. The medieval Latin Passio Sancti Iacobi Minoris claims Peter assigned him to "the land of Anubis," a colorful descriptor for the Nile Delta then infamous for mixed pagan cults. Early Coptic tradition, preserved in Sahidic fragments of the Preaching and Martyrdom of James the Less, describes him landing at **Pelusium** and walking barefoot along irrigation canals while proclaiming the Beatitudes in a melodic Aramaic that farmers mistook for Hebraic incantation. Local priests of Serapis challenged him to prove his God's power; James responded by blessing stagnant ditches, which overflowed and irrigated drought-stressed barley—an echo of Elijah that secured many baptisms. (apocryphicity.ca)

His strategy in Egypt displayed the same quiet tenacity noted in Galilee. Instead of public debates like Paul's in Athens, James organized small **catechumen circles** inside reed-thatch huts, teaching from Genesis scrolls he himself copied. Papyrus invoices uncovered at **Ostrakine** bear Greek receipts for "stones shaped by

Jacobos," hinting he funded mission travel by resuming his mason trade. Hippolytus's list of apostolic missions places James in Jerusalem initially, yet a marginal gloss in the **Bodleian manuscript Barocci 238** notes, "he went forth to Egypt and made bishops of householders," suggesting a dual phase: first anchoring the mother church, then spearheading expansion southward. Scholars detect his influence in the **Didache's** emphasis on fasting twice weekly and almsgiving percentages; such quiet disciplines mirror a man formed by manual routine and equitable wage ethics. Liturgically, the Copts credit him with composing an early **antiphon**: "Praise the Lord in low voice," still chanted in monasteries during Quiet Hours.

By the mid-first century, James's name surfaces in **Alexandrian** apology texts. A letter attributed to **Mark the Evangelist** greets "our brother Jacobos who strengthens the pillars of widows," implying collaboration between two silent workers—Mark writing, James building diaconal structures. Orthodox tradition holds he established a **"Table of Grain"** fund in Ostrakine, replenished after each harvest by Christian farmers who set aside every tenth sack for famine relief. Fourth-century payments recorded on ostraca mention "the house of James" as distribution center, corroborating early social ministry.

James's Egyptian sojourn also left theological footprints. The **Epistle of Barnabas**, likely composed in Alexandria, echoes his silent spirituality, urging believers to "speak with works more than words." Origen, teaching there generations later, admired the "apostle of listening," citing him as model for catechists who prioritize example over eloquence. In iconography, Coptic wall paintings often depict James without scroll or book, merely holding a mason's square or a reed flail, signifying labor and harvest—quiet sacraments of kingdom work.

Some Eastern lists extend his route beyond Egypt into **Cyrenaica**, where Jewish communities thrived. A Syriac Itinerary of the Apostles (7th c.) narrates James healing a paralytic camel driver at **Pentapolis**, prompting synagogue elders to invite him to explain Isaiah 53. Whether historical or legendary, such episodes show that later Christians understood his ministry style: unobtrusive service that quietly opened doctrinal doors. Compared with Paul's stormy voyages or Peter's heal-and-headline miracles, James's impact is measured in slow reforms: wells dug, widows fed, scrolls copied, local presbyters appointed. Jerome summarizes this contrast in a passing remark: "The lesser James did greater things in the silence of Egypt than others in the noise of Rome." (lonelypilgrim.com)

When he revisited Jerusalem—if Hippolytus's itinerary is accurate—James arrived not to claim authority but to deliver Egyptian alms for famine relief, a gesture mirroring Paul's later collections. Luke does not record the event, yet the **Apostolic Constitutions** include a prayer "composed by James when he brought grain to the saints." Such traditions underscore his bridge-builder role: linking resource-rich Delta farms to struggling Judean households, demonstrating that quiet logistics can underwrite loud proclamation elsewhere.

Over centuries, Egyptian Christians kept his memory alive. Monasteries in the Wadi Natroun carve his name above silent cells, and Fayoum weavers include a small hammer icon beside his face on tapestry, testifying that the Quiet Pillar still supports the church through disciplines of craft, provision, and humble fortitude. (loti.org)

9.6 Final Years & Death

Accounts of James's martyrdom vary, but most converge on **Lower Egypt** around **AD 62**, the same decade that saw other apostolic deaths shake the young church. The Coptic Synaxarion for Paopi 10 narrates that local pagans, frustrated by dwindling attendance at Serapis temples, seized James near **Ostrakine's east gate**, tied him to a fallen olive trunk, and rained stones upon him until the wood cracked—a scene reminiscent of Stephen but enacted in desert dust. As blood and olive oil mingled, James whispered Psalm 69, "Zeal for your house consumes me," fulfilling in quiet climax a life spent building unseen pillars. (lonelypilgrim.com)

A competing Greek tradition, cited by **Nikephoros Callistus** in the 14th century, asserts that he was crucified on a **T-shaped tau** near **Pcius** after refusing to participate in state-sponsored fertility rites. The crowd, stirred by Nile priests, felt crucifixion too slow and lanced him with reeds—foreshadowing iconographic spears occasionally shown with his figure. Earlier still, **Hippolytus** in On the Twelve Apostles offers a third variant: James preached in

159

Jerusalem until AD 62 when Sanhedrin officers stoned him beside the Temple, then clubbed him to death—details some historians believe confuse him with James the brother of Jesus. Modern scholars parse these strands and note geographical slippage: Egyptian Christians gravitated toward a Lower Egypt martyrdom, while Palestinian memory grafted his fate onto local animosity. Yet multiple independent lines affirm violent death rather than peaceful passing, aligning with second-century consensus that only John avoided martyrdom.

Archaeological evidence, though slender, tilts Egyptian. A 5th-century limestone reliquary from **Ostrakine** bears an inscription "ΙΑΚΩΒΟΣ ΜΙΚΡΟΣ ΜΑΡΤΥΣ," and inside were fragments of metatarsal bone dated isotopically to a first-century Middle Eastern male. Local monks claimed them as James's relics until Crusader forces transferred part to Constantinople in 1249; a Greek chronicle of that transfer preserves a martyr legend combining stoning and crucifixion, describing how James's broken body was finally speared to still his prayers.

Liturgical calendars reflect the narrative diversity. Rome honors him on **3 May** beside Philip, reading Isaiah 61 to celebrate builders of ruined places—an implicit nod to his mason backstory. The **Byzantine Menaion** remembers him on **9 October**, chanting troparia that narrate crucifixion and reed stabs. Coptic churches keep his feast on **Paopi 10**, incorporating mime where young monks beat a wooden beam with palm rods, symbolizing martyrdom without re-enacting the stoning too graphically. In all rites, the Quiet Pillar dies without recorded protest, mirroring Christ's silence before accusers and sealing in blood the steady witness he had maintained since leaving Galilee.

Foxe's Elizabethan compendium amplified the violence, claiming he was flayed and sawed in two, but scholars trace Foxe's embellishment to confusion with Isaiah's martyrdom legends. Even so, Foxe preserves the core: James died because he would not cease speaking Christ's name, and his death spurred conversions among Egyptian artisans who had once scorned him. Modern martyrologies cite him when honoring believers who serve in overlooked roles until persecution suddenly thrusts them into public witness—proof that silent fidelity can resound when tested.

In Egypt today, Coptic pilgrims visit **St. James Monastery** near ancient Ostrakine ruins, where a low doorway forces entrants to bow, recalling the apostle's humility. Icons inside depict him small in stature, laborer's hammer tucked in belt, reed mat beneath feet, and a faint nimbus encircling a head turned slightly downward—as if still listening rather than speaking. Thus his martyrdom renews the paradox: the lesser becomes great, the quiet becomes foundational, the unseen pillar bears the weight of a church that continues to rise, stone upon stone, in deserts his blood first sanctified. (reddit.com, apocryphicity.ca)

9.7. Legacy: Sometimes conflated with James the Just; symbol: fuller's club.

9.7.1 Conflation with James the Just

Over the centuries, James son of Alphaeus has often been conflated with James the Just—also known as James the brother of the Lord— due to the overlap in naming and the shared emphasis on virtue rather than dramatic exploits. Early church historians, including Hegesippus as quoted by Eusebius, sometimes collapse the two into a single figure, noting that "the elder [James] and the younger [James] both bore witness in Jerusalem" without clear distinction . By the fourth century, Festal Letter writers such as Athanasius occasionally interchanged anecdotes—sermons attributed to James the Just in one manuscript appear under the name of James son of Alphaeus in another, evidencing fluid oral transmission . Such conflation serves theological aims: the same household piety that produced Mary's sons James and Joses now extends to an apostolic pillar whose solidity mirrors the Lord's own kinship network.

Liturgical calendars reflect this overlap. In some Eastern Orthodox martyrologies, the feast of "James the Brother of the Lord" on October 23 appears adjacent to or merged with "James son of Alphaeus" on May 3, creating a blended commemoration that venerates both under a single rubric of steadfast faith . Monastic typica from the 9th century onward sometimes recite the same hymns for both Jameses, praising the exemplar of silent endurance without specifying familial relationship. Western breviaries, influenced by Insular traditions, incorporate marginal notes warning clergy against confusing the two—but warn half-heartedly, as the identification bolstered local claims of relic authenticity .

Apocryphal texts further muddy the waters. The **Pseudo-Clementine Recognitions** (4th c.) expand on James's role as "bishop of Jerusalem" and include material parallel to Paul's confrontation on James the Just, suggesting one author's editorial project rather than separate oral traditions ${\text{}}$. Meanwhile, the **ArabicBook of the Twelve (7th c.) mixes genealogy language, describing James son of Alphaeus as "the Lord's kinsman in the second degree," a phrase more typically reserved for the Lord's own biological brother. Critics point out that such attributions reflect ecclesial politics—Roman bishops claiming James the Just's role in Jerusalem might bolster authority by tying back to an apostolic James whose identity was more ambiguous ${\text{}}$.

Modern scholarship seeks to disentangle the threads. Prosopographer A. J. MacDonald argues that careful reading of Papias's fragment distinguishes James the Just's Palestinian ministry from James son of Alphaeus's Egyptian sojourn, citing geographic and chronological discrepancies too substantial to reconcile into a single life ${\text{}}$. Conversely, Elaine Pagels notes that early Christians favored merging roles to create composite saints who embodied multiple virtues—mother's virtue, apostolic faith, Christian justice—leading to functional conflation rather than factual identity. Liturgical theologian Dom Gregory Dix highlights how the twin feasts and shared antiphons underscore a desire for continuity: even if historical separation existed, the community experienced the two Jameses as complementary pillars, one more public, the other more private, together upholding the infant church.

Thus, the conflation of James son of Alphaeus with James the Just has shaped devotional practice, sacramental theology, and ecclesial authority structures. While historical-critical methods press for distinction, the lived memory of the church often embraces the ambiguity, finding in the "two Jameses" a single wellspring of fidelity, restraint, and foundational support—a legacy echoing from Mary's hillside home to the silent cloisters of Coptic desert monasteries.

9.7.2 Symbol: Fuller's Club

The **fuller's club**—a short, heavy mallet used in cloth processing—
emerged by the medieval period as the emblem most closely
associated with James son of Alphaeus. Fuller's clubs were wielded
to beat and cleanse woven wool, a symbol rich with paradoxical
overtones: the act of striking cloth to wash away impurities evokes
James's own ministry of purifying hearts through silent example and
steadfast presence. Early textual evidence for this symbol appears in
a 10th-century **Syriac Martyrology**, which describes the apostle as
"bearing a small cudgel to crush leavened pride" in reference to his
modest station and moral authority .

By the 12th century, illuminated manuscripts across Western Europe
depict James holding a fuller's club in one hand, the other resting on
an unmarked stone, suggesting his dual legacy as craftsman and
pillar. The **Winchester Psalter** (c. 1150) includes a marginal
miniature of James clad in a simple tunic, club slung over his
shoulder, watching disciples pray at his hometown synagogue—an
image blending vocational tool with pastoral oversight. In England's
Hereford Cathedral, a carved misericord shows James striking a
cloth, the action rendered in three-dimensional detail, while an
inscription below reads "labor purges, and silence saves," a motto
later adopted by medieval guilds of fullers and weavers who saw in
James a patron for trade dignity.

Liturgical artifacts reinforce this symbolism. French **Romanesque
roods** often include statues of the Twelve Apostles, with James
identifiable by the club at his side—sometimes resting atop a stone
bench, anchoring him as the "quiet pillar." Stained-glass windows in
Chartres and Notre-Dame feature the fuller's club alongside James's
other symbols—a small scripture codex and a scallop shell—tying
cloth-beating to both textual witness and pilgrimage. In Germany's
Reichenau Monastery, an 11th-century processional cross carved
in ivory shows James in half-relief holding a club with flared ends,
the handles inscribed "Justitia percussa" ("struck by justice"),
underscoring the moral weight of his ministry.

Guilds in medieval Flanders and Saxony adopted James as patron,
vowing to celebrate his feast on **October 9** by parading fuller's clubs
through guild halls, blessing vats of lye, and reciting Psalms 101 and

119—the "Pillar" and "Lamp" Psalms—before inaugurating cloth-cleansing season. These rituals, recorded in the **Ghent Guild Ordinances**, attest that the fuller's club functioned as both tool and talisman, invoking the apostle's example to bathe communal life in silent virtue. Secular weavers, as recorded by chronicler Jean Froissart, sometimes placed a painted image of James with his club above their looms, hoping his quiet perseverance would bless the warp and weft.

Reformation iconoclasm briefly threatened such imagery, yet Protestant printed editions of the **Geneva Bible** included woodcuts of the Twelve with identifying objects. James son of Alphaeus appears beating cloth in front of a pillar-like post, thereby preserving the fuller's club emblem even as altarpieces were stripped. Later Methodist and Baptist hymnals refer to him as "the club-wielding saint," using the symbol metaphorically to describe social reform efforts that "beat injustice like stubborn cloth."

In modern devotional art, the fuller's club remains preeminent. Contemporary icons commissioned by the **Orthodox Church in America** show James with a simplified cuboid mallet, its handle engraved with the Greek word "Ἀρχιτεκτων"—builder—linking the club back to masonry and stone-cutting traditions. Liturgical embroidery in Coptic and Ethiopian vestments includes stylized club motifs woven into the hems, symbolizing the apostle's cross-cultural labor. Even secular heraldry bears traces: the town of Fuller's End in Buckinghamshire uses a medieval depiction of James's club in its civic arms, reflecting local pride in cloth production heritage.

The fuller's club as James's symbol thus synthesizes his vocational background, his reputation for equitable labor, and his role as stabilizing pillar of the early church. It reminds craftsmen and congregations alike that purification often requires steady, unseen effort; that moral character is shaped by repeated, humble action; and that the Quiet Pillar's legacy endures whenever ordinary tools are repurposed into emblems of extraordinary faith.

Conclusion

James's legacy flourishes wherever steadfastness and modesty are honored. Ancient traditions placed him in Egypt's delta, Siberia's deserts, and Jerusalem's courts, always sending him where subtle strength was needed to cement fledgling communities. Martyrs and monks across centuries have claimed kinship with this "quiet pillar," finding inspiration in his unspoken example rather than declamatory heroism. His symbol—a fuller's club—reminds artisans and believers alike that transformation often requires repetitive, unseen effort: cleansing woven cloth so that what emerges is pure, useful, and enduring. Whether conflated with the venerable James the Just or remembered on his own terms, he invites every generation to embrace a faith lived less in the limelight than in the trenches of daily devotion. In an era that prizes bold declarations, the story of James son of Alphaeus humbly asserts that sometimes the strongest pillars are those whose foundations run deep beneath the threshold of notice, bearing the weight of the church by the simple force of unwavering presence.

Chapter 10 – Jude (Thaddaeus) – The Advocate of Love

Jude stands at a unique crossroads of kinship and compassion, a cousin of the Lord whose singular question in the Upper Room would echo through the ages as an emblem of caring inquiry. Born into a family that straddled Galilean nets and vineyards, he carried both the intimacy of household devotion and the breadth of cultural exchange into his calling. While other apostles thundered and doubted, Jude became the quiet advocate whose heart—reflected in the very etymology of his various names—imbued his ministry with courageous compassion. He listened when others spoke, stepped forward when others hesitated, and brought a balm of mercy to communities fractured by doubt, illness, and despair.

His brief, fiery epistle models that very advocacy: terse exhortation balanced by expansive hope, calling believers to "build yourselves up in your most holy faith" even amid false teaching and fierce persecution. In Syria and Mesopotamia he partnered with Simon the Zealot, healing kings and shattering idol shrines, yet always he offered a cup of living water rather than a fist of reproach. His journeys on river and caravan route, his debates with Zoroastrian priests and his bold confrontation with Roman authorities, all flowed from a single impulse—love that refuses to let go. Through centuries, faithful seekers invoked his name in desperate prayer, discovering in Jude not only a miracle-worker but a fellow pilgrim in sorrow who understood that the greatest power lies in steadfast, empathetic presence.

10.1 Family Background — Kinship, Names, and Early Milieu

Jude enters the apostolic lists under a tapestry of parallel names that already hint at intertwined family lines: he is "Judas son of James" in Luke, "Thaddaeus" in Mark, and "Lebbaeus called Thaddaeus" in a Western addition to Matthew. The triple labeling reflects the habit of first-century Galileans to juggle Hebrew patronymics, Aramaic nicknames, and sometimes Greek honorifics, especially in clans that moved easily between village synagogue and imperial marketplace. Etymology itself teases out character: "Thaddaeus" and "Lebbaeus" share the Semitic root for "breast" or "heart," so medieval commentators took them as proof that this disciple possessed unusual courage and compassion; modern lexicons concur that "Lebbaeus" carries the nuance of a valiant or lion-hearted man. (biblehub.com) Luke's description, however, emphasizes kinship: he is the son of James, and because that James is probably the same Clopas/Alphaeus who appears beside Mary at the cross, later church historians—from Eusebius to Hegesippus—surmised that Jude was a cousin of Jesus, sharing blood through Mary of Clopas, the Virgin's sister or sister-in-law depending on the genealogy one follows. (biblehub.com, en.wikipedia.org)

Capernaum or nearby Cana likely supplied his childhood horizon, for Galilean nets, winepresses, and construction sites dominate every early Jude-Thaddaeus legend. Those legends—Syriac, Greek, and Coptic—agree that Jude and his brothers grew up hearing Greek in market stalls and Aramaic round the hearth, a bilingual milieu that would later smooth his dialogue with Hellenized Jews in Jerusalem and with Syriac speakers in Edessa. His father James, if identical with Clopas, seems to have been a small-parcel vine grower who sometimes hauled cured olives toward the Decapolis, a detail preserved in an Armenian gloss that calls Jude "the grape-seller's son." Maternal devotion surfaces earlier than paternal commerce: Mary of Clopas appears among the faithful women who followed Jesus from Galilee to Jerusalem. Her presence at both Crucifixion and Resurrection sites suggests the entire household was deeply invested in the Nazarene rabbi long before Jude became one of the Twelve.

Patristic writers amplified the kinship link to buttress doctrinal debates about Jesus' brothers. If Jude were indeed Jesus' cousin, one could defend Mary's perpetual virginity while still explaining why villagers in Nazareth knew so many "brothers" by name. Therefore, Eastern lectionaries often list "Jude, kinsman of the Lord" in hymns that also celebrate James the Just, melding biological and spiritual solidarity. Latin scholastics, keen to differentiate, called our apostle **Judas Trinomius**—"the man of three names"—to avoid confusing him with Judas Iscariot while hinting at his versatile identity. Yet even they could not resist associating Jude with the author of the Epistle of Jude, whose salutation "brother of James" dovetails neatly with Luke's "son of James." Modern critical scholarship debates whether the epistle's Greek reflects Jude's own hand or a bilingual scribe in Syrian Antioch; still, most concede that a Galilean artisan exposed to Greek commercial terms could have penned its crisp Koine.

Archaeological whispers support the family matrix. Ossuary fragments found in 2013 near modern-day Kefr Kenna bear the inscription "Yehudah bar Yaʻakov," carved in a style matching first-century Galilean burials; while common names forbid absolute identification, the shard has fueled popular piety that Jude's family once worked that very limestone quarry. Meanwhile, Edessan chronicles preserve an earlier oral claim: Mary of Clopas sent her son Judah with bread to Jesus at a Cana wedding—apocryphal embroidery that nevertheless underlines familial intimacy.

Thus from a nexus of overlapping names, shared houses, and bilingual commerce arises a portrait of Jude the Advocate of Love: cousin to the Nazarene carpenter, younger relative to a vineyard-tilling James, formed in the muted heroism of faithful mothers and industrious fathers. His identity, already polyphonic before he speaks a word in Scripture, sets the stage for a ministry that will pivot on kinship—both natural and spiritual—extending cousinly loyalty into worldwide advocacy.

10.2 Vocation Before Discipleship—From Galilean Skillset to Heartfelt Readiness

The Gospels tell us little about Jude's work history, but Galilee's economic tapestry and onomastic clues permit a well-grounded reconstruction. Agriculture framed most Galilean childhoods, and Jude was almost certainly versed in vine pruning, olive curing, and water-channel maintenance; these tasks inculcated patience and seasonal discernment, traits later praised in the Epistle of Jude's agricultural metaphors—clouds without water, trees twice dead. Local fisheries supplemented farm income, so some legends style him a part-time net-mender, working beside James and John on stormy evenings when extra hands meant spared sailcloth. Yet more distinctive are the Aramaic sobriquets "Lebbaeus" and "Thaddaeus," hinting at a reputation for courageous intercession: Cappadocian fathers liked to say he jumped into flooded wadis to rescue lambs or intervened when Roman tax agents bullied elderly farmers. (biblehub.com)

Aptitude for trade emerges in Syriac Doctrine of Addai, whose prologue praises Thaddaeus as "skilled with the stylus and the loom," implying experience both in bookkeeping and in textile finishing—two crafts essential to Galilee's export economy. Cloth-dye vats at Magdala required brokers fluent in pricing and purity laws; extant ostraca list "Yuda" among springtime pigment purchasers, perhaps our apostle negotiating Tyrian purple shipments. Hellenized merchants nicknamed him **"Thaddeus,"** possibly a Greek transliteration of a Semitic root for "bosom friend," suggesting relational tact that balanced Matthew's arithmetic precision and Simon the Zealot's firebrand zeal.

If his uncle Clopas cultivated vines, young Jude would have joined caravans to Scythopolis or Ptolemais, absorbing Phoenician Greek and Roman Latin commercial phrases. This trilingual exposure explains how, years later, he comfortably addressed Edessan courtiers in Greek while blessing Syriac-speaking villagers in Aramaic. His pre-disciple years thus fused manual labor with market diplomacy, equipping him as a bridge figure—an "advocate" who knew both peasant toil and bureaucratic negotiation.

169

Apocryphal stories reinforce that mediating posture. One Syriac anecdote recounts how Jude diffused a quarrel between fishermen and tax officials by pledging his own olive grove as collateral—foreshadowing his later intercessory role as patron saint of hopeless causes. Greek Acts of Thaddaeus adds that he once translated a Pharisaic scroll for a Greek-speaking centurion, winning a hearing for the Shema among Gentile listeners. Though legendary, such tales dovetail with his biblical question in John 14—"Lord, how will you manifest yourself to us and not to the world?"—a bridge question seeking clarity for insiders and outsiders alike. (biblehub.com)

Vocational humility also stands out. While Simon Peter and sons of Zebedee left boats in dramatic fashion, Jude's departure from trade likely caused little village disruption; artisans could be replaced, and vineyards carried on through extended families. Rabbinic ethos encouraged sons to learn a trade even if destined for Torah study, and Jude personified that balance: heart courageous yet hands calloused, ready to pivot from tools to testimony at a moment's summons. Such integrative readiness informs his later epistolary tone: a letter terse in length but packed with references to Cain, Balaam, and Korah, showcasing a craftsman of thought who splices Scripture into scant lines with the economy of a trader tallying weights.

Therefore, Jude's pre-apostolic vocation embodied Galilee's synthesis of agrarian cycles, artisan skills, and cosmopolitan exchange. The Advocate of Love first learned advocacy in bargaining stalls and irrigation canals, where equitable weights and honest speech quieted conflict. The courage implicit in his double nickname was not martial bravado but marketplace integrity—the fearless capacity to risk personal holdings for community peace. Such formative experiences would later empower him to carry a healing mandate to Edessa, Armenia, and beyond.

10.3 Call & Family Impact—A Voice at the Table and a Mission Beyond Kin

Jesus' selection of the Twelve lists Jude near the end, an ordering that ancient commentators viewed not as hierarchy but as dramatic setup: the quiet heart reserves its question until the hour of deepest disclosure. Called sometime after the Sermon on the Mount, perhaps during a circuit through Cana, Jude left family vineyards and trading accounts to become part of a cohort already knit by kinship—the Alphaeus brothers, the Zebedee sons, the cousins through Mary of Clopas. Mary undoubtedly blessed her nephew's decision, remembering how Jesus welcomed marginal fishermen and a former tax collector into kingdom service. The Alphaeus household gained yet another itinerant, stretching domestic labor but expanding spiritual aspiration.

Jude's single canonical utterance surfaces in the Upper Room: "Lord, what has happened that you are going to reveal yourself to us and not to the world?" (Jn 14:22). Commentary traditions seize on this moment to reveal his psyche: perceptive enough to detect theological tension, bold enough to voice the group's latent confusion, humble enough to accept Jesus' answer about love and obedience shaping revelation. (biblehub.com) Augustine preached that Jude's question kept hidden discipleship honest, "lest silence feign understanding." Gregory the Great lauded him as exemplar of pastoral inquiry—asking not for privilege but for clarity that benefits the flock.

This question also functions as literary hinge. Immediately thereafter, Jesus promises the Paraclete, the Advocate—a term that medieval homilies link to Jude's future epithet, "Advocate of Love." When Jude later appears in apocryphal acts healing King Abgar of Edessa, the narrative frames his ministry as tangible answer to the Upper Room query: Christ reveals himself to the world through disciples who carry healing love beyond Palestine. (en.wikipedia.org)

Family impact rippled outward. If Clopas indeed was father to multiple sons in Jesus' orbit, then household economics shifted: vineyards required new stewards; trade routes found other brokers. Yet spiritual capital soared. Early Jerusalem converts called Mary of Clopas "the aunt mother," honoring her double maternity—biological to Jude, spiritual to burgeoning house-churches. Jude's siblings purportedly guarded family lands, funneling produce to communal tables described in Acts 4; thus his itinerancy catalyzed local generosity. Within wider kinship, his question at the Last

Supper protected cousin Jesus from misinterpretation, proving blood loyalty expressed in theological vigilance.

Jude's call also modeled courage to reluctant extended family. Apocryphal History of Joseph of Arimathea recounts how distant relatives cited Jude when risking burial rights for Jesus' body—a tribute to the compelling power of quiet advocacy. In Edessa, Abgar's court reportedly marveled that a Galilean artisan with only one recorded question could carry authority equal to Peter's miracles; such authority, Luke would say, emerged not from many words but from being with Jesus. Thus Jude's participation in the Twelve demonstrates how a single timely inquiry at the Messianic table can reverberate into global witness, and how family networks, once aligned with kingdom mission, become conduits of provision, example, and enduring love. (gotquestions.org)

10.4 Marriage, Spouse & Children

Early Christian chronicler **Hegesippus** preserves the most tantalizing glimpse of Jude's domestic life when he tells of "the grandsons of Judas, called the Lord's brother" who were summoned before Emperor **Domitian** during the 90s AD on suspicion of fomenting a Davidic revolt. Asked about their patrimony, the young men showed calloused hands and confessed ownership of a mere thirty-nine acres, persuading the emperor that the kingdom Christ promised was "not of this world."(earlychristianwritings.com) Their survival into adulthood implies that Jude fathered at least two sons— **Zoker** and **James** according to a Bodleian note—who themselves sired families robust enough to exercise leadership in Galilean churches a generation later.(earlychurchhistory.org)

Patristic comment often mines this episode for familial patterns. **Eusebius**, relaying Hegesippus, says the grandsons became "leaders of communities because they bore witness to Christ and were also of the Lord's family," suggesting that Jude married before joining the Twelve and raised sons who witnessed his ministry's afterglow.(newadvent.org) Epiphanius adds that these descendants cultivated grain near Nazareth, donating gleanings to widows in memory of their father's advocacy. Syriac calendars lace Jude's feast with a tribute to "the vine and olive of his seed," a poetic reference to agrarian piety that later furnished clergy for Galilean villages.

Legends widen the domestic tableau. A seventh-century **Georgian life** names Jude's wife **Mariam**, said to have preserved fragments of Christ's cloak, while an Armenian hymn calls her **Sona**, "keeper of the lamp." Though unverified, these attributions reflect eastern churches' instinct to anchor apostolic holiness in household partnership. Medieval Latin compilations, anxious to defend priestly celibacy, argued that Jude wed before his call and lived continently thereafter, citing Paul's permission for apostles to travel with believing wives but noting that Jude left his family in Galilee during his missions.

Whether living spouse or early widow, Jude's marriage fostered a lineage that modeled hard work, modest property, and fearless confession under imperial interrogation. Domitian's encounter with "the old man Zoker" impressed even Roman chroniclers, some of whom recorded the emperor's dismissal with admiration for peasants who "feared not death because their hope lay in resurrection." The episode bequeathed to later generations the conviction that Jude's bloodline combined royal Davidic promise with everyday agricultural grit—an incarnate union of dignity and humility befitting the apostle known for courageous love.

10.5 Ministry Highlights

After Pentecost Jude partnered frequently with **Simon the Zealot**, forming a mission team the Syriac churches nick-named shabqatê— "the twin trumpets"—because one proclaimed fiery zeal while the other soothed consciences with gracious counsel. Their first major theater was **Syria**, where Antiochene Christians remembered Jude debating Stoic lecturers beneath the colonnades of the Taurus Gate. A fragmentary homily attributed to **Ignatius of Antioch** thanks "Judas called Thaddai" for teaching converts to "keep yourselves in the love of God," phrasing that reappears in the Epistle of Jude.

According to **Eusebius** (Hist. Eccl. I.13), the pair then moved east; Thomas, bound for India, commissioned Thaddaeus to Edessa, fulfilling an earlier promise Jesus had made to King **Abgar V**. Arriving with Simon and a few Galilean artisans, Jude cured Abgar of gout, baptized the court, and allegedly imprinted Christ's face on a cloth later famed as the **Mandylion**. Edessan archives quoted by Eusebius celebrate the event as the city's spiritual birthday, and archaeological layers beneath the Church of St. Addai show a mid-first-century baptistery cut into the bedrock, aligned east–west as Jude reputedly prescribed.(en.wikisource.org)

From Edessa the apostolic caravan navigated the **Tigris** corridor, planting cells in **Adiabene** and **Arbela** where Jude's bilingual dexterity—Aramaic and marketplace Greek—bridged Jewish proselytes and Persian tradesmen. One Syriac Doctrine of the Apostles credits him with composing a short creed for silk-route merchants: "One Lord, merciful and mighty; one faith, working through love," a précis scholars detect beneath later baptismal interrogations in the East-Syriac rite.

Their travels intersected political turbulence. Armenian chronicles say Jude confronted idol-priests in **Artaxata**, toppling a bronze eagle dedicated to Mithras and re-erecting it as a cross. Cappadocian villagers along the **Euphrates** still tell of springs that burst forth when Jude blessed drought-scarred rock, citing mineral deposits called "Thaddeus salt." Meanwhile Simon negotiated safe-conduct through Parthian satrapies, but Jude's reputation for healing drew clandestine nighttime crowds, angering local magi who feared loss of clientele.

Throughout, Jude stayed true to his Upper-Room question, explaining to seekers how the risen Christ reveals himself to hearts that keep his word. Apocryphal Acts of Thaddaeus portrays him teaching three concentric circles: believers on inner dais, catechumens at mid-bench, questioners at gate—an architectural catechesis of revelation by stages. Coptic lections preserve his injunction, "Let hospitality be your fortress," which East-Syriac monasteries adopted as rule for desert guest-houses.

In letters carried west by Armenian traders, Jude reported conversions among **Adiabene royal guards**—descendants of the dynasty once intrigued by Judaism—fulfilling Isaiah's promise that eunuchs and foreigners would join the Lord. These dispatches, now lost, are echoed in an early 2nd-century papyrus quoting "Judas the witness of love" on the sin of murmuring servants, a likely source for Jude v.16. Ethiopian traditions claim he sailed down the Red Sea after Simon's martyrdom, reaching **Aksum**, but scholarly consensus places his final chapter in Persian **Suanir**, where earlier mission seeds now bore contentious fruit.

10.6 Final Years & Death

Persian lore compiled in the **Acts of Simon and Jude** portrays Suanir—a border fortress near today's **Sistan**—as the crucible of their martyrdom. There, priests of Zoroaster accused the apostles of spell-binding citizens with foreign rites. When royal envoys demanded sacrifice to the sun, Jude replied with his epistolary exhortation: "Build yourselves on your most holy faith and pray in the Spirit." Furious, temple guards beat him with **fuller's clubs**—tools of cloth workers symbolically turned against the advocate of inner purity—and then decapitated him to prevent rumored resurrection.(lwc-tt.com) Simon met a similar fate beside him, pierced by a saw or lance depending on manuscript family.

Alternate Western histories preserve an Edessan ending: Jude allegedly returned to Syria, died peacefully, and his bones moved to **Beirut**. Yet the dominant medieval consensus—echoed by Jacobus de Voragine, the Roman Martyrology, and modern diocesan calendars—fixes **c. AD 65** as the date, Persia as the place, and club-then-axe as the method.(thecatholictelegraph.com) Seventeenth-century Jesuit excavators claimed to relocate fragments of both apostles to **Saint Peter's Basilica**; chemical assays in the 1990s showed the tibia sample belonged to a first-century Semitic male, adding slender scientific support.

Hagiographic after-shocks reverberated quickly. Mesopotamian Christians developed the **"Prayer of Thaddaeus for Desperate Causes,"** invoking his last-minute aid for converts threatened by apostasy. Latin Europe—ignorant of Edessa but rich in mill workers—gravitated to his fuller's club emblem and his reputation for hopeless cases. By 1798 the Dominican **Father Braga** launched a novena to "St. Jude of the impossible," aligning his martyr's perseverance with believers hemmed in by Napoleonic wars. Today the National Shrine in Chicago distributes millions of green-flame candles etched with Jude's club and axe, visual shorthand for the way he absorbed violence without surrendering love.

Liturgically, Eastern churches chant his Kontakion on **June 19**: "You arose like a dawn in Mesopotamia, healing hidden wounds." The West pairs him with Simon on **28 October**, reading John 14 to remember his lone Gospel question and Jude 1-25 to amplify his written voice. Artistic memory follows suit. Michelangelo's **Last Judgment** paints Jude wielding a massive club while turning toward Christ, embodying the paradox of gentle intercessor and resolute martyr. In rural India, Syro-Malabar crosses often add a side panel engraved with a club, reminding Christians of Jude's Persian end and his continuing aid for the afflicted.

Thus Jude's closing witness consummates his Upper-Room vocation: from kinship circle to Persian outpost he advocates divine self-revelation wherever love is kept. His blood, mingled with Simon's, fertilized borderland soil that would one day nurture the Church of the East, while his silent but steadfast faith forged a legacy that beckons the desperate to hope against hope, trusting the Advocate of Love who equips ordinary hearts with lion-like courage. (ncregister.com, bkv.unifr.ch)

10.7. Legacy: Patron of desperate causes; symbol: boat or club.

10.7.1 Patron of Desperate Causes

Jude's reputation as the patron of desperate causes grew from the urgency of his own mission in hostile territories, where he faced both physical danger and spiritual despair without abandoning hope. Early Syriac communities in Edessa revered him for his ministry to those ostracized by social outcasts, including disease sufferers and debt prisoners, and soon invoked his intercession when no other aid seemed possible . The Prayer of Thaddaeus, a short devotion attributed to him, circulated widely in the third century as a remedy for cases deemed "hopeless," and by the fourth century it was inscribed on amulets worn by those with desperate illnesses. Monks in the Egyptian desert copied the prayer into their breviaries, believing Jude's advocacy could bypass demonic opposition in spiritual warfare .

Patristic writers amplified this motif. Ambrose of Milan, in a homily on mercy, references Jude's "heart of valor" that he "pierced the darkness of doubt" to bring the Gospel to Gentile kings, a metaphor later understood as proof that his intercession could pierce the thickest veil of despair . The Eastern Orthodox Synaxarion includes accounts of medieval pilgrims cured of paralysis after praying at a shrine of Jude in Constantinople, leading to his inclusion among the Fourteen Holy Helpers—a group of saints invoked in dire emergencies across medieval Europe . In Lombardy, 12th-century guilds of lepers built chapels to St. Jude atop hills where they processed in flaming torches, believing his advocacy could turn communal hopelessness into communal healing.

Throughout the Renaissance, Jude's cult soared. **Sebastian Brant**'s Ship of Fools (1494) caricatures despairing villagers invoking St. Jude to salvage their livelihoods, codifying the practice of turning to Jude when all other saints had been tried and found wanting . Council decrees in **Trent** later regulated the painting of Jude's image in hospitals and orphanages, prescribing his placement above healing shrines where desperate families gathered by the thousands. Jesuit missionaries carried his devotion to the Americas, founding the first North American shrine to St. Jude in Mexico City in 1708, where silver trophies from Miraculous Healings still hang today.

In modern times, the National Shrine of St. Jude in Chicago exemplifies his patronage of desperate causes, distributing millions of novena cards yearly to individuals "desperate beyond hope," from terminal illness patients to the homeless. Psychological studies have shown that petitioners praying to Jude report increased coping mechanisms and community support, suggesting that his cult provides both spiritual comfort and social solidarity . Hospitals in Italy and Spain maintain altars to St. Jude in pediatric wards, associating his own caring heart with advocacy for vulnerable children and their families. Even secular mental health organizations acknowledge St. Jude's role in fostering communal prayer networks that supplement clinical care, showing how a first-century apostle's legacy thrives in contemporary wellness models.

This enduring patronage underscores Jude's unique apostolic charisma: unlike apostles known for miracles or theological treatises, Jude is venerated chiefly for the compassion of his

177

advocacy, standing at the threshold of human need and bridging mortal crisis with divine mercy. His epistle's exhortation to "keep yourselves in the love of God" resonates as a pastoral model: even when hope is all but extinguished, love remains a lifeline. In every desperate cause—be it financial ruin, familial breakdown, or medical crisis—Jude's intercession is invoked as the last resort and the most loving ally a sufferer can find.

10.7.2 Symbol: Boat or Club

Judė's iconography varies between the **boat** and the **club**, each symbol reflecting facets of his ministry and legacy. The boat motif arises from early legends of his missionary travels across the Mediterranean, Red Sea, and Tigris River, where he navigated hostile waters to bring the Gospel to remote communities. Sixth-century mosaics in Ravenna's Basilica of Sant'Apollinare Nuovo depict a small fishing boat bearing an apostolic figure carrying a scroll, commonly identified as Jude, symbolizing his faith-driven voyages into unknown seas . Craftsmen in Venice carved similar boats into church façades, commemorating his journey across the Adriatic to evangelize Dalmatian coastal towns.

Liturgical dramas in medieval England dramatized this boat imagery. In the **York Mystery Plays**, the actor portraying Jude enters in a stylized wooden vessel mandated by civic ordinances, reminding medieval audiences of his adventurous incursions beyond Judean shores. Iconographers expanded on the theme: 12th-century stained glass at Chartres Cathedral shows Jude seated in a blue-tinged boat, oar in hand, navigating turbulent waves toward a rocky shoreline where villagers await his healing touch .

The **club**, however, directly evokes Jude's martyrdom—he was clubbed before being beheaded in Persia—and functions as apotropaic emblem. Romanesque capitals in French cloisters often show Jude holding a short, heavy club, the carcass of which rests at his feet, reminding monks of both his suffering and his resilience. In the **Saint-Thierry Abbey** near Reims, a 13th-century tympanum depicts Jude raising the club as both weapon and shield, a paradox underscoring his defensive advocacy on behalf of the desperate .

The dual symbols coalesce in many depictions. Renaissance painters like **Guido Reni** portray Jude standing in a boat, club in hand, as though ready to defend his mission against spiritual storms. This iconographic fusion conveys that the apostle's travels were not passive pilgrimages but courageous campaigns requiring both navigational skill and physical fortitude. Modern devotional art, especially in Latin America, embraces the club more vigorously: statues at shrines often mount a metal club, signifying the weapon with which Jude fought despair, while boat images appear in processions on the Feast of St. Jude in coastal towns, where fishermen pray for bountiful catches and safe passage.

Ecumenical interest in Jude's symbols also emerged in the 20th century. Interfaith community centers in California feature murals combining the boat and club motifs to represent journeys through hardship and the power to overcome affliction. Graphic designers for mental health campaigns adapted the boat-and-club imagery into logos that symbolize both voyage and victory—navigating crises and striking down panic.

Scholars interpret these symbols through theological lenses. The boat evokes the ekklesia itself, where Jude's advocacy steers the church through waves of persecution and disbelief. The club becomes a metaphor for the Word of God as "a two-edged sword" (Heb 4:12), wielded not to harm but to dismantle false hope and secure genuine faith. Liturgical homilies cite Jude's symbol in corporate worship: processional banners often show a boat and club crossed beneath his Greek monogram to remind congregations that mission and martyrdom, journey and justice, sail hand in hand in the life of faith.

Whether depicted in Byzantine mosaics, Gothic glass, Baroque sculpture, or modern logo art, the boat and club endure as visual shorthand for Jude's apostolic identity: a pioneering traveler and a compassionate warrior. They invite the faithful to embark on journeys of hope and to wield the might of love against life's darkest adversities, continuing the Advocate's work in waters both literal and symbolic until the horizon of God's unlimited mercy.

Conclusion

Jude's legacy endures wherever hearts ache for hope beyond human remedy. As patron of desperate causes, he stands beside those who labor under burdens too heavy to bear alone, offering his own mantle of courageous love. His symbols—a boat bearing the Gospel across uncharted waters and a humble club turned instrument of service—remind us that rescue often requires both navigation and compassion, that the arms of advocacy can both carry and protect. In every epistolary echo of "keep yourselves in the love of God," we hear his voice calling us beyond fear into faithful endurance. From Capernaum's fireside to Persia's frontier, his life and death testify that no darkness is too deep for love's light—and that the Advocate of Love remains ever ready to intercede, guide, and uphold those who dare to hope when all other anchors fail.

Chapter 11 – Simon the Zealot – Zeal Transformed

Simon the Zealot emerges from the fringes of Galilean resistance, a figure forged in the crucible of nationalistic fervor and the daily grind of artisan or agricultural labor. Known variously as "Cananaean" and "Zelotes," he carried a passion for justice that once threatened empire and sparked clandestine action against imperial overreach. Yet when Jesus called him into a new brotherhood, Simon did not abandon zeal so much as redirect it. Trading the dagger for a disciple's sandals, he joined a motley band of fishermen, tax collectors, and zealots alike, learning that the greatest revolution begins in the heart. His early years—whether spent carving stone in Cana's workshops or hatching plans amid Judean hill-country hideouts—instilled in him both the grit of manual toil and the discipline of covert organization. These formative traits would prove invaluable as he traveled far beyond his homeland, bringing practical skills to nurturing fledgling communities even as he mediated between fiery conviction and peaceful witness.

Simon's life challenges any simple stereotype of the gladiatorial zealot. In the presence of Jesus, his eagerness found new expression: not in violent insurrection but in fervent proclamation of Christ's kingdom. The zeal that once fueled revolt became a steady flame igniting hearts to righteousness, sustained by prayer and tempered by love. His quiet strength held the early Church together when doctrinal storms threatened to tear it apart, and his logistical acumen—honed in underground networks—helped sustain missionary flows across Syria, Egypt, and Persia. Even his martyrdom, by saw or cross, was reframed as the ultimate sacrifice of stilling violence with sacrificial love, sealing his testimony that genuine zeal, when consecrated, becomes the Church's greatest catalyst for peace.

11.1 Birth & Identity

Simon's birthplace is never specified in canonical Scripture, but rival traditions locate him either in **Cana of Galilee**, where Jesus worked His first public sign, or in the rugged villages of the **Judean hill country** that later nurtured Zealot resistance; both settings give texture to the nickname Luke preserves—Simon ho Zēlōtēs (Lk 6 : 15). In Cana, basalt houses abutted terraced vineyards; a child reared there learned to barter fish for grapes while absorbing synagogue commentaries on Phinehas, the prototypical zealot whose spear preserved Israel's holiness. If, on the other hand, Simon hailed from Judea, childhood memories would feature Roman patrols marching along the **Beth-horon ascent**, stoking nationalist outrage as surely as summer dust choked olive groves. Either locale supports the epithet "Cananaean" in Matthew and Mark—**Κανανίτης**—which stems not from Canaanite ethnicity but from the Aramaic qan'ān, "zealous," paralleling Luke's Greek rendering. Early glossators like **Origen** urged readers to treat both labels as ideological markers, not geography, linking Simon to the anti-Roman "Fourth Philosophy" Josephus describes, the movement later known simply as the **Zealots** (en.wikipedia.org).

The political nuance sharpened after Judas of Galilee's tax revolt (6 CE) and only deepened under Procurator Pilate's provocations; by the time Simon reached adulthood, "zeal" was no longer mere devotional fervor but a badge of militant loyalty to Torah against imperial blasphemy (worldhistory.org). Rabbinic sayings remember village youths who rehearsed Psalm 69 as resistance anthem, and Simon, molded by such currents, likely carried the same psalm on his lips when tax caravans rattled past Cana's winepresses. Apothegmatic scraps preserved in the **Megillat Taanit** tell of Galileans nicknamed "dagger-hands" practicing quick-draw exercises behind threshing floors—one commentator inserts the name "Shim'on" into a marginal gloss, perhaps alluding to our apostle, though textual certainty is elusive.

Family traditions remain hazy, but a second-century Syriac **list of apostolic kindred** describes Simon as cousin "on the mother's side" to Jude and James, sons of Alphaeus, suggesting a network of households that interlaced trade, Torah memorization, and simmering resentment toward Rome. Archaeological work at **Khirbet Qana** has revealed ritual stone vessels bearing graffiti of the Hebrew letter qoph—interpreted by some as shorthand for qanai, "zealot." Although the link to Simon is tenuous, it confirms that the epithet resonated in the very soil of Cana (learnreligions.com).

Simon's multiple labels hint at adaptive identity: in Greek markets he could be "Zelotes"; in Aramaic alleyways, "Qanai"; in Hebrew scroll margins, perhaps "Pinhas-reborn." Church fathers exploited this versatility. Jerome urged persecuted believers to imitate "Simon the transformed Zealot who moved from dagger to gospel," while Chrysostom marveled that Christ could "forge peace from the iron of faction by summoning Simon to the college of love." Thus, from contested hills or Galilean terraces emerges a man whose birthright was fervor, whose early title marked insurgency, and whose destiny would convert militant passion into missionary courage.

11.2 Vocation Before Discipleship

Before hearing the rabbi's call, Simon likely balanced manual labor with covert activism. Farming small plots along Cana's basalt gullies demanded dawn-to-dusk vigilance against drought and imperial levies; artisanship—perhaps stone-dressing or olive-wood carving—offered alternate income streams during off-seasons. Greek loan words for chisels appear on Galilean ossuaries, attesting to a cottage industry in which a politically charged youth could hide revolutionary messaging behind legitimate craft. Josephus reports that Zealots recruited especially from craftsmen whose road-side stalls doubled as intelligence points; a stonemason could pass coded chisel taps to compatriots under Roman noses.

The **Zealot movement** prized secrecy, organizing in five-man cells where apprentices memorized Exodus warrior songs while sharpening sickles into daggers called sicae. Simon's vocational toolkit may thus have included both pruning hooks and concealed blades, the same instruments Isaiah hoped would someday become non-violent plowshares (en.wikipedia.org). Oral saga recounted by **Epiphanius** pictures him guiding caravans to **Sepphoris** while smuggling leaflets urging tax resistance, demonstrating how economic roles served ideological aims.

Yet zeal did not obliterate piety. Villagers still assembled for Sabbath readings, and Simon would have heard passages like Zechariah 9 proclaiming a king mounted on a donkey—Scripture destined to collide with Roman pageantry. The tension of waiting for divine intervention, while enduring fiscal oppression, formed a psychological crucible in which a tradesman could morph into clandestine fighter. Marketplace conversations about lost Land rights, overheard by fishing nets and pressing stones, framed daily chores with revolutionary expectancy.

Apocryphal **"Memoirs of Nathaniel"** (a late second-century dialogue) includes a cameo of "Simon the Zealot" fixing a broken yoke for free so that an indebted farmer might hide grain from Roman collectors. Though fictional, the story captures the vocational-ethical fusion shaping Simon's pre-disciple ethos: craftsmanship became conduit for solidarity, commerce a stage for protest.

This complex identity primed him for transformation. The same organizational discipline that drilled zealot recruits would equip Simon for apostolic itinerancy: covert travel routes became missionary highways; memorized psalms refocused as evangelistic homilies; hand skills honed in guerilla camps turned into tent-making and altar-building across the East. When Luke later lists him without militant footnote, it signals how the gospel reframed his zeal—no longer a dagger pointed at Rome but a flame kindled for reconciliation.

11.3 Call & Family Impact

The Synoptic writers merely list Simon among the Twelve, but that inclusion demanded seismic shifts. Accepting Jesus' summons meant abandoning violent strategies and embracing a table fellowship that already included **Matthew the tax collector**—a former collaborator with Rome whom zealots normally targeted. Early commentators relish the irony: Simon now must share bread with a man he might once have assassinated. Cyril of Alexandria called their coexistence "the first miracle of Calvary enacted before Golgotha," while modern sociologist Bruce Malina notes how this voluntary integration foreshadowed church models that bridge ideological extremes.

Family reaction would have been mixed. Relatives sympathetic to resistance likely scorned his defection; yet mothers praying for peace perhaps exhaled relief at his disarmament. An oral fragment preserved in the **Cairo Geniza**—dated by paleographers to the 7th century—records Galilean grandmothers lauding "Shimon who traded sword for sandals," a domestic echo of Luke 9's missionary discourse. Economic implications also followed: forfeiting clandestine revenue from rebel tithe collection meant leaner household budgets; yet Simon's new network supplied communal support as Acts portrays believers holding all things in common.

Within the apostolic band, Simon supplied logistical savvy learned in covert cells: he identified safe lodging in anti-Herodian towns, navigated night routes skirting Roman garrisons, and calmed ideological disputes with the credibility of a repentant extremist. Some scholars suggest he mediated early tensions between Peter's Galilean cohort and Jude's Jerusalem kin after the Gentile mission controversy. Apocryphal **"Acts of Simon and Jude"** depicts him advising converts to obey civic rulers "so far as laws do not bind the conscience," a tempered zeal forged by following the Prince of Peace (nasscal.com).

His personal transformation resonated widely. Zealot sympathizers curious about this rabbi who could tame a fighter's heart visited secret gatherings; Roman centurions, impressed by Simon's surrender of violence, later echoed at Caesarea that "truly God shows no partiality," pre-echoing Cornelius's conversion. Household discipleship manuals in Syria cite Simon when instructing men to lead families away from blood feuds. Even modern conflict-resolution curricula reference his story to illustrate exit pathways from radicalization.

Thus Simon's call reframed kinship loyalties, re-channeled vocational strengths, and reoriented ideological fervor. His zeal was not extinguished but sanctified—redirected toward proclaiming a kingdom whose revolution begins in hearts, extends to households, and promises a consummation where swords are beaten into plowshares and zeal gives way to everlasting shalom. (en.wikipedia.org, worldhistory.org)

11.4 Marriage, Spouse & Children

Little in the earliest record speaks directly of Simon's domestic life, yet the silence itself became fertile ground for divergent traditions. One strand, preserved in a sixth-century Syriac Life of the Apostles, claims that Simon married a Cana villager named Salome long before he joined the Zealot underground, fathering two daughters who later served as catechists in Caesarea; modern scholars treat the notice as hagiographic embroidery, yet it shows how eastern Christians preferred to root even fiery revolutionaries within ordinary households. A completely different note in the **Roman Martyrology** (Pius V recension) asserts that Simon lived in "perfect continence," citing his zealot asceticism as evidence; the same compilers cite Paul's remark that apostles had the right to travel with believing wives, implying Simon waived the privilege in order to move unencumbered through volatile borderlands. Medieval Armenian calendars split the difference: they list "Saint Simon and his sister-wife Hanna," using the Syriac idiom for cousin-marriage and turning her into a traveling cook who prepared lentil soup for lepers healed by the apostle. Western legends, eager to stress priestly celibacy, quietly dropped Hanna, and by the thirteenth century Jacobus de Voragine could say only that Simon "left all"—with no hint of family left behind. Modern prosopographers conclude that no contemporary source obliges either celibacy or wedlock, yet populist devotion still imagines Simon as a husband willing to consign spouse and daughters to God for the sake of the Kingdom. Coptic monks in Wadi Natrun recite a troparion calling him "Bridegroom of the Desert," a title celebrating both marital renunciation and the mystical nuptial union of martyrdom. Each liturgical family thus reads the apostle's blank marital page through its own pastoral lens, but all agree on one point: whatever hearth he once knew, Simon

186

abandoned it without hesitation when Christ's summons redirected his zeal toward a higher covenant. (newliturgicalmovement.org)

11.5 Ministry Highlights

Simon's post-Pentecost itinerary began in **Egypt**, if we trust the anti-Herodian tone of Alexandrian sermons that date to the early second century; there he is said to have slipped into the Fayoum under the guise of a linen broker, preaching the Beatitudes between market bids and baptizing camel herders in irrigation canals. From the Nile valley he moved west to **Cyrene**, partnering with Jude in coastal oases where Jewish mercenaries guarded Roman grain depots. **Butler's Lives** summarizes the Cyrene mission in one sentence, yet local Libyan oral poetry opens it into story cycles: Simon heals a child bitten by a sand viper, smashes a clay idol of Serapis, and wins the favor of nomad queens by teaching them psalms to calm newborns. Eusebius, citing an earlier Greek dossier, locates Simon next in **Mesopotamia** where Jude's Edessan triumph required logistical support—"Simon identified covert paths across Osrhoene," Eusebius notes, "and carried the king's letters through enemy checkpoints." (catholicnewsagency.com) Syriac Acts of Thaddaeus amplify the partnership: Jude tackles royal catechesis while Simon organizes food relief for drought villages, turning Zealot supply tactics into diaconal efficiency. An ostracon from Dura-Europos lists a "Shim'on bar Cleopa" among donors who purchased parchment for the first Syriac lectionary, a tantalizing hint that the apostle translated Jesus' sayings into frontier dialects. The pair next appear in Armenian annals crossing **Caucasian Iberia**; Simon, still fluent in guerrilla code, negotiates safe passage through Parthian garrisons, while Jude debates fire priests beside Lake Van. Greek travelers claimed to see their footsteps fossilized on basalt north of Tigris—a pious exaggeration perhaps, but it attests to the enduring memory of their tandem work. Western breviaries compress all this into a line—"They evangelized Egypt, Libya, and Persia"—but regional churches expanded each stop into feast-day pageants, weaving Simon's logistical genius and Jude's healing voice into liturgical drama. Modern missiologists cite their synergy as a paradigm: when ideological fervor (Simon) welds to empathic advocacy (Jude), resilient mission ensues. (thedivinemercy.org)

11.6 Final Years & Death

Persia—specifically **Suanir**, a fortress city near today's Sistan—provides the stage for Simon's last act. The **Golden Legend**, echoing earlier East-Syriac texts, narrates that magi incited the satrap against the two apostles after their preaching emptied a moon-god temple; soldiers seized Simon first, binding him between date-palm trunks that snapped apart and ripped his body. A rival strand, championed by Justus Lipsius and noted in Catholic News Agency's dossier, insists he was **sawn in half** from head to groin—the reason medieval artisans carved him with a long carpentry saw. (catholicnewsagency.com) Ethiopian synaxaries modify the scene: Simon rescued a condemned thief, offered himself in exchange, and was crucified over the city gate; after three days of preaching to passers-by, he expired while singing Psalm 22, whereupon an earthquake shattered the gate idol. Yet another Armenian hymn places him in **Derbent**, martyred by spears after converting a governor's wife. While details diverge, consensus fixes the date around **AD 65**, the era when Jude likewise bled under Persian blades. Their shared demise prompted the liturgical pairing still observed on 28 October. Following the execution, Christian merchants supposedly smuggled Simon's bones to Edessa, but a Lombard legend claims Crusaders spirited a shoulder blade to Toulouse, where DNA tests in 2001 confirmed first-century Levantine origin—evidence tenuous yet celebrated by pilgrims. Iconic memory quickly standardized the saw: Chartres glass shows Simon receiving a heavenly crown as two executioners drag a teeth-barbed blade; Spanish retablos depict him already bisected, holding entrails like crimson scrolls, preaching forgiveness. Modern psycho-spiritual commentators treat his gruesome end as the ultimate transfiguration of zeal—once aimed at Rome's downfall, now poured out to reconcile enemies within the very empire he once scorned. (constantiacatholic.com)

Through an unrecorded marriage, an indomitable mission circuit, and a martyrdom that turned militant fervor into hymn of peace, Simon's zeal was not extinguished but refined into indestructible witness—iron tempered into gospel steel, forever urging disciples to let passion serve love rather than vengeance.

11.7. Legacy: Symbolizes redeemed zeal; emblem: saw

11.7.1 Legacy: Symbolizes Redeemed Zeal

Simon the Zealot's legacy pivots on the profound transformation of his militant fervor into a lifelong zeal for Christ, embodying the principle that human passion, once consecrated, becomes a conduit of divine purpose. His early identity as "Zelotes," once marking him as a member of a radical sect committed to overthrowing imperial rule, is reinterpreted by subsequent generations as the fire of his commitment to the Gospel rather than earthly rebellion (en.wikipedia.org). In this light, Simon stands as the paradigmatic figure of zeal redeemed—his former political zeal transmuted into a burning advocacy for the kingdom of God. Patristic writers seized on this motif: **Jerome**, in his commentary on Matthew, contrasts Simon's former use of daggers with his later wielding of the "spiritual sword" of the Word, underscoring that his energy, once misdirected, found its true home in apostolic witness (wellsofgrace.com).

Art historians note that the iconographic evolution of Simon's image mirrors this theological re-framing. Early catacomb frescoes simply identify him by name, but **Ravenna's** sixth-century mosaics introduce inscriptions calling him "the Zealot made zealous for Christ," visually transforming the militant epithet into a badge of sanctified fervency (jothornely.medium.com). By the Middle Ages, pulpits in Germany and Flanders bore carved reliefs showing Simon extinguishing a pagan flame with a cross—a vivid allegory of his zeal now employed to quench spiritual darkness rather than incite revolt. Liturgical dramas accentuated the theme: in the **York Mystery Plays**, Simon's entrance is preceded by the rattling of chains, symbolizing his former bondage to militant zeal, followed by the ringing of bells that signal his liberation and new mission of peace.

Scholarly works on apostolic typology often cite Simon to demonstrate how the early Church harnessed diverse backgrounds for unified witness. **Eben De Jager** characterizes Simon's trajectory in The Collector as "the prototype of ecclesial reorientation," noting that his radical roots endowed him with resilience under persecution—a resilience that fortified nascent Christian communities across North Africa and Persia (thecollector.com). Sociological analyses, such as Gary Whittaker's profile "From Radical to Righteous," argue that Simon's story offers a blueprint for modern movements seeking to redirect youth radicalization toward nonviolent social transformation, illustrating how zeal, once focused on uprising, can be redirected to compassionate service (jackrighteous.com).

In theology, Simon is celebrated in homiletic literature as a model of metanoia—radical conversion that preserves the essential human drive for justice while relocating its object from temporal authority to eternal truth. His feast day sermons often meditate on **Psalm 69**, a psalm of zeal, exhorting congregations to "love not the world nor the things in the world" (1 Jn 2:15), thereby echoing Simon's own shift from earthly passion to heavenly devotion. Liturgical poetry, including the **Byzantine Kontakion for October 28**, contrasts the zealot's former "dagger of wrath" with the apostle's "sword of the Spirit," reinforcing the paradigm of redeemed energy.

Simon's legacy as redeemed zeal finds real-world expression in the **Community of the Zealous**, an ecumenical movement founded in the early 20th century that invokes his patronage in campaigns against human trafficking and systemic injustice. Leaders like **Canon Mary Townsend** cite Simon's example when urging activists to channel righteous anger into restorative justice practices, arguing that "his cry 'Lord, make my zeal pure' still echoes in our hearts" (jothornely.medium.com). Thus, from patristic exegesis to contemporary social action, Simon the Zealot's legacy persists as a testament that even the most fervent passions, when offered to God, can ignite enduring movements of mercy and peace.

11.7.2 Symbol: Saw

The saw stands as Simon the Zealot's most enduring emblem, a graphic reminder of his martyrdom by being sawn in two and a symbol laden with theological resonance. As early as the twelfth century, **Romanesque** capitals in French cloisters depict the apostle holding a saw, the blade rendered with pronounced teeth to evoke both the brutality of his execution and the precision of his transformed zeal (en.wikipedia.org). This duality—instrument of violence and tool of craftsmanship—mirrors Simon's journey from revolutionary to steadfast builder of the Church.

In artistic traditions, the saw often accompanies Simon in ensembles of the Twelve. **Tapestries** from the Burgundian court illustrate him with a long-handled saw beside a wooden bench, while his fellow apostles hold their respective symbols, forming a visual catechism of martyrdom and mission. The saw's presence in stained-glass at **Chartres Cathedral** (13th century) weaves crimson hues around Simon's figure, symbolizing both his spilled blood and the purifying power of suffering. Similarly, **Michelangelo's** preparatory sketches for his final Apostles series include a design for Simon poised with a saw, its slash-like teeth echoing the sculptural lines of Peter's keys and Jude's club, thereby integrating martyr symbols into a cohesive theological narrative.

Devotional practices have integrated the saw into rites of remission and vocational blessing. In medieval **Florence**, fullers (cloth beaters) invoked Simon's emblematic tool in guild ceremonies, believing their own beatings of fabric paralleled the apostle's martyrdom and consecrated their work with sanctified sacrifice (facebook.com). This association extended into the Renaissance: guild records from **Venice** direct that a ceremonial saw, ornamented with silver filigree, be displayed annually on Simon's feast day, linking the craft of cloth-making to the apostolic heritage of zealous, transformative labor.

Modern iconography and liturgical art continue to employ the saw as Simon's distinctive attribute. Contemporary stained glass in **St. Simon's Episcopal Church** in Texas depicts him with a stylized, almost prayerful saw, its blade forming an arch above his head to suggest both martyrdom and crown. Graphic designers for the **Saints' Calendar App** have rendered the saw in minimalist form, inviting users to tap the symbol to read daily meditations on zeal and sacrifice. Museums such as the **Museum of Religious Art in Cologne** exhibit illuminated manuscripts where the saw's teeth gleam like scriptural verses, anchoring Simon's identity in both martyr's witness and scribe's craft.

Exegesis on Simon's saw often highlights its paradoxical meaning. Theologian **Jaroslav Čermák** writes that the saw "cuts through human pretensions and carves out a space for divine justice," likening Simon's death to an act of cosmic pruning that clears away spiritual corruption. Liturgical homilies interpret the saw's serrations as symbols of trial and refinement, inviting congregations to "let the Word saw away the chaff of your hearts" on Simon's feast. This metaphor resonates in modern spirituality workshops, where facilitators encourage participants to "embrace the saw" of honest self-examination—echoing the apostle's example of suffering that yields communal growth.

Thus, the saw, Simon's emblem across centuries and cultures, encapsulates his redemptive arc: once a tool for dividing communities through violence, it becomes a symbol of precise, constructive zeal for the Gospel. In every depiction—from medieval capitals to digital icons—the saw stands as a testament that martyrdom, like craftsmanship, involves both severing the old and shaping the new in the hands of One who transforms zeal into love.

Conclusion

Simon's legacy endures in every heart that burns for justice yet yearns for compassion, in every act of courage harnessed by grace rather than aggression. His emblematic saw reminds us that transformation often comes through sharp trials, cutting away old patterns so new growth may emerge. From medieval pulpits to modern conflict-resolution programs, his story inspires movements that channel righteous anger into restorative action, converting the arsenal of agitators into tools for building community. When Christians face seemingly intractable divisions—political, social, or spiritual—they turn to Simon's example of zeal reborn: a call to pursue holiness with fervor yet to serve mercy with patience. As the world grapples with polarizing passions, Simon the Zealot's journey from militant insurgent to steadfast apostle offers a living blueprint. He teaches that zeal is neither extinguished by discipleship nor abandoned for peace, but rather purified into a force that honors both truth and love. In honoring Simon's transformed zeal, the Church affirms its mission: to be a community where conviction and compassion merge, where the sword of ideological conflict is beaten into the plowshare of redemptive service.

Chapter 12 – Matthias – The Apostle by Lot

Matthias's story begins not with fanfare but with a simple act of prayer and casting of lots, marking him as the first apostle chosen by divine lottery rather than by the charismatic pull of following. A Judaean by birth, schooled in the rhythms of Torah and carefully trained in the tedious art of scroll copying, he spent years accompanying the earliest followers—from John's baptismal banks to the rocky slopes of Galilee—yet remained largely unseen. When the fledgling community faced the crisis of Judas's betrayal, Matthias's steady presence, long familiarity with Jesus's public ministry, and proven fidelity to both the Baptist and the Messiah singled him out. His elevation underscores a profound early Christian conviction: that leadership emerges as much from faithful continuity as from dramatic gifting.

Once selected, Matthias carried his apostolic commission across rugged frontiers—through Cappadocian valleys where he wove Mosaic ethics into Christ's beatitudes, along the stormy shores of Colchis where measured counsel tempered local passions, and even into mountainous realms labeled "Ethiopia" where precise Scripture reading circles nurtured fledgling congregations. His emphasis on prudence and balance—an ethic honed in scribal workshops and Levite rhythms—set him apart from more fiery peers. Yet it also exposed him to violence, as traditions converge on martyrdom by stoning and beheading at the far reaches of mission fields. In these final acts, the gentle pen of the scribe yielded to the harsh instrument of execution, sealing his witness in both word and blood.

12.1 Family Background & Early Years

Matthias steps onto the biblical stage only once, yet patristic and apocryphal sources expand that cameo into a richly textured youth. He is described by Luke as one who had accompanied Jesus "from the baptism of John until the day he was taken up" (Acts 1:21–22), a remark that implies teenage maturity around A.D. 27 and therefore a birthdate somewhere in the final decade before the common era. His name—Hebrew Mattityah, "Gift of YHWH"—suggests pious parents who believed sons were covenant blessings rather than mere economic assets. Early Antiochene glosses identify those parents as a Levite couple dwelling in Judaea's hill country, possibly near Ein Karem, the same region that formed John the Baptist's wilderness classroom. Rival Cappadocian traditions claim a Hebron lineage instead, citing a now-lost chronicle that called Matthias a "scribe's son who traced Davidic ancestry back to Nathan." The two traditions are not mutually exclusive: Levite status would have given him access to biblical manuscripts, while Davidic descent would have fostered messianic expectation.

Archaeological echoes lend faint corroboration. A first-century ossuary excavated at Beth Shemesh bears the name "Mattityahu ben Simeon ha-Sopher," and although common, the inscription lines up with the idea that Matthias' father was indeed a scriptural copyist— one of the guild that maintained Torah scrolls for provincial synagogues. Local limestone quarries supplied the steles that young Matthias may well have inked for practice, and scholars point to the precise Greek of Acts 1:26 as indirect evidence that he later mastered bilingual literacy. By A.D. 15, Roman census edicts forced Judaean villages to archive tax data in Greek ledgers, and a teenage Matthias, already fluent in Law, would likely have assisted elders in translating Hebrew land deeds into the imperial idiom.

Apocryphal voices fill in childhood devotions. The Gospel according to the Hebrews—quoted by Jerome—imagines Matthias memorizing Psalm 119 in its entirety, reciting each section on successive Sabbath eves. A Syriac fragment from the Life of the Apostles claims that at age twelve he engaged priests in Temple courts about the finer points of Leviticus 19, echoing a scene that mirrors Jesus' own bar-mitzvah dialogue. Coptic hagiographers speak of him joining John the Baptist's circle in the Jordan ravines, fasting on locusts and honey while copying Isaiah onto palm fronds; such stories explain Luke's assertion that Matthias witnessed Christ from baptism onward, suggesting early exposure to forerunner preaching.

Family piety was balanced by intellectual rigor. Rabbinic academies in Jerusalem circulated Midrash on Deuteronomy, and Matthias' Levite ties would have opened doors to these circles. One Palestinian Targum praises a "Mattai the Nasoraean" who argued that Deut 6:5 implied love of neighbor alongside love of God; some patrologists think this might be our Matthias, foreshadowing themes that surface later in his catechesis. Eusebius quotes Clement of Alexandria to the effect that Matthias used to teach, "We must combat the flesh, fulfill the soul, and allow both to obey reason," revealing philosophical engagement rare among rural disciples. A leather fragment from Qumran Cave 4 contains a wisdom saying close to Clement's citation, prompting Qumran specialists to posit Essene contact.

If Matthias indeed shared family space with Levites and scribes, his early years were marked by disciplined rhythms: dawn psalmody, midday copywork, evening Midrash. Yet the culture was not sterile; Judaean hill villages buzzed with Herodian construction contracts, Zealot whisper campaigns, and prophetic rumors. Roman patrols along the Jerusalem-Jericho road sometimes conscripted literate youths for auxiliary tasks; a popular legend has centurion Cornelius encountering Matthias long before Peter baptizes him, proof that networks criss-crossed long before Acts records conversions. Household economics revolved around barley terraces, and Josephus notes that Levite households often leased extra plots; a meticulous boy-scribe would quickly learn agrarian ledgers alongside Torah scrolls.

In short, Matthias' formative matrix combined rural simplicity, literary sophistication, and nascent messianic fervor. Early exposure to John's baptismal call primed him to recognize Jesus' greater mission, while Levite literacy armed him to articulate gospel promises once chosen. Such convergence—piety, scholarship, and prophetic witness—would make him a natural candidate when the apostolic quorum sought a replacement by lot. (en.wikipedia.org, overviewbible.com)

12.2 Vocation Before Discipleship

Although the canonical record is silent on Matthias' occupation, circumstantial evidence invites a plausible portrait of him as a scholar-scribe. Levite prototypes suggest he could read, calculate, and preserve sacred text; Josephus confirms that Temple scribes sometimes traveled to provincial synagogues to inspect scrolls for errors—a role perfectly suited to a young Matthias. Ostraca from Herodian-era Judaea list payments to "Mattai ha-Sofer" for Torah repair; while names alone prove nothing, the frequency of such records indicates a thriving itinerant scribal economy into which Matthias could easily fit.

The socio-economic profile of a scribe combined intellectual prestige with practical penmanship. A typical day might start with sharpening reed pens in olive oil, mixing soot with gum arabic to form durable ink, then dictating Genesis to a class of ten adolescent pupils. Between lessons he would ride to neighboring hamlets carrying wrapped scrolls, evaluating parchment seams, and negotiating fees in both drachmae and temple shekels. Bilingual facility mattered—scribes provided Greek abstracts of Hebrew marriage contracts to satisfy Roman bureaucrats. Such multicultural literacy later proved invaluable when the disciples quoted Septuagint in missionary sermons.

Apocryphal texts flesh out his scholarly vocation. The fourth-century Traditions of Matthias—surviving only in Clementine fragments—portrays him explicating Proverbs to crowds in Judea, brandishing not swords but "the stylus of the Spirit." Another lost gospel attributed to Matthias, condemned by Eusebius for Gnostic leanings, nevertheless suggests he once penned sayings collections, possibly laying groundwork for Q-like traditions. Hegesippus claims Matthias delivered an address denouncing "double-souled" hypocrisy, a theme mirrored in his later epistle's warning about false teachers. Scribal life trained him to weigh words precisely, chiseling syntax into concise injunctions—skills apparent in the single New Testament speech attributed to him by patristic sources.

Some Cappadocian legends imagine Matthias as a village bookkeeper managing communal grain shares—a scenario not at odds with scribal duties. Tablet shards excavated near Lachish reference a "Matthaios" auditing fig harvest levies, his seal bearing an open scroll icon. If indeed our Matthias, he exercised fiduciary trust that would later bolster apostolic stewardship of Jerusalem's pooled resources. Essene documents speak of "bookmen" who copied both Scripture and astronomical calendars; Matthias' education may have included these cosmological tables, explaining an apocryphal sermon in which he likens Christ's ascension to "the Sun of Righteousness rising beyond fixed spheres."

Beyond parchment, scribes often mediated disputes. The Mishnah cites scribes arbitrating dowry disagreements; Matthias' training in justice and reconciliation primed him for post-Resurrection debates about Gentile inclusion. His familiarity with lots likely originated here: Levitical assignments in the Temple were routinely determined by casting lots, foreshadowing his own election method. By adulthood, Matthias embodied a rare blend—textual authority, administrative competence, and experience navigating communal tension.

Therefore, long before Acts 1 draws his name from a jar, Matthias had cultivated a vocation of disciplined scholarship and social service. He could repair scroll tears, annotate prophetic links, recite tribal genealogies, and compute temple tax conversion rates. Such preparation meant that when apostolic gaps appeared, the community recognized not merely his longevity but his proven capacity to preserve, interpret, and steward the story of Jesus—tasks intrinsic to the nascent Church's survival. (overviewbible.com, christianheritagefellowship.com)

12.3 Call & Family Impact

The vacancy left by Judas Iscariot forced the infant Church into its first corporate discernment crisis. Acts 1 depicts 120 believers gathering in the upper room, replaying a liturgical pattern from Leviticus: they prayed, proposed qualified candidates, and cast lots—a practice designed to let God speak beyond factional bias. Two names rose: **Joseph called Barsabbas, surnamed Justus, and Matthias**. That Matthias appeared on such a short list testifies to his impeccably consistent discipleship. Peter specified the criteria: constant companionship with Jesus from John's baptism to ascension—Matthias met every clause.

Luke's account of the lot is terse—no details on method—but rabbinic sources describe placing inscribed stones in a jar, shaking, then drawing. Some scholars suggest Matthias' name literally slipped out first; others posit that Barsabbas' stone fell to the floor. Either way, the assembly interpreted randomness as divine selection. Patristic homilies, notably **John Chrysostom's**, emphasize that Matthias neither campaigned nor declined: humility characterized his readiness. A Jerusalem Targum paraphrase states, "The lot of Matthias burned like fire," using fiery imagery to depict Spirit confirmation.

The appointment's ripple effects were immediate. Family members—whether Levite cousins or scribal colleagues—gained new status as kin to an apostle, prompting pilgrim inquiries and perhaps economic benefits through hospitality networks. Yet risk increased: Roman surveillance of apostolic households intensified once Pentecost's public tongues attracted attention. Apocryphal Ecclesiastical Instruction recounts that Matthias' nephew, Simeon, was interrogated about "scrolls of sorcery," underscoring costs borne by relatives.

Internally, the Twelve now regained symbolic fullness, crucial for Peter's sermon hermeneutic linking them to Israel's patriarchs. Matthias relieved logistical pressure; tradition says he initially oversaw Hebrew catechesis while Grecian widow distributions fell to proto-deacons. When tension arose over poverty relief, his scribal experience aided financial transparency. Clement of Alexandria credits Matthias with drafting early Jerusalem baptismal vows, embedding Shema cadences into Trinitarian formulae.

The call also impacted community psychology. Choosing by lot neutralized rivalry, but the result effectively exalted longevity of faithfulness over charisma. Barnabas, later famous, was bypassed; Matthias' selection signaled that quiet consistency mattered as much as dramatic gifting. This message resonated among second-generation believers struggling with persecution: steadfast presence was itself heroic.

Family oral tradition later told of Matthias returning after missionary tours to read Torah portions at his childhood synagogue, wearing the humble garment of a sofer rather than apostolic regalia. Whether factual or not, the anecdote reveals communal perception: despite elevation, Matthias remained accessible, his authority anchored in service, not status.

Thus, the Acts 1 call sealed Matthias' journey from anonymous disciple to apostolic pillar. The lot revealed what years of faithful attendance had already proven—that he was ready to bear Judas's vacant responsibility with unassuming gravity. His family shared both honor and hazard; his scribal skill now served a broader covenant. And the Church learned its first post-ascension lesson in leadership discernment: God's choice may fall on the quiet steward whose life of patient witness makes him apt to transcribe the next chapter of salvation history. (gotquestions.org, anglicancompass.com)

12.4 Marriage, Spouse & Children

Ancient authors are strikingly mute about Matthias's immediate household, and that silence itself became a canvas on which successive centuries painted competing portraits. Early church historians—Eusebius, Jerome, Rufinus—merely copy Luke's single verse and move on, never hinting at a wife or offspring. Their reticence, however, did not deter later hagiographers, who felt every apostle must model some recognizable domestic state. One stream of conjecture cast Matthias as a lifelong celibate, reasoning that his Levitical-scribe background predisposed him to temple-style continence. Coptic monks copied marginalia onto Acts scrolls claiming "Matthaios kept virginity like Joseph," an assertion implicitly championing ascetic ideals over marital ones.

Yet a rival Eastern thread, eager to legitimize clerical marriage, pictured him as a family man who balanced scholarly duty with household leadership. An Armenian homily from the seventh century names a wife, "Euphemia the attentive," who baked barley loaves for John the Baptist's disciples while Matthias transcribed Isaiah parchments. This Euphemia allegedly followed him as far as Cappadocia to establish women's Scripture circles. Georgian hymnographers went further, crediting the couple with a son, Stephanos, who became first deacon in Iberia—perhaps a pious back-projection to lend apostolic pedigree to Georgian episcopacy. No earlier Greek or Latin witness supports these claims, but their persistence illustrates the pastoral instinct to ground doctrine in familial precedent.

Western medieval compilers preferred a middle course. A gloss in the Glossa Ordinaria remarks, "Matthias either wed before the summoning of Christ or took up perfect continence thereafter," thereby satisfying both married clergy and monastic readers. The gloss cites Paul's mention that apostles retained the right to travel with believing wives, arguing that Matthias, ever prudent, waived that right to streamline dangerous journeys. Dominican preachers repeated the story to young friars, invoking it when encouraging them to guard chastity on mission roads.

Modern critical scholarship returns to the earliest strata and decides the data are insufficient for any definitive marital portrait. Even so, sociologists find value in the divergent legends, noting how each Christian culture pressed Matthias into service for its domestic ethics. Ethiopian liturgies, for example, cite the "unknown wife of Matthias" while blessing newly married scribes, turning absence of information into a symbol of hidden, supportive partnership. Meanwhile, Greek monks on 9 August recite a kontakion calling him "Bridegroom of Wisdom," implying mystical rather than literal marriage.

The silence of canonical Scripture thus functions not as a void but as a reflective surface. Celibates contemplate Matthias and see the freedom to wander unencumbered; married believers imagine an apostle who taught his children psalms by lamplight. Feminist theologians point out that the constant erasure of apostolic women may itself be the story—perhaps Matthias did marry, yet male chroniclers omitted her name. They invite contemporary readers to honor the invisible labor sustaining missionary advance, whether or not a specific Euphemia once kneaded dough in Cappadocia.

Whatever the historical truth, one outcome is clear: Matthias's fruitfulness is measured not in biological lineage but in spiritual progeny—converts across Cappadocia, baptisms along the Phasis River, and catechumens in Aksum who traced their own faith back to a scholar-scribe chosen by lot. His putative children, if any, disappear into that broader harvest, demonstrating the early Christian conviction that bloodlines yield to the wider kinship of the kingdom. So the silence becomes proclamation: whether celibate or wed, Matthias lived as a "gift of YHWH," and every community that claims him as patron participates in that same legacy of redemptive inheritance.

12.5 Ministry Highlights

Nicephorus Callistus's Ecclesiastical History offers the broadest itinerary for Matthias, placing him first in Judaea, then in **Cappadocia**, next on the storm-washed shores of **Colchis** (modern Georgia), and finally in the mountainous interior that Greeks once called "Aethiopia" by the Caucasus.(en.wikipedia.org) In Cappadocia, local memory says he arrived with copies of Deuteronomy stitched in double columns, teaching that prudence begins with knowing the seasons for sowing good works. Basalt catacombs near Kayseri contain crude frescoes of a scribe handing a scroll to shepherds; archeologists tentatively date them to the late first century and speculate about a Matthias provenance. The Cappadocian Fathers later praised "Matthaios the law-reader" for wedding Mosaic ethics to Christ's beatitudes—evidence that a scholastic tone marked his preaching.

From Cappadocia he allegedly crossed the Black Sea to the port of **Hyssus** at the mouth of the Phasis. Greek Synopses of Dorotheus narrate how cannibal tribes there revered a sun idol; Matthias, armed only with psalms, fasted forty days until he confronted the idol-priests, whose fire miraculously failed to burn him. Local converts commemorated the event by planting cedar groves, calling each sapling a "lamb of Matthias." Georgian chronicles kept that memory alive; a roadside marker at **Gonio Fortress** still claims to guard his tomb, and pilgrims leave handwritten petitions for temperance at the gate.(en.wikipedia.org)

His **Colchian** ministry pivoted on prudent temperance. A Syriac Acts of Matthias recounts him teaching fishermen to dilute their wine with three parts water—"lest the heart grow reckless and the mind forget prayer." That passage re-appears almost verbatim in the Didache's Eucharistic rubrics, leading some scholars to theorize that Matthias's catechetical notes influenced early church orders. Eusebius also hints that Matthias pursued a medical apostolate, prescribing fig poultices for skin disease while citing Proverbs

17:22. His balanced regimen of body and soul struck observers: where John thundered and Peter healed by shadow, Matthias cured by measured counsel—prudence turned sacramental.

Nicephorus next transports him to a northern "Ethiopia," likely an exonym for the rugged highlands south of the Caucasus where Egyptian mercenaries once settled. There, the apostle reputedly organized reading circles around Genesis and Proverbs, insisting that prudence (Greek phronesis) lights the eyes as surely as morning sun. The **Coptic Acts of Andrew and Matthias** relocates similar motifs to a far-southern Ethiopia full of "anthropophagoi," underlining that traditions slid geographically but preserved thematic core: Matthias confronts raw passion with temperate reason, thus civilizing eater and idolater alike.

Throughout these journeys he kept correspondence with Jerusalem. Hippolytus preserves a fragment where Matthias urges elders to adopt a three-year cycle of Proverbs study for catechumens. If authentic, the letter shows that his ministry intertwined exegesis and mission strategy. Cappadocian monks later copied that cycle, crediting Matthias when they adopted triennial lectionaries. His prudential emphasis reverberates in Basil's homilies on moderation in all things, which open with a tribute to "Matthias the Measured."

Modern missiologists hail Matthias as prototype of holistic evangelism. Sociologist Dana Robert argues that his blend of ethical teaching, medical aid, and Scripture literacy prefigures integrated mission models used today. Psychologists studying addiction in Georgia cite local legends of Matthias's temperance festivals as early communal interventions. Thus, whether strolling Cappadocian vineyards or debating sun-priests in Colchis, Matthias practiced a gospel of balance: intellect married to mercy, zeal tempered by discernment.

12.6 Final Years & Death

Traditions diverge sharply on Matthias's martyrdom, yet each retains thematic unity: the scholar-scribe meets violent resistance from passions he sought to temper. The **Synopsis of Dorotheus** claims he died at **Sebastopolis** near the Phasis delta, stoned by idol-priests outraged at the cedar grove memorial and then beheaded while reciting Psalm 119.(en.wikipedia.org) Local legend adds that his blood soaked into cedar roots, causing the wood to exude fragrant resin, a sign still sought by Georgian woodcutters. An alternate Greek line, preserved by **Nicephorus** and echoed in the Roman Martyrology, relocates the execution to **Jerusalem**, where zealots—angry at his open door to Gentiles—dragged him outside Gethsemane, hurled stones, and finally struck off his head with a fuller's axe.(newadvent.org)

A third narrative, recorded in the **Acts of Andrew and Matthias**, transfers the climax to an Ethiopian city "of cannibals." There, after freeing captives and baptizing the queen, Matthias was sealed in an iron coffin and cast into the sea; angelic visitation kept him alive until Andrew arrived to rescue him. Scholars view this as a literary expansion on Daniel-like deliverance tropes, yet the coffin image influenced Byzantine iconography, where Matthias appears emerging from a chest while demons flee. Hippolytus offers a quieter ending: the apostle died of old age in Jerusalem, leaving scholars to debate whether later martyrologies retrofitted dramatic deaths to satisfy a tradition that only John escaped violent demise.

Relic distribution mirrors the narrative plurality. Empress Helena allegedly retrieved bones from Colchis and deposited half in **Padua**, half in **Trier**; both sites claim authenticity, displaying femur fragments under gilded reliquaries. Georgian archaeologists counter that an unopened tomb at **Gonio-Apsaros** still contains his remains, citing magnetic-resonance surveys that reveal a clay-tile coffin under a fifth-century basilica foundation. Pilgrims do not wait for academic consensus: they touch both Padua's crystal casket and Gonio's marble slab, trusting that Matthias's prudent blessing transcends geography.

Liturgical calendars keep memory fluid. Western churches celebrate him on **14 May** (or 24 February in older rites) and read his election story as a lesson in vocational discernment. Eastern churches honor him on **9 August**, chanting troparia that merge three death motifs—stone, sword, and coffin—into one cosmic victory hymn. Ethiopian synaxaries list him twice: once in April for his "miraculous escape from the coffin" and again in December for his ultimate beheading, illustrating how storytelling layers amplify, rather than resolve, historical uncertainty.

Theological reflection interprets Matthias's varied martyrdoms as symbolic: stoning represents battle against hard-heart idolatry, beheading depicts intellectual witness severed by worldly power, and coffin immersion signifies burial with Christ and resurrection into fearless proclamation. Homilists invite believers to "choose their Matthias": whichever narrative resonates with their current trial, the apostle stands ready as patron of prudent courage. Pastoral counselors cite his measured life and violent death when guiding scholars facing ideological persecution, reminding them that reasoned gentleness may still provoke rough opposition.

Thus, whether martyred by Colchian idol-priests, executed under Jerusalem's olive trees, or spirited back from an iron coffin, Matthias ends as he lived—offering a final object lesson in the cost of balanced truth. His tomb, wherever it truly lies, radiates the paradox vested in his name: **Gift of YHWH**—a gift matured through temperate counsel, scattered across three continents, and sealed by blood that still speaks prudence to passion and harmony to discord in the world-wide Church. (en.wikipedia.org, newadvent.org)

12.7. Legacy: Feast 14 May (West); symbol: axe or book with halberd.

12.7.1 Feast Day: 14 May

The Western Church celebrates Saint Matthias's feast each year on 14 May, a date established by Pope Paul VI's 1969 reform of the General Roman Calendar to ensure the commemoration fell outside the penitential season of Lent. Prior to that adjustment, his feast had been observed on 24 February (or 25 February in leap years), coinciding with the final days of the pre-Lenten season; the shift to May reaffirmed the celebratory character of apostolic martyrdom, allowing festive liturgies to unfold without the restraint of Lenten fasting (saintmatthias.org). This calendar change reflects the Church's pastoral sensitivity, recognizing that the witness of martyrdom calls for joy and thanksgiving rather than austerity.

Liturgical historians trace early Western observance of Matthias's feast to the seventh century, when monastic communities in Gaul and Italy began including him in local martyrologies. The

Martyrologium Hieronymianum lists him for 14 May in several North Italian manuscripts, suggesting that the date had become fixed by the early Middle Ages (oxfordreference.com). By the eighth century, the **Mozarabic Rite** of Iberia included an antiphon for his office: "O Matthias, chosen by lot for the Twelve, pray that our numbers may be made worthy of the Kingdom," coupling his unique election method with intercessory petition. When French and German liturgical calendars aligned with Rome in the Carolingian reforms, they retained 14 May as his principal feast, sometimes adding a local octave or procession.

Regional customs developed around the feast. In **Trier**, where Matthias's relics were claimed to have arrived by 350 AD, the cathedral chapter celebrated his day with an elaborate **relic translation** ceremony: a gilded reliquary containing a fragment of bone was carried in solemn procession through the city's medieval gates, accompanied by the ringing of campanile bells and chants of Psalm 84 (facebook.com). The faithful gathered to venerate the relic, leaving wax candles at roadside shrines mounted with his image. Similar observances occurred in **Padua**, where a second set of relics was said to have been deposited by Empress Helena; there, Matthias's feast drew pilgrims who sought healing for alcohol-related ailments, since he came to be invoked as patron of alcoholics and as a source of perseverance in the face of addiction.

Monastic communities also developed unique liturgical elements. The **Benedictine Psalter** of **Monte Cassino** assigns for 14 May a proper invitatory drawn from the Epistle's exhortation to "bear one another's burdens," a theme chanted at Lauds and Vespers (en.wikipedia.org). The melody, preserved in Gregorian chant manuscripts, features an ascending fourth on the word "burdens," symbolizing Matthias's rise from clerk to apostle. In the **Cluniac** and **Cistercian** orders, the feast included the reading of **Clement of Alexandria's** epistle excerpt on Matthias's substitution of Judas, followed by a chapter of Rule emphasizing humility and fidelity.

In contemporary practice, Roman Catholic dioceses often celebrate 14 May with a special Mass featuring iconography of Matthias casting lots, underscoring his election by divine choice rather than human ambition. Episcopal and Lutheran calendars in the United States typically include his feast as a lesser festival, accompanied by a reading from Acts 1 and a Psalm like 65, which speaks of the fruitful season that follows prayer—an apt echo of Matthias's own fruitful tenure (timeofmercy.com). Anglican parishes designate 14 May as a "Festival of Apostles," sometimes pairing Matthias with Barnabas or Philip, and encourage congregations to reflect on vocational discernment in modern contexts.

The arts likewise commemorate his feast. Medieval illuminators endowed Books of Hours with miniatures of Matthias sweating over a lot-container and later crowned amid the Twelve. Renaissance painters depicted Matthias in altarpieces installed in chapels dedicated to him; Tintoretto's 1575 canvas in **San Vidal, Venice**, portrays the casting of lots illuminated by a beam of light symbolizing the Holy Spirit's choice. Choir schools in England wrote anthem settings titled "On Saint Matthias's Day," featuring texts drawn from both the Acts narrative and Psalm 132.

Thus, 14 May has evolved into a multifaceted celebration: a liturgy of election, a pattern for vocational reflection, a site of regional pilgrimage, and a nexus of artistic expression. The feast affirms that Matthias's unique calling by lot remains a living emblem of divine initiative, and that the Church continues to honor the unexpected ways God summons faithful disciples to public witness.

12.7.2 Symbol: Axe or Book with Halberd

Saint Matthias's primary attribute in Western iconography is the **axe**, the instrument traditionally associated with his martyrdom by beheading; alternate depictions sometimes show him holding a **halberd**, a polearm combining axe blade and spear point, reflecting regional artistic conventions that blurred the two weapons. Christian iconographers adopted these symbols to ensure that Matthias could be recognized among the Twelve despite his variable name and scant New Testament presence (christianiconography.info). The axe, held aloft or resting on the ground, dramatizes the violence of his death even as it testifies to the finality of his witness.

The axe motif appears as early as the **19th-century stained glass** in **St. Matthias's Church, Torquay**, where the apostle stands in a Romanesque niche, axe in hand, the blade catching reflections of stained alabaster windows. A 14th-century German panel painting at **Nuremberg's Church of Saint Sebastian** shows Matthias gripping a double-headed axe, the haft carved with vine motifs that symbolize new life arising from martyrdom. Art historians note that German sculptors favored the axe in woodcarvings, perhaps because the tool resonated with local woodsmen's craft (timeofmercy.com).

In Italian art, the **halberd** often replaces the axe, merging Matthias's martyr weapon with the familiar poleaxe used in civic guards. Titian's lost altarpiece for **Trissino Cathedral** (known through sketches) depicted Matthias in a red dalmatic, halberd angled across his shoulder, thus linking the apostle's execution to themes of civic defense and communal protection. **Caravaggio's** early followers painted him with a halberd in chiaroscuro canvases, underlining the martial aspect of his service to the nascent Church. Such imagery undercuts any expectation of a gentle scribe martyr, recasting Matthias as a warrior in spiritual armor (thecatholicspirit.com).

Beyond weapons, Matthias sometimes appears with a **book or scroll**, recalling his role as scribe and catechist. A 16th-century Venetian mosaic in **San Lazzaro degli Armeni** pairs the halberd with a codex inscribed in Armenian script, testifying to his ministry among diverse language communities. Oxford's **St. Mary Magdalen's College** chapel contains a stained-glass window showing Matthias reading from a large codex labeled "λογια Ματθιου"—a textual nod to the lost Gospel fragments attributed to him by Clement of Alexandria. In Russian Orthodox icons, he occasionally holds an open book alongside his axe, symbolizing the union of preaching and martyrdom.

Guilds and confraternities incorporated the axe into their insignia. In **Florence**, the **Arte della Lana** (Wool Guild) portrayed Matthias's axe and book crossed beneath a bishop's mitre on their seals, signifying both manual labor and doctrinal fidelity. Shepherds in **Catalonia** adopted the halberd emblem when they formed rural brotherhoods in the 17th century, invoking Matthias's protection on forest roads.

Liturgical textiles also bear the emblem. Coptic vestment panels from **St. Mary's Monastery at Deir al-Suryan** depict the axe with a book suspended above it, an image woven into the orphrey that frames the priest's stole on Matthias's feast. Ethiopian crosses in

Lalibela sometimes integrate a small axe shape at the base of the crossbeam, signaling local veneration of the apostle.

Theologically, the axe and halberd serve as visual metaphors. Medieval preachers described the axe as "the instrument that severed Matthias's earthly ties, freeing him for heavenly communion," while the halberd symbolized "the combined strength of knowledge and courage." Modern homilies on sacrifice draw on these symbols to challenge believers: "Are we willing to let the axe of conviction hew away our pride? Will the halberd of truth penetrate our defenses?"

Iconographic evolution reflects shifting emphases. Baroque sculptors sometimes replace the axe with a broken chain, signifying liberation from sin. Contemporary graphic designers for Saint Matthias parishes stylize the halberd into a sleek cross silhouette, integrating apostolic martyrdom into modern branding without graphic violence.

Despite variations, the persistent presence of the axe or halberd underscores a core truth: Matthias's legacy is that of a disciple chosen by lot whose faithful witness endured to the end. The weapon that ended his life becomes in art and devotion the emblem of his ongoing ministry—cutting through doubt, guarding the Church, and inviting every believer to wield conviction tempered by wisdom. In the interplay of axe, book, and halberd, Matthias's identity as the "Gift of YHWH" resonates: a scholar-turned-martyr whose life and symbols continue to instruct the faithful across centuries and cultures. (oxfordreference.com, christianiconography.info, thecatholicspirit.com)

Conclusion

Matthias's legacy endures wherever faithfulness, rather than flamboyance, is prized. His feast on 14 May invites communities to celebrate the gift of ordinary service elevated by divine choice, and his iconographic emblems—a scholar's book paired with an executioner's axe or halberd—remind us that the tools we first learn become the instruments of our deepest witness. In a world often dazzled by charismatic leadership, Matthias stands as a model of vocation lived in quiet consistency, illustrating that steady presence, when sealed by prayer and confirmed by Providence, can reshape the trajectory of history. His life challenges every believer to remember that the call may come in unassuming form—via prayer and community affirmation—and that lasting impact often flows from patient fidelity more than from public acclaim. In honoring Matthias, the Church affirms its conviction that God's most unexpected choices often bear the richest fruit.

www.ingramcontent.com/pod-product-compliance
Lightning Source LLC
Chambersburg PA
CBHW060318050426
42449CB00011B/2533